The Adulteress's Child

The Adulteress's Child

Authorship and Desire
in the Nineteenth-Century
Novel

Naomi Segal

Polity Press

Copyright © Naomi Segal, 1992

The right of Naomi Segal to be identified as author of
this work has been asserted in accordance with the
Copyright, Designs and Patents Act 1988.

First published in 1992 by Polity Press
in association with Blackwell Publishers

Editorial office:
Polity Press
65 Bridge Street
Cambridge CB2 1UR, UK

Marketing and production:
Blackwell Publishers
108 Cowley Road
Oxford OX4 1JF, UK

238 Main Street
Suite 501
Cambridge, MA 02142
USA

ISBN 0 7456 0509 5

A CIP catalogue record for this book is available
from the British Library and from the Library of Congress.

Typeset in 10 on 12pt Galliard
by Graphicraft Typesetters Ltd., Hong Kong
Printed in Great Britain by T.J. Press (Padstow) Ltd, Padstow, Cornwall

This book is printed on acid-free paper.

To David

When women bear children, they produce either devils or sons with gods in them.

D. H. Lawrence, *Studies in Classical American Literature*

Contents

Acknowledgements

*T*his book is dedicated to my son David, now four years old, who is beautifully and even riotously healthy. I also wish to thank a large number of other people for helping to bring it into being. First, the eighty or so women who were kind enough to let me interview them or who patiently filled in questionnaires for me in 1988. Secondly, the staff of Polity Press, especially my editor, John Thompson, for their patient forbearance for more years than I would have wished, and their efficiency and speed at processing the typescript. Third, St John's College for a two-term sabbatical in 1990–91 which enabled me to carry out the bulk of reading and writing in peace. My personal gratitude goes to friends who were more than available during some difficult months, especially to Frances Pine, Ann Caesar, Stella Rosenoff and Teresa Brennan, whose warmth as well as intellectual stimulation helped me to keep alive the link between experience and theory. As always, I thank my mother and father, whose love is ever-present, and who have guided and supported me through happy years of childhood and adulthood, and my daughter Rachel who makes sense of everything. Finally, this book also belongs with my love to David Forgacs.

1
Introduction

*H*ere is a puzzle. I have twelve socks loose in a drawer; six of them are red and six are blue. In the dark, how many do I need to take out in order to have a pair?

The answer is three, because I need the number of possible colours plus one, which is certain to give me two of the same colour: a pair. But a curiously large proportion of people asked this puzzle, after reaching the first stage of the logic – that I need the whole of a group plus one – give the answer 'seven'. Their reason is that I need one red sock and one blue sock to make up a pair. When pressed, they laugh and realize the error but not perhaps the pervasiveness of the assumption on which it is based.

We all know that a pair of socks is two which are identical in form and colour. But most people think of a pair rather in terms of a couple, in which complementarity is supposed to be the basis of juxtaposition: two things not of a kind but of two mutually adjusted kinds, a complete set, a pigeon pair, male and female plugs.

This book is a study of mothers and their children in the nineteenth century novel of adultery. The central woman in these novels is, before and beyond her insertion into the desire of the male protagonist, significantly part of another, primary couple – not so much the couple of husband and wife in which she is subordinated by convention, as that in which she is the larger, the more powerful, the sole adult: the couple of mother and child. What is her role in this couple, and how is it described and circumscribed by the male author? What stake does the reproductive act of authorship have in her reproduction as an imagined body? And what difference does it make to the politics of the text if her child is a son or a daughter?

Until recently at least, childcare advice in books and magazines universally referred to the child as 'he'. A reason commonly cited (in the years when this began to be an issue) was that it would be most confusing, since the mother must be a 'she', to deal in two alike pronouns all the time. A similar point is made in a study of 1977 by a literary critic discussing the narrator of Jane Austen's novels: 'so truly is this impersonal narrator the "spirit of the story", that one cannot ascribe him/her a sex, and it is misleading to use either "him" or "her" for this function; I use "him" throughout this study in the same way one uses "man" for "mankind" (in Jane Austen's case it usefully makes a clearer distinction between the author and the narrator).'[1] In both these instances the anxiety to make a complementary pair of mother and infant, author and narrator is something special – it never takes possession of people writing about doctors and patients or about Balzac and *his* spirit-of-the-story narrator. Here (unlike the case of the socks, in which something rather different is at stake) the commentator is dealing with a woman in the position of subject in a pair in which the second figure functions as her other; she is in both cases in the place of the mother. What each commentator does is pre-empt the possibility of a different-complementarity of two females. They make the other a male because in this way, I suggest, the mother is stripped of her status as subject.

We all know women are the second sex. There is one couple in which the first, the author, is always a woman, and this is the mother–child couple. But if many of us are not mothers, all of us are or have been children and, since transference is the key trope which shapes our reasoning, we continue to be and think as children as long as we live. Thus when we speak of the mother–child pair we will put ourselves in the shoes of Oedipus, not Jocasta, the infant marked by the phallus and not the legislative mother. For the mother is never perceived as legislative. Law, reason, power, language are real in so far as they are construed as coming late, coming from the father, 'being inserted' disruptively into a pair that drops apart to let the father 'insert' the child into the symbolic. Dorothy Dinnerstein has argued that the childcare system wherein infants are nearly always mothered by women causes the child (and the remembering adult) to find all initiatives of power from women uncanny and overwhelming, and to prefer to attribute the canny, motivation, reason to males. A sentence in which the mother is subject is almost impossible to form. If she appears in that position, we tend to mark the limit of her function with an other who is masculine – son or son *manqué*.

The difficulty of perceiving or theorizing the mother as a subject is very general. Observe the switch in the second sentence of the following remark by Julia Kristeva: 'we direct towards the mother not only our needs for survival but above all our earliest mimetic aspirations. She is the other subject, an object that guarantees my being as a subject.'[2] The rapid changeover here shows how the mother's subjectivity is strictly constrained by the child's desire for her as mirror. Her being as a subject is allowed to be no more than a mimetic function – effectively she is, by her very moves or initiatives, put back into the passive, the object position.

In my concluding chapter I shall return to this issue and try to suggest a cause in our earliest knowledge of the mother and her knowledge of us. For now I want to offer some more examples of how the paternal experts in psychoanalysis and childcare constrain the possibility of the mother's knowledge. In Freud the authority of the analyst as father survives the concept of countertransference. It has been well observed how in the 'Dora' narrative, Freud not only fails to incorporate the desire of Dora for Frau K., so that their mutual communication – always over the question of teaching and speaking sexuality – is marginalized in favour of the more easily palatable possibility of Dora's desire for Herr K. and a consequential chain of transference from her father onto the analyst. Several commentators note how this squeezes out not just Dora's homosexual desire but also the repressed tie to her mother, in which Freud willingly colludes. John Forrester has suggested that the most deeply repressed countertransference is that in which Freud would have to recognize himself as taking up the role of mother to Dora: 'as likely as not, for both of them, the secret lay in the picture of the Madonna – but they didn't find the words to say it.'[3] What silences both the daughter and the analyst is the impossibility of the mother's subject position. The whole phenomenon of Freudian countertransference is a masculine move, based upon a knowledge that must be that of the father.

The analyst's knowledge is, as Lacan insists, a fiction in which the patient partakes by suspending disbelief. But this very observation implies that the analyst can (and should) know something the patient does not: the true limits of that supposed knowledge. Thus here too the analyst has an advantage without which countertransference could not function in the cure. The unconscious feelings of the analyst differ from the transference of the patient in that it is his job to pre-empt them, make them conscious, make them work for him.[4] Placed initially in the object position, he overturns this by his pre-emptive knowledge, making himself master of the unconscious processes of both self and other, the patient's because these are the object of the work, and his own because they similarly serve the cure. Feeling is changed into knowledge, and precisely as he sites the origin of everything in the patient's psyche, he makes his own the organ of control. The patient ends up, like the mother, a subject that is more precisely an object: initiating only at the price of ignorance. The analyst develops in this sea change nicely from infant to father.

When Laplanche and Pontalis describe the good psychoanalyst using countertransference, controlled by reason and awareness, as a way of learning more about the patient, they base this argument on Freud's remark that 'everyone possesses in his own unconscious an instrument with which he can interpret the utterances of the unconscious in other people',[5] but there is something disingenuous in this generalization. Everyone may possess it but it is not given to everyone to perform this operation, turning outward the inward or bringing ego where id was. The knowledge this assumes is the paternal prerogative of the analyst.

This is well demonstrated in the work of that least authoritarian of psychoanalysts, Donald Winnicott, whose influence on childcare has been considerable. In his article 'The theory of the parent–infant relationship', he sets up a parallel between analyst and mother.[6] While the analyst must (as slowly and patiently as need be) bring discovery and knowledge 'within the patient's omnipotence' (p. 585), the mother must help the infant form a delusory but essential sense of omnipotent control out of a mass of real, unprocessed experience. She must enable the infant to perceive everything as its projection. This is achieved from an original partnership in which 'the infant and maternal care together form a unit' (p. 586). Maternal care – which, he argues, begins prenatally in the mother's state of intuitive identification with her child (this is of course contentious) – consists of 'the maternal ego implementing the infant ego and so making it powerful and stable'. The mother must be able first to make a total and devoted adaptation to the infant and later to have a 'good enough' sense of when and how to let go, to *fail to adapt*, when the infant needs the space to separate and perceive itself as developing independent mastery.

In both these stages, the mother, however respectfully described, is allowed to be successful only to the degree that she acts without knowledge. 'It should be noted,' Winnicott observes, 'that mothers who have it in them to provide good enough care can be enabled to do it better by being cared for themselves in a way that acknowledges the essential nature of their task. Mothers who do not have it in them to provide good enough care cannot be made good enough by mere instruction' (p. 591). The mother may be mothered, by an adviser or a husband, so that she is 'held' in a 'holding' position, but she cannot be taught. Still less can she be aware what she is doing. 'It is a very strange thing that mothers who are quite uninstructed adapt to [the] changes in their developing infants quite satisfactorily' (p. 593). Or rather perhaps it is not so strange, since the accumulated knowledge of an experienced mother may make her *too* good at her primary task so that she anticipates the child's needs and fails to let go exactly when required; in this case, 'by being a seemingly good mother, [she] does something worse than castrate the infant' (p. 592). She must at all costs act by feeling, an 'understanding of the infant's needs based on empathy'. The analyst, 'unlike the mother, needs to be aware'. The comparison between them depends on a fundamental difference of knowledge.

What also follows is that, while a failure to form the bonding identification with the foetus and neonate is not explicitly deplored, there is no way to compensate for such failure. These are skills that cannot be learned, and that also need to be precisely limited, for the mother, as we have seen, must not be too good; 'good enough' is not so much a reassuring minimum as an exact, indefinable measure. Only the expert can see when the porridge is just right.

Elsewhere, Winnicott defines how the mother is to act as mirror to her infant:

> What does the baby see when he or she looks at the mother's face?
> I am suggesting that, ordinarily, what the baby sees is himself or herself. In other words the mother is looking at the baby and what she looks like is related to what she sees there. All this is too easily taken for granted . . . I can make my point by going straight over to the case of the baby whose mother reflects her own moods or, worse still, the rigidity of her own defences. In such a case what does the baby see?
> . . . The mother's face is not then a mirror . . . the baby . . . will not look except to perceive, as a defence . . . If the mother's face is unresponsive, then a mirror is a thing to be looked at but not to be looked into.[7]

Here too, consciousness militates against success. The exactitude of mirroring required has, it appears, to depend on the mother's ignorance of what she is feeling and doing. She must act always without the intentionality of desire. In Lacan's pun on *le désir de la mère*, we find in addition to the child's desire of the mother not the mother's own impulse but only the child's intimation of what the mother desires, conceived as the phallus; the child wishes to be the phallus for the mother because this is what, it is said, the child 'knows' her to desire. Here again her status as a subject is never more than a secondary fiction. And coming, as does Freud's argument, from an irredeemably phallocentric theory, this succeeds only once again in turning around the mother's subjectivity into an object function that serves fathers and sons.

If the fathers and the sons think thus about mothers, what about the daughters, and the mothers themselves? There is a curious fact about the many feminist studies of the mother–child relation published in the late 1970s and early 1980s. Those which dealt with the mother–daughter pair spoke from the position of daughter; those which spoke from the position of mother were almost all written by the mothers of sons. Judith Arcana's pair of popular studies, *Our Mothers' Daughters* (1979) and *Every Mother's Son* (1983), show a typical morphology. The first, shorter by about a third, is a consciousness-raising act of reassessing the position of the feminist daughter: how are we to understand our mothers? It concludes on a note of optimism based in an upturning of the power roles: daughter will re-educate mother, teaching her 'mother–daughter sisterhood [as] the consciousness we must seek'.[8] In this it is similar to many other discussions of mother–daughter reconciliation, which begin by biting back expressions of anger and end with the offer of elder sisterhood. What precisely happens to bring this about? 'Sixty-three per cent of the women I studied,' Arcana declares, 'said that they consciously tried not to model themselves as women after their mothers' (p. 9). Individual interviews in this book (and by implication the questions that provoke them) show that the daughter–mother pair is perceived as a metonymic phenomenon: behind the resented mother is a social structure of which she herself is a victim-daughter. The tendency to read back the dyad as a chain without origin is characteristic of all these analyses. To blame the mother is so tempting that the only way it can be avoided is to cast her as unknowing once again, herself a helpless daughter, dominant only as the channel of others' control.

Arcana's second book could, no doubt, only be written after the first. Its title borrows a ready-made phrase, and has a subtitle which already delimits the woman's function: 'the role of mothers in the making of men'. Dedicated to the author's son, 'who is both the question and the answer' – so where is the place of her authorship? – it begins with a chapter called 'The Book of Daniel' and proceeds to others named 'Raising sons', 'Making men' and 'Fathers'. In the perplexity that is the woman's encounter with her beloved enemy, the boy elbows for his space and she debates how she is to give him it. The other best-known studies from the mother's place similarly come from mothers of sons – to cite only the most famous, in their very different spheres: Adrienne Rich, Jane Lazarre, Mary Kelly, Julia Kristeva. What they have to say is indeed urgent. And I confess it, I decided on this topic for a book when I discovered my second child was going to be a boy. The reason is not far to seek. There is something uncanny – for some women an anticipated triumph, for others a new crisis – about our known body reproducing itself as a gendered other. How are we to hold power over the creature that will soon hold power over us? What is it for a feminist to be fulfilling Freud's promised second-best by giving birth to the penis through her 'not-all' genital? How is she then to nurture a good man in a world that requires her to produce soldiers and pornographers? Or how to follow Winnicott's injunction to know exactly when to stop holding and start letting go lest the child be castrated? Architects of our own rejection, we can perhaps only find some mode of control over this bizarre process of loss and self-loss if we make a study of it in writing. So the mothers of sons frame and date each nappy and tooth and the mothers of daughters seem not to record, not to puzzle over, their girls' moves or their own passion for them. Is this because, as the Lacanians would argue, the arrival of the phallus here as elsewhere precipitates the accession to language – we speak with, of and after the male input? Are the daughter–mother studies gestures of separation which must precede the real debate of how to contend with and speak fitly of our once-only and brief position of power over a male? Why does the mother of the daughter not write?[9]

Chodorow's non-Kleinian object-relations theory, in *The Reproduction of Mothering* (1978), has been hugely influential over the last ten years.[10] She argues that mothers cathect male and female children differently: their relation to their daughters is characteristically pre-oedipal and narcissistic, a relation of like to like; with their sons they encounter an other to whom they respond sexually, oedipally. Mothers thus collude in the process whereby, as is so frequently argued, men become men by separating from the woman who mothers them, recognizing her as different in all the ways patriarchy sets, and aligning themselves with the father in a joke that excludes her. In this same argument, a girl separates less radically, encounters the mother as another herself, stays with her on the social margin, servicing those who more nearly have the phallus. Viewed positively, by Chodorow or Gilligan for example, this means an aptitude for alliance, a warmth and readiness to feel; viewed negatively it means failure to take off, at worst a Freudian neurosis or Lacanian psychosis.

The view that mothers cathect their sons and daughters differently is, I believe, based on the same knee-jerk reaction that thinks of a pair as having to consist of one red sock and one blue sock, as a mother requiring a son to complete her sentence, and make passive sense of her position as subject. Three books give three different reasons for it. Dinnerstein in

1976: 'the mother . . . is likely to experience a more effortless identification, a smoother communication, with a girl baby than with a boy baby. With him, there is more difference and separateness, more of a barrier to be bridged.' Luise Eichenbaum and Susie Orbach in 1983: 'built into a mother's experience with a son from the beginning of his life is the knowledge that he will become his own person in the world. She accepts the fact that he will become a man and move out into the world to create and commit himself to a family of his own. But although she expects her daughter to have a family too, she expects this to be an extension of her own family rather than a separate entity.' Rosalind Coward in 1984: 'some women have described the experience of finding their sons utterly different from the outset, a difference based just on the strangeness of the body. Baby boys have bodies which do not invite identification but rather fascination for women.'[11]

All these arguments represent something real but feel peculiarly like excuses. The separateness Dinnerstein cites is what follows, not what causes, the perception of a gendered other. Eichenbaum and Orbach get into a tangle in which the exchange of women which prescribes that, as Luce Irigaray puts it, women's genealogy is dissolved into men's,[12] is whisked away to be replaced by the loss of the son into his own family and the daughter still under your roof. The strangeness Coward cites is just the beginning of the enigma: what can we be sensing as masculine in the boy baby's body, which is just as soft (including his penis) as a girl's – as the protagonist of Verity Bargate's novel *No Mama No* discovers to her surprise?[13] In each case, the fundamental reasons for our differing reaction (if indeed we have a different reaction) are left unexplored, as if once again it were not the mother's place to have knowledge of what she does.

If we women do find it difficult to take up knowledge of our experience of motherhood, that is surely because of something at once deeply unconscious and abstract in our encounter with the question. We are of course embedded in a system which perceives maternity as a function: the mother receives, carries and gives forth to the paternal family a child stamped with its name. In this she plays a role less in a pair than in a chain. I shall try to argue that there are two genealogical chains in which the mother may function. Either she is positioned in a patrilinear structure, giving a son to her father or husband, or she functions in a matrilinear structure, offering a daughter to her mother. In the first case, the male child makes her a negative, a producer of what she is not; she is, as Freud prescribes, the temporary owner, the partial maker, of a penis which proves her sex a no-thing. In the second case she reproduces herself, finds herself confronted by an other that belies the premise of pairing by complementarity. To the woman she makes she has the crisis of seeing a self in the object position that makes her subject. It is not very surprising that this is rarely written. We have little language that can encompass this relation of otherness, for it prescribes that the grammar of pronouns must be surpassed into a naming free of the *nom du père*. Both the name of the mother and the no of the mother – that is, the mother as authority in the world or as internalized superego – have little place in the discourse of patriarchy. The power of motherhood, its dual function as knowledge and as desire, is as yet largely unwritten.

In the three central chapters of this book, I shall examine fictions written by men. The nineteenth century, a period of the major development of the European novel, sees the 'maturing' of fiction out of the hands of women with whom its earlier productions are identified into those of men who remain, in the canon, its chief progenitors. In Chapter 2 I shall look at a set of Romantic fictions in which the protagonist plays son, seeking a way into manhood by offering his confession to another man, usually internalized as frame-narrator, always also implied as the text's reader. In his own narrative, the protagonist shows how he avenges the childbed death of his mother on a woman whom he loves and kills. As I suggested in an earlier book, *Narcissus and Echo*, what is implied here is a son–mother relation in which otherness, separation, means mutual murder. However, implied behind the central deadly bond of male and female is a possible pairing of woman with woman embodied in the elder sister at whose birth the mother did not die, or the women who refuse the prescribed hostility of rivals to form a kind of alliance with another in which the man finds himself exchangeable. Between women, then, there is a partnership or chain in which the phallus may be differently passed on from the way patriarchy prescribes. (We see this possibility also in the Naomi–Ruth partnership analysed at the end of this chapter.)

In the two main chapters, I shall be looking at seven novels which stand at the apex of realism, where the author uses the spirit-of-the-story voice of an omniscient narrator, is God/father to his text, and where he typically writes a tale of transgression, the novel of adultery. Here we find the woman functioning as one of two possible kinds of mother. In the first set of cases, she is a mother of sons. Desired by the hero, she has a husband presented after the model of cuckolds as despicable, laughable, no serious rival for desire. But her son is more precisely a threat. When the author chooses to oppose a real barrier to desire, he makes the son fall ill, the mother succumb to pangs of guilt, the paternal God appear as proscriber of illegitimate love. The woman is thus replaced in the chain from which the young man's desire might have seemed to emancipate her, and she becomes once again the mother who cannot know her own desire. Even if the hero 'overcomes' her love of the son, it is by reinstating her in the maternal position as the central, non-functioning link in a patriarchal genealogy. By only a small adjustment, the homosocial bond is kept intact.[14]

There is a second version of motherhood in the novel of adultery. Women who have children in fiction are a small enough group, commonly becoming pregnant (often as the result of a super-potent wedding-night) in order that they can suffer obstetrical trauma. Women who give birth to daughters are an even smaller subgroup, and a strikingly high number of them are adulteresses. Emma Bovary has her Berthe, Hester Prynne her Pearl, and Effi and Anna their two Annies. Similarly, Chateaubriand's Atala and Gide's Alissa are the daughters of adulteresses, and their suicidal failure of desire is (the texts suggest) formed out of their mothers' male-mediated legacy. And other fictional mothers of daughters are also transgressors: Thérèse Desqueyroux, Nadja, Germinie Lacerteux, even (though the reason for that is more diffuse) the lost heroine of *Le Grand Meaulnes*. This phenomenon is common enough in male-authored texts to warrant an explanation. There is something, it appears, in the women perceived as desiring which deserves punishment. They have disqualified themselves from the uniquely gratifying form of motherhood that Freud identifies in the birth of a son. More surely chastised than the mothers who grieve over their sick sons and recognize God's right-minded displeasure in the threat to their primary pairing, these women are ajudged fit only for the disappointment of reproducing themselves. Emma Bovary's horror at her labour issuing only in the production of a female child is well known. Anna Karenina is condemned to love her son by Karenin and hate the love-child she gets from Vronsky. But where the negativity of this structure is more anxiously explored, something more emerges. A bond among women, incarcerated or condemned, survives to suggest an alternative ideal beyond repetition.

All these fictions are men's readings of the mother–child couple. They present two possible structures: the woman transferred from one paternal chain to another, or the woman marginalized into a cellular space in which the paternal is in abeyance, a matrilinear chain held up as negative utopia, harem, *gynaeceum*, prison.

The rites and taboos of primitive patriarchy (which will be examined in Chapter 5) are little different in motive from the highest capitalist exchange of women: in both systems, a chain must be maintained in which the female is the link between males, a non-functioning moment in the oedipal development of boys to men. In Harold Bloom's waste land of reading, poetry is begot by a just war between fathers and sons, strength passed on by the resolute refusal to inherit meaning; these texts have no mothers and no sisters.

The literary canon is formed on this model of male parthenogenesis. Women's texts enter and are interred. It is not fortuitous that adultery formed the central subject of men's writing in the nineteenth century. In the era of the *embourgeoisement* of the tragic, to desire another man's wife makes you a troubadour of the everyday. It also allowed for the true test of realism, the act of Tiresias that makes the author claim the desire of the woman as if it were his own. 'Madame Bovary, c'est moi' is, if anachronistically, one answer to Freud's negatively rhetorical 'Was will das Weib?' Giving voice, or taking it away? We shall look later at what goes on in the Flaubertian technique of *style indirect libre*.

In the fictitious mothers of sons we see one wishful version, her love is his one way or the other, directly or indirectly she welcomes him to her bosom. In the mothers of daughters we shall see a less avowed wish: to see in what occult manner she loves the child more exactly of her flesh, in whom no mark of the husband remains, the scarlet letter that shows up and shares the unique 'wound' that makes her mother. It will remain for the final chapter to analyse what these wishes may mean, for women, children and men.

The adulteress is the woman who, by placing desire where maternity belongs, in her 'inside body', incarnates a scandal to both fathers and sons; that is the scandal of their own, never autonomous desire and its relation to a never quite subordinated other. I began this Introduction with the question of the impossibility in writing of the mother's know-ledge or desire; before going on to examine detailed examples of patrilinear and matrilinear adulteresses, I want to conclude the Introduction with a comparison of two quasi-mythical mothers from that most male-authored of all texts, the Hebrew Bible. The mothers in the Bible appear there of course because they give birth to men: the repeated topos of annuncia-tion to a woman apparently beyond child-bearing age culminates each time in the reward of the birth of a son. But within this circumscription, we can compare two very different versions of the myth of ideal mother-hood, the patrilinear Sarah and the matrilinear Naomi.

In a study of mothers in the Hebrew Bible, Esther Fuchs takes from Robert Alter the following topos of the biblical annunciation type-scene: it 'consists of three major thematic components: the initial barrenness of the wife, a divine promise of future conception, and the birth of a son'.[15] She goes on to discuss the developing variants in the stories of Sarah, Rebecca, Rachel, Hannah and the Shunamite woman. In each narrative, the autonomy of the woman is increasingly recognized and portrayed, although all the women continue to be presented as wives those desire is consonant with the continuance of the male lineage and whose satisfaction is at one with their role as essential link. The only hint, perhaps, of the quirkiness of biblical genealogy is in God's repeated preference of younger sons over older, a preference both Rebecca and Rachel anticipate. For these two women, as for Hannah and the Shunamite, the husbands (like the priest and prophet Eli and Elisha) play the role almost of cuckold, well fooled by a more perspicacious woman and a God she comes to address directly. But I am not aware that the figure of Naomi has been discussed as a late and matrilinear version of this topos. In the comparison I wish to make, the story of Naomi's progress from aged barrenness to the nurturing of a baby not even related to her is a matrilinear process that depends on the voluntary alliance of women.[16]

First, Sarah. The death of Sarah follows immediately after the narrative of the binding of Isaac. Rabbis have interpreted this juxtaposition as an indication of how deeply wounded she is by the willingness of her husband to sacrifice the son of their old age. Male poets have written of 'the mother's weeping' that 'lives for ever' long after 'the slaughtered one is forgotten, the slaughterer too.'[17] In their eyes, typically of the mother of the patrilinear bond, she holds the maternal role to be her whole existence; its near-transgression must cause her death. But we could look somewhat differently at the timing and significance of Sarah's death.

Abram the founder of Judaism is promised that his seed will become a great nation as numberless as the stars, but he is eighty-five and his wife Sarai ten years younger and they have no children. Sarai then decides to offer her handmaid Hagar to Abram as a surrogate mother: 'go to my maid; perhaps I will get children through her' (Genesis 16:2).[18] When Hagar conceives, she despises her mistress and Abram allows Sarai to send her away into the desert. Found wandering by a fountain, she is consoled by an angel who tells her that her son will be a misanthrope but father to another great nation; she returns and gives birth to Ishmael.

In this first phase we see Sarai's attempt to fulfil her wifely role indirectly founder on the perennial risk of surrogacy: the barren woman displaced by another in the significant chain. But thirteen years later God changes their names to Abraham and Sarah and promises that she will indeed bear a son. At the first announcement, Abraham laughs to himself; at the second (by divine messengers) Sarah, overhearing, laughs to herself. She is well past the menopause, her husband is almost a hundred: 'now that I have passed the age of child-bearing, could I have such pleasure, with my husband an old man too?' (Genesis 18:12). God's response to Abraham's laughter is to prescribe the name Isaac ('Yitzhak: he shall laugh') for the child; his response to Sarah's is to chide her for thinking anything – from hearing laughter in the heart to inducing conception in a woman of ninety – is beyond his powers.

Thus the woman's moment of irreverence is stifled in the gratifying production of the son who will breed multitudes. The first of the matriarchs, she earns her place as the mother of the nation as it were replacing Eve the sinner. Her name means princess, sovereign. Almost an equal to Abraham – who twice saves his own life at the risk of her virtue by the quasi-incestuous expedient of pretending she is his sister – she takes her place on the first throne of legitimate motherhood. For a second time we see her cut herself off from other women by casting out Hagar and Ishmael so that Isaac should not have to share his inheritance. Against Abraham's wishes, but approved by God who repeats that the lineage must go down through Sarah's son, she insists on their departure, aligning herself exclusively within the triadic male chain. It is soon after this that God sends to tempt Abraham and demands that he sacrifice his only and beloved son.

The love-test is made between men. With good reason commentators have called this a version of the Oedipus complex. As Ruth Kartun-Blum has shown, almost all male Israeli poets of recent years (and no female ones) have written a version of the binding of Isaac, so urgently and elliptically does it restate the conflict and tension between father and son.[19] The father takes his obedient boy (whose age may be over thirty, if we judge by Sarah's age at her death) up the mountain with the knife and the kindling but no lamb. Both son and father dazzle by their appalling submissiveness; jointly accepting that 'God will see to it that he has a lamb for the burnt offering . . . they [go on] the two of them together' (Genesis 22:8). What few of the poets point out, taking here the viewpoint of the heartlessly sublime patriarch, there that of the innocent, benighted son – to whom some donate a rebellious streak as the poetry gets younger – is what really makes this scene oedipal. The inner struggle of each man and the more violently suppressed mutual murder of their conflict are both swallowed up by the repeated unity of their agreement upon the gesture of sacrifice to their greater maker, the Lord. Thus in the structure, parricide is replaced by filicide all down the line. They deserve the reward of the ram caught patiently in a thicket, a fit victim for the common motion of partnership they have willingly offered the deity. The final blessing and multiplication of the patrilineage follows immediately upon the burning of the ram.

In the next chapter Sarah dies in Kiryat-arba (the city of the four) and Abraham mourns and buries her. Touchingly, it is said, she cannot outlive the shock of realizing her husband almost murdered their child: this is understood as the poignantly human reaction to the excessive sublimity shared by the men in whom no movement of rebellion to divine ordinance is perceived. Thus male readers find her death apt and moving, while women may feel her utter subordination to the patrilinear chain as somehow distasteful. But I think there is something else to find in Sarah's death. The binding kills not so much the son as the mother, not because the son almost died but because he did not die. In unbinding Isaac and offering up the ram in his place, Abraham gives life to his son a second and more important time. Exactly as in the Oedipus, where the boy dances gracefully into his father's embrace on the joint understanding that, after all, in all that matters the male lineage reproduces itself without significant intervention of the woman (for her desire is not what really counts, since the mutual murder of father and son is more surely productive than the lonely labour of the mother), here their triumph makes her entirely redundant. The princess is not on the throne after all, her beauty offered up to Pharaoh and Abimelech as a sibling exchange to keep the men from each other's throats, her body required to start the generations, but not needed once the four – God, father, son and male animal – have come together to exclude her.

The story of Naomi appears much more tangentially in the biblical text, in the final section, the Writings. It is usually read as the triumphant tale of Ruth's motherhood as a reward for loyalty as much to God's people as to her beloved mother-in-law, but I want to look most closely at the fate of Naomi, from declared barrenness to what can be read as a miraculous lactation sealing an indirect fertility. Naomi is the inverse of Sarah in several ways. As opposed to Abraham who from the start is destined for plenty and fruitfulness, her husband takes his family out of their native land by reason of famine. Wife and mother of two sons, she has everything she wants until the famine brings the death of all her menfolk within ten years. Only 'the woman was left, out of her two sons and her husband' (Ruth 1:5): here the woman becomes protagonist by an almost scandalous default,[20] and the order of the bereavements stresses not only the later loss of the young men but perhaps also the greater disappointment to her to be left without hope of grandchildren.

Naomi has failed after all to do what was the source of Sarah's pride: despite her fertility she has not passed on her husband's seed as a mother should. She is alone in the foreign land of Moab and decides to return now that (precisely in the hour of her bereavement) the famine is lifted in her own country. Her two daughters-in-law follow her. She instructs them to return to their families, since widowhood releases them from the genealogy of their husbands: unlike her they have no obligation to Elimelech's line. Rather, it would be incumbent on her to produce more sons for them to marry if she could, but

> have I any more sons in my womb who could be your husbands? Go back, my daughters, go. I am too old to be with a husband. Even if I said, there is still hope for me to be with a husband at night and I gave birth to sons, would you wait for them until they grew up, would you remain widows for their sake without taking husbands? No, my daughters, I feel very bitter on your account that the Lord's hand has gone out against me. (Ruth 1:11–13)[21]

In this speech Naomi begins her move towards a matrilinear position. Left without menfolk, she stands central in a triad of women, and what she says to the two younger ones shows a lively consciousness of the obligations women bear to each other. She realizes, first of all, that she has only had them on loan: they belong not just to their people and the second husbands that may be found for them but more precisely 'each woman to her mother's house' (Ruth 1:8). She perceives her duty to compensate their widowhood with almost comic literalness, but in portraying her inability to make men for them a second time she is doing two most impressive things. Firstly she is seeing herself as their double, her motherhood provoked imaginatively by their need for motherhood; secondly what she is (extraordinarily) offering is to bear sons *to give to them*. Naomi is wishing to put Orpah and Ruth in the position of husband to her: she would secure their lineage if she could.

Naomi's doubling of the young women's needs is a nice reply to the cross-generational bonding of Abraham and Isaac: it differs by being a matter of choice or gift to women with whom she has no blood-tie, only an analogy of loss. The reproduction of sons becomes a homage to other women, another kind of surrogacy which does not involve replacement.

Both Orpah and Ruth are moved by Naomi's speech, but while Orpah reluctantly agrees to leave, 'Ruth stuck close to her' (Ruth 1:4). Ruth's famous plea of loyalty repeatedly stresses that the social and religious 'conversion' undertaken is above all personal in motive: 'do not implore me to leave you or to turn back from following you, for where you go, I shall go, and where you lodge, I shall lodge; your people are my people and your God is my God. In the place where you die, I shall die and there I shall be buried. May God do such things to me and more, for [only] death can bring a parting between me and you' (Ruth 1:16–17). While this passionate declaration has the ring of love and its final terms especially are reminiscent of what became the Christian wedding-vows, Ruth is offering Naomi not so much a kind of marriage, a complementary pair, as the tie of mother and daughter. For her sake she is replacing her 'mother's house' by migration and an unknown grave.

From this point on Naomi habitually calls Ruth 'my daughter', though the narrator is careful to stress at every opportunity her foreign origin and their in-law relationship, as if to draw attention to the voluntary nature of their attachment. Ruth is first characterized to Boaz in terms of her loyalty to Naomi and when the latter sends her to him she describes him with an ambiguous possessive: 'this man is a kinsman of ours, one of our redeemers' (Ruth 2:20).[22] The arrangement is initiated by Naomi and the levirate redemption, carefully detailed as the required negotiation by which Boaz can lay claim to Ruth, is the way for the man to '[buy] all that belonged to Elimelech, and all that belonged to Chilion and Mahlon, from the hand of Naomi' (Ruth 4:9). Thus when Boaz takes up the genealogical duty to continue the line of Elimelech, he is the link by which Naomi fulfils her promise to give Ruth a husband.

Ruth re-enters the male genealogy and is celebrated by the [male] elders as worthy to take her place alongside the matriarchs Rachel and Leah, but unlike them and Rebecca (and Sarah if we recall the claim of siblinghood made by Abraham) she is attached to her husband by no preceding blood-tie. She marries and bears a son, the ancestor of King David. The child is received by 'the women' who declare to Naomi: 'blessed be the Lord, who has not left you without a redeemer today; his name will be cried aloud in Israel. He will be a restorer of your spirits and will support you in your old age, for your daughter-in-law, who loved you, gave birth to him – she who was more good to you than seven sons' (Ruth 4:14–15). Here the female chorus (heard almost nowhere else in the Bible) mitigates the reward of a male child, though not negatively: for the pleasure of a son can be surpassed by the love of a daughter by choice. Furthermore, the gifts promised through him to Naomi are realized by another startling reversal: 'Naomi took the boy and laid him in her bosom and became his nurse' (Ruth 4:16). The terms here do not specify, but can be understood to hint at, a miracle of lactation. Naomi takes the place of mother to him, restoring a kind of fertility that replaces all she had lost. Not only does she become, in this way, a mother to Ruth's child, who bears no direct kinship to herself, but by another remarkable reversal she is also described in the formula of paternity: 'a son is born to Naomi' (Ruth 4:17).[23] Mother-hood and fatherhood come to rest in her. Genealogy becomes maternity, and the patriarchal line is replaced by a mutuality of women.[24]

Ruth is the eponym of this Book (one of the only two in the Bible named after female protagonists) but, as a variant of the annunciation topos, it is really the tale of Naomi's reversed barrenness. In the end it is rather Ruth than her mother-in-law who is the surrogate mother: she is the bearer of the child, but it is really Naomi's. The mystery of daughterly passion is embodied in acts that are both courageous and modest: Ruth's initiatives are bold but take the form of replies, obedience. We can see her original move of attachment to Naomi as being an emotional reply to the latter's offer of bearing a son for her sake. At the end she performs the ultimate courtesy: recompensing with fine exactitude the offer of Naomi, Ruth passes her motherhood to her. The first promise of exchange is answered by a choice of filiation, and on the basis of this mother–daughter bond they twice exchange a man between them – first Boaz, then his son – keeping intact the primary pairing of women across generations that marks the matrilinear contract.

Something else emerges from the comparison between Sarah and Naomi. The two figures are distinguished in addition to the differences of patrilinearity and matrilinearity by an opposition between endogamy and exogamy. When the two sexes mate, we observe, blood-kinship is a repeated adjunct, more or less pre-empting choice: like royalty, Isaac or Jacob are just lucky if they also manage to fall in love with the predestined cousin. Where this topos is missing, Abraham twice creates it by saying that Sarah is his sister, thus familiarly linking heterosexual desire (it is because Sarah is so beautiful in other men's eyes that she can be both a danger and a sop) to incest. But in the story of Naomi and Ruth, a mating of the same sex, stress is constantly laid on the foreignness of Ruth and, as a direct and implicitly essential link, the extent of her choice. Ruth acts knowingly and voluntarily in choosing Naomi, and Naomi only slightly less so in accepting Ruth. The exchange of Boaz is a like gift, a moment when the older woman offers and the younger woman takes up the masculine mysteries of the Hebrew legal system. Ostensibly the objects of exchange, they have pre-empted the structure by choice and desire. Finally, culture is crowned by nature when the infant is shared by them, one giving birth, the other nurturing so that the 'restoration of life and nourishment in old age' predicted as the boy's future gifts to Naomi are similarly pre-empted and shared. In these terms, the baby boy is almost feminized. Or rather, he resembles the Judaic

God, whose defining privileges – creation and providence – are so patently displaced from those of the female body. Both male figures are miraculous precisely in so far as they appropriate women's gifts and offer them back when women no longer have them: to the old woman the child will give life and nourishment, just as God may restore gestation and lactation.

The miracle of the annunciation, with all its variants, can be understood, as Fuchs suggests, as a sign of God's utter control and men's superiority – 'the implication is that Yahweh violates nature's rules and gives the barren woman a child because of her husband's magnanimity and despite her pettiness' (p. 121) – since those faculties that define the female remain in God's hand and are allocated only according to patrilinear needs.[25] But it could also be read as hiding another motive. Barren women are aberrations, fit objects for the intervention of a mutant God. Before the end of fertility, or in the massive majority of women, the functions here donated as a reward are simply there. Miracles distort and reroute nature: they must do so in order to illustrate the *extremis* of the principle of masculine providence, for the mythic male parthenogenesis that is the base structure of monotheistic patriarchy is a drastic compensation for the fear of expendability. The most deeply repressed fact of the whole structure (which, like all repressed facts, returns in dreams or texts to haunt us) is that women are not always or only links in the passing-on of a male line. They give birth to daughters, can love them and be loved by them, and this can be a matter not of the 'sterile narcissism' of like to like, but of choice, knowledge and desire.

2
Récits

P sychoanalysis seeks the unconscious of literature, but we know too that literature is the *'unthought'* of psycho-analysis.[1] Feminism is perhaps the unconscious of both. For both these masculine discourses are organs of control in which gender functions as the unspoken of their chief subject, sexuality. The woman reader is un-intended by a text which at best dictates its own subversion. The hysteric speaks her body and becomes herself a sign. Literature is an oedipal drama in which father and son negotiate over the absence of the woman: undesired mother, impossible daughter.

It is a long time since literary criticism used psychoanalysis in a bio-graphical bid to expose the unconscious of the historical author. If in-stead it has tended to psychoanalyse the text as the symptomatic utterance of the narrator, this is not because the ontological status of the latter is any more 'real', but because any piece of language functions as a piece of evidence. I take it that the narrator in the texts I am interested in acts as a function of the author's desire. The narrative is a motivated phantasy, but whose phantasy is a question we may and perhaps must leave unde-termined. In this chapter I shall be looking at a group of fictional texts published in France between 1731 and 1936: Prévost's *Manon Lescaut* (1731), Chateaubriand's *René* (1805), Constant's *Adolphe* (1816), Gautier's *Mademoiselle de Maupin* (1835–6), Musset's *La Confession d'un enfant du siècle* (1836), Mérimée's *Carmen* (1845), Nerval's *Sylvie* (1853), Fromentin's *Dominique* (1863), Gide's *La Porte étroite* (1909) and Bernanos's *Journal d'un curé de campagne* (1936).[2] Although historically they fall across three centuries, I want to argue that the genre they share, that of the confessional *récit*, is essentially a Romantic mode and is so because the unconscious stance it takes is that of the oedipal son.

For a man to write fiction is to take up in phantasy the position of oedipal father. Authorship is always the wish to be God, and God is no one's child. As European fiction approaches the 'manhood' of realism in the early nineteenth century it aspires more exactly (and ever more so-phisticatedly) to the final goal of monotheistic authority: the male God giving birth to himself. In Stendhal, Tolstoy and Flaubert we shall later see how the paternal control of the son-self is variously achieved: author-ship becomes a relation with the reader in which the latter (in parallel with the protagonist) is the aspirant, the child bidding to understand, to acquire the wisdom of the text, with knowledge and irony as the chief stakes of control. Compared with these texts, the *récit*, even where it post-dates them, performs a dream of immaturity. There is, in every case, an implied author (sometimes doubled in the text by the frame-narrator or editor) who knows more than the foolish protagonist: some man stands in the position of conferring or denying access to the symbolic order. But the stress is always on the doomed paradise of infancy. Authorship, it seems, insists on being represented as a gathering-up of wisdom; as Nerval's narrator, now wiser and sadder, puts it in his closing frame, 'delusions fall one after another like the rind of a fruit, and the fruit is experience.'[3] But we know better than to believe him. The wastrel ideal, as he presents it, was more worth having than sturdy friendship. More is left unfinished at the point of writing than is resolved.

The confessional *récit* is, then, a deferral of authorship. The protago-nists, even when they write, are never writers. An always more or less explicit autobiographical function makes the author's position ambivalent. Like Dominique, the author keeps a private place at the top of his house where the nasty past is caressed as misplaced guilt – in place of a mad-woman, the attic houses a foolish genius, and the attic is the text.

The *récits* I have listed display the following set of family resemblances: they are written by, of and (by implication) to men; in the protagonist's confession, he recounts the story of his failure to a paternal interlocutor and frame-narrator who serves him as double and invites him to enter the patriarchal order; his story always involves a woman, usually older than him, and she tends to die, leaving him to tell the tale. But, even in the extreme cases when he has literally murdered her, his guilt is lodged in her; *femme fatale* or over-powerful mother, she is to blame for his failure.

In nearly every one of these texts, the protagonist's mother is dead; typically she has died giving birth to him. 'I cost my mother her life when I came into the world', so René begins his confession.[4] The trau-matic moment of the childbed death is the premise from which his history proceeds: the infant hero has both murdered and been abandoned by the mother, and his consequent attitude to the mother's surrogate is a complex of resentment and guilt. The beloved functions as a substitute mother upon whom a vengeful repetition of the childbed death will be practised. But as first, incestuous substitute she is also (in *Réne* literally) his sister. Implicit in this sibling structure is a hint that the mother–daughter pair will not entail a childbed death: that, even if sometimes problematically, mother and daughter can coexist, forming a kind of couple that mother and son cannot. If the incestuous, oedipal model of sexuality is pervasively represented as a mutual murder, there seems to be imagined between women – in a way that I think is something other than voyeurism – a grouping of women in knowledge and desire that is the inverse of the deadly relationship of man and mother.

I have argued elsewhere that there is a division along gender lines of the characters in the *récit*. Whereas the male characters tend to cluster around the protagonist as doubles, father- or brother-figures who embody his fears, guilts or desires, it is required of the central female character that she serve him as his mirror. As *femme fatale*, for instance, she is used to carry and explain his misdeeds: Des Grieux or Don José invoke Manon and Carmen as the grounds of their own crimes, even down to the murder of the beloved herself. Or the passionate devotion of an Ellénore or a Brigitte is presented as reflecting a complex, agonized, interesting ambivalence on the part of their lovers. Good women fade away or run to convents in order to leave mourning, enervated men alive and articulate. What happens in all these texts is that the mirror fails to give back what the gazer wants. The woman turns out (precisely within the retrospective account of her which is meant to kill her a second time, since it is addressed to the men's world that wants him) to exceed the role assigned her, to have skills and breadths which confound containment. And one important way in which this appears is in her relations with other women.

The male characters as doubles to the protagonist are his projections, just as he himself, both as young fool and as wiser narrator, is a projection of his author's desire. The woman, mirror or failed mirror, performs a very different function. it is because she starts out as radically other that making her into the frame for a reflection is so urgent. What happens when the woman herself has an other in the text?

Female gods exist only in polytheism, but the mother is unique. In the *récit*, as in *Star Wars*, it seems at first glance as if the universe contained only one female. These narratives frequently stress that the beloved woman is both destined and at the same time curiously arbitrary: glimpsed at first as nondescript, ordinary, she is a woman whose beauty is evident to other people but not to the protagonist. The future beloved is, as Gide's Michel observes, someone he knows both 'very little' and 'too well to see her with fresh eyes . . . I had seen her grow up.'[5] In other words, she stands for the sister/mother, who is never what Swann calls one's 'type'.

Quintessential sign, the mother as love-object is both wholly arbitrary and entirely determined. And the possibility of her plurality or doubleness is often perceived as a threat.

We have seen how childcare experts and literary critics alike find it difficult to structure a double for the mother. Her offspring and her narrator have to be 'he', by a logic of opposites that does not occur to the writer on male authors or authority figures. This may derive unconsciously from the sense that a male subject logically projects his other as his phallus – had, phantasized, lost, desired – where a female subject has 'no thing' to project. Or it may again be the incapacity of the transferential imagination to attribute enough subjectivity to the woman to let her relate to an other. Whatever the reason, in both the *récit* and the novel of adultery, the question of the plurality of women is crucial and unresolved.

This is especially apparent in the *femme fatale* narratives, *Manon Lescaut* (1731) and *Carmen*. It is a premise of such stories that desire, invested in the woman and hinted to emanate dangerously from her, makes her uncanny. The fatal woman is always a kind of deity, adorable and for that reason repulsive to nature (read 'culture'), which has a horror of matriarchal religions. In looking at these texts, we shall find two versions of devil-worship: the first blonde and humbly desired by a postulant boy who speaks in the idiom of his ecclesiastical training, the second loaded with the glitzy trappings of devilry and able to assume the politics of her race and sex. But both these women are deities only so long as they stand alone.

If Manon is to be blamed for all Des Grieux's delinquencies, she must be (and this is what most scandalized contemporary readers) his divinity. Whereas the worldly frame-narrator finds her merely enigmatic – an attractive example of 'the incomprehensible nature of women'[6] – the young hero perceives her immediately on their first meeting as 'the mistress of my heart' (p. 19). A simple, clever, shy boy training for the priesthood, he becomes both cunning and articulate as soon as he lays eyes on her and attributes this miracle to her presence: 'people would not speak of love as a divinity if it did not often work prodigies' (p. 20). Abandoning his pious friend Tiberge, he runs off with Manon to Paris, 'defrauding the rights of the Church' (p. 25) in more than one sense.

For if Des Grieux is a seminarist, Manon is that staple of eroticism, the false nun. Her family are sending her to a convent, apparently to curb her wild ways. At the beginning, the abduction is mutual; it is only later

22

that mutuality becomes a problem. After an initial idyll in which their desires seem reciprocal, Manon leaves Des Grieux, having first arranged that his father and brother will take him safely home. For him, the shock of her first departure is read as a betrayal not simply because it denies their amorous twinship, but because there should be no one else perceptible on Manon's horizon if there is no one else on his.

The second time they meet, Manon's youthful beauty gives her the look of 'Love itself . . . an enchantment' (p. 44). In abandoning a promising career to run away with her, Des Grieux deifies her 'in a profane mixture of amorous and theological terms' which prove her 'too adorable for a creature' (p. 45). Throughout the text, it is to her that he attributes the 'ascendant of my destiny dragging me to my doom' (p. 20) for, as he declares more sulphurously, 'the sight of Manon would have made me fling myself from Heaven' (p. 61). In a famous scene of sophistical argument with the long-suffering Tiberge, Des Grieux demonstrates the superiority of both the pains and the rewards of passion over those of religion.

More than once, however, Des Grieux the narrator derides Manon for her seeming heartlessness with the epithet *infidèle*, which means both 'faithless' and 'infidel'. His idolatry of her is really a gilded cage in which her fidelity is to be suspended. It is not a million miles between the matriolatry that is supposed to hold her still on her pedestal and the simple old-fashioned exchange of women on which all patriarchies depend but which the 'primitive' ones display more explicitly. In one sense, the whole of *Manon Lescaut* is structured as a steady progress towards the wild side: Des Grieux begins as a theological student and ends spread naked over a makeshift grave in a prison colony. In another it merely traces the crude sexual politics of a culture that runs on internal as well as external colonialism but disguises these structures at home. Throughout the story, and especially in the act of narrating, where Des Grieux offers the death of Manon and desire to the fathers and the Church who long to receive him, Manon is the stake of exchange. She must, for the sake of society, function as the link between men, both as the dangerous lure of desire and in her required disappearance, but above all in her paradoxical culpability. In order to carry the blame, she must change from false religious to redeemed whore (exactly as Des Grieux does) and this transformation hinges on a change from seeming one alone to being one of many.

When Manon leaves Des Grieux for the rich banker B . . . , the latter has no serious role to play: the two spend his money without a second thought once they have got together again. A more real arrangement of sharing begins when Manon's brother Lescaut comes to live with the couple: in this triangle, Des Grieux plays the role of slightly wise child, and when Manon leaves him again (this time for the wealthier and more corrupt G ... M ...), it is clear that he has no kind of control over the placing of the woman. On the contrary, Lescaut and Manon play father and mother in the family economics, and perhaps the most scandalous aspect of her second 'betrayal' to Des Grieux is her energetic willingness to work to support him. In all these changing structures what is constant is the singularity of Manon as central female in a male world that both manipulates and is manipulated. For the crisis central to a million lovelorn stories about women's infidelity to men is something that, deep down, changes little: at the very moment she appears to be making a devastating choice, she is simply shifting the old structure along a bit, not undermining anything that counts.

Manon reaches her apogee at a point where the couple seem at last settled and content. In a passage inserted late, supposedly to give positive amplification to her frolicsome character, she confounds both Des Grieux and his current rival, an Italian prince. Each man in the course of this episode has a mirror held up to him by Manon, literally and non-literally, and while the prince goes away growling, Des Grieux clearly fails to register that he has been made a fool of. Manon is, as it were, knocking their two heads together – but she is still dancing in a prescribed formation. A short while after, she reverses the stakes, and this has a quite different effect.

They plan to play a trick on the son of G ... M ..., who is now pursuing Manon. Des Grieux waits for her at the theatre. But instead when he is told a 'pretty young lady' (p. 133) is waiting for him, he finds a woman with 'a pretty little face which was not hers' (p. 134). She hands over a letter from Manon signed 'your faithful lover' (p. 135), which is reproduced in *style indirect libre*, explaining that 'in order to console me for the disappointment [of not being able to see her that night], she had managed to procure me one of the prettiest girls in Paris, who would be the bearer of this letter' (p. 134).

The surrogate acts as postie but the real object of transmission is the man. The scandal of Manon's 'unfaithfulness' is surely less serious for Des Grieux than the loss of her uniqueness. That she is happy to share him with another woman implies something so shocking to his logic that he transforms it instantly into a plurality he can control. The very vocabulary of the passage – repeated use of the epithet 'jolie', as if to belittle a beauty which is *not* divine, the verb 'procure' which editors of the text immediately infer (how?) reproduces Manon's own word, since 'it is here the technical term'[7] – reinforces the sudden and total demotion of Manon from divinity to whore. Des Grieux commands the girl to 'go back to her, tell her from me that . . . I cast her off for ever and at the same time I renounce all women, who could never be as adorable as she, and who are doubtless just as cowardly and hypocritical' (p. 135). He flings himself weeping in his chair, calls the girl to him, and asks her to try and console him:

> 'Come and dry my tears, bring back some peace to my heart, come and say you love me, so that I can get used to being loved by someone other than my unfaithful one [mon infidèle]. You are pretty: perhaps I could love you in return.' That poor child, who was no more than sixteen or seventeen years old and looked rather more modest than others of her type, was extremely taken aback by such a bizarre scene. She approached me nevertheless and tried to give me a few caresses, but I flung her away at once with both hands. 'What do you want from me?' I cried, 'you are a woman, you belong to a sex I loathe and have finished with for ever. The loveliness of your face threatens me with another betrayal.' (pp. 136–7)

Now the reader's first view of Manon Lescaut (through the eyes of the frame-narrator and mediated by a woman whose ambiguous invitation has hints of the brothel) was exactly similar to the way this girl is described: situated among a group of prostitutes but in her loveliness and modest refinement standing out from them. At Des Grieux's own first meeting with her she is said to be a little younger than him (he is seventeen) but 'much more experienced' (p. 20), and he means sexually experienced, as subsequent remarks show. In both these ways we can see that the surrogate girl is presented by the narrator and the author as a double for Manon, but one who, precisely in her innocence, makes Manon a whore. Des Grieux notes with a certain rising triumph how the girl approaches, departs, starts, stops, tries dumbly to service him according to his demands. In this manipulation he is co-opting Manon's instructions. Controlling by the voice, he becomes puppet-master to a whole sex and with this gesture ensures that that sex is despicable.

Des Grieux finishes sulkily: 'Go back to M. de G . . . M . . . : he has everything he needs to be loved by beautiful women . . . As for me, I have nothing but love and constancy to offer, so women despise my miserable poverty and treat my simplicity as a plaything' (p. 137). He has won. By comparing himself to G . . . M . . . , he restores the male chain, and guarantees that the image of himself as women's thing cannot be taken seriously: the very idea that what he offers women in general is 'love and constancy' is an absurdity. He is now able to play at being their toy – in other words, to use them.

A few moments later, he goes to see Manon. Approaching her room, 'I advanced towards the door of my faithless one [mon infidèle] and, despite all my fury, I knocked with the respect one shows on entering a temple' (p. 140). But as soon as he sees her peaceably reading, he showers her with reproaches, rants and raves, succeeds in frightening her into throwing herself at his feet. Her attempts at apology and explanation go unheard. By the time Manon explains her conscious motive for sending the girl – '[she] came, I found her pretty, and as I knew that my absence would make you unhappy, I sincerely hoped that she could cheer you up for a little while; for the faithfulness I want from you is the faithfulness of the heart' (p. 147) – the radical generosity of her gesture is lost.

The potential exchange of the man among women is one way, then, in which the woman may try to emancipate herself from her hazardous position on the pedestal. But it is easy to see how the plurality it assumes can be reread by the man as a *così fan tutte*. From this point in the text, Manon becomes a simple, well-meaning girl whose utterances are always flattering. Des Grieux risks nothing by her.

If we take this earliest *récit* as a model for subsequent variants, we can see several issues emerge. The powerful woman, mother and *femme fatale*, stands alone as the negative deity on whom the patriarchal chain depends: she is at the same time indispensable and under a control that marks her as doomed. Fiction written from the son's place positions her as the exchangeable stake between himself and the fathers; her infidelities are movements along a continuum from nun to whore. What is not said is that both nuns and prostitutes are often communities of women – communities so close that (as we shall see in Chapter 5) it is not un-common for them to menstruate synchronically. In these texts the woman is separated by men's gaze or discourse from the group to which she may ally herself. Her most extreme gesture (of sharing or exchanging the man with another woman) is reinterpreted as damning her out of uniqueness into the brothel – a female space that is not so much a hive as an economic machine run on the ideology of men's excessive desire. In the other texts to be examined in this chapter we shall (abandoning chro-nology for thematic similarity) find four variants on this scheme. In *René* and *Adolphe*, blatantly oedipal stories, a radically isolated woman finds her only plurality in a posthumous fantasy of doubling. In *La Confession d'un enfant du siècle* and *Journal d'un curé de campagne*, a theme of mother–daughter bonding through prostitution turns into the figuration of sainthood. In *Dominique* and *La Porte étroite*, two sisters unite momentarily to override and exchange the man's desire. And most radically, in *Mademoiselle de Maupin* and *Sylvie*, women come together in knowledge to overturn any conception of their rivalry.

But first a brief word about the other *femme fatale* narrative, *Carmen* (1845), in which the negative valency of the woman's divinity is much more visible. Carmen is so much a gypsy that she powerfully assumes the demonology with which others brand her – but by the end of the narrative her skill at soothsaying is turned against her to support the fatality of the plot: she is made to predict, more or less to endorse, her own murder as the just deserts of her wilfulness.

Like the more overtly incestuous *Colomba*, this text is a drama of endogamy. Don José presents himself as an outsider, the frame-narrator emphasizes how blond he is under his deep tan, but if he takes up the right of life and death over Carmen that she seems to be offering him, this makes him a gypsy. In the language of the text's glossary, one name used for the gypsy people means 'the married ones'. The question of Don José's identity as white man is given over into the hands of the dark woman: if she is to carry his sins for him, he cannot survive outside her gang. In this sense – just as, to prove his manhood and win the fair-skinned Lydia, Orso must follow his demonic sister Colomba into a prescribed vendetta – Don José becomes Carmen's brother when he desires her.

But Carmen has no sisters. Like Manon, she appears in the frame-narrative individuated from a group of loose women, the *grisettes* who swim naked at dusk at Cordoba. She is dressed modestly but her eyes are black and large. When Don José first encounters her he is on guard outside a cigar factory in which, owing to the intense heat, the women strip off 'because they like to be comfortable, especially the young ones'.[8] The soldier represses his desire to enter this interesting hell until the devilish Carmen gives him the chance. A few hours later, he is called out to investigate a murder: Carmen has slashed crosses in the face of another woman who called her gypsy witch. As she raises her mantilla, a single eye gleams; he calls her 'sister', places her between two dragoons, and is quickly seduced into letting her escape. Her place as his demon is established here, down to the black gaze that survives when he stabs her, by her act of separation from the world of other women.

Her work companions are not gypsies and are violently prejudiced against them; we also never see her in companionship with any gypsy women. Other than a little girl here or an old woman there, she is always, like Princess Leia or Tiger Lily, the brains of a gang of men. The only hint of the possibility of a sisterhood appears at the end of the text. In the closing section, characteristics of gypsy culture are enumerated by the frame-narrator. The wild, shy, cunning gaze of the men fits much of what we have seen of Carmen; but she differs point by point from everything he says of the women:

> In Germany gypsy women are often very pretty; beauty is extremely rare among the *gitanas* of Spain. When very young they can pass muster as having a sort of pleasing ugliness, but once they are mothers they become repellent. The dirtiness of both sexes is incredible . . . occasionally in Andalusia a few girls who are a bit prettier than the rest take a little more care of themselves . . . there is no example of a *gitana* ever having shown an interest in a man from outside her race, etc. (p. 661)

This disquisition teaches us nothing about Carmen. On the contrary, by defining the people to whom she cleaves and making no place for her among its women, it isolates her as effectively as her two black eyes were reread as one uncanny one. If the woman has no place among her gender group, she is nowhere.

In *René* (1805), the hero is in love with his sister, but he tells the story of her guilty, suppressed and unrequited passion for him. Her isolation as the only woman in the universe is so total that when he returns from a whistle-stop world tour thinking his problems would be solved if only he could fall in love, our thoughts like his turn unavoidably to her. While incest is much more explicitly advertised in Chateaubriand's other *récit*, *Atala*, its temptation is the repressed core of *René*. The boy's mother has died giving birth to him: he was 'pulled forth [tiré] from her bosom with iron' (p. 185); his older brother is the father's favoured heir. Amélie, the sister, joins him in brief bliss in the edenic gardens of their estate; then they are cast out, and she immediately talks of joining a convent. 'She said I was the only tie that kept her in the secular world, her eyes gazing sadly upon me' (p. 191). Thus desire for the brother keeps her in the all-male family, and this desire is modelled irresistibly upon the mother–son bond culturally identified as sexual. We see little of Amélie's own bereaved daughterhood or of her assimilation into the world of the convent when she eventually joins it.

Rather than retire to a monastery which he imagines uncongenial, René goes travelling; both at his departure and on his return, Amélie seems relieved not to see him. He languishes alone, praying for 'an Eve drawn [tirée] out of myself' (p. 215). But metaphorically the birth that follows is the more conventional one of male out of female. He threatens suicide and Amélie rushes back, happy to right the mother's originary wrong by restoring his life. In ecstasy he recognizes that 'she was the only person in the world I had ever loved, all my feelings blended into her, with the sweetness of my childhood memories . . . She was almost a mother, she was something more tender' (pp. 217–18). From this point, he watches her decline, as his repression becomes her 'secret'. She finally departs to enter the nunnery, leaving behind a letter in which she accepts the 'necessary refuge' (p. 221) of the convent by the sea, and offers her brother the image of his own future:

> . . . A wife, children, would occupy your days. And what woman would not long to make you happy? The ardour of your soul, the beauty of your genius, your noble, passionate manner, that proud and tender look, all these would combine to assure you of her love and fidelity. Ah, with what bliss would she not clasp you in her arms and press you to her heart! How all her looks, all her thoughts would hang upon you to pre-empt your least trouble! She would be nothing but love, nothing but innocence before you; you would feel you had recovered [tu croirais retrouver] a sister.
> . . . At night, from within my cell, I shall hear the murmur of the sea lapping the convent walls; I will dream of those walks I took with you deep within the woods, when it was as if we could hear [nous croyions retrouver] the sound of the ocean in the shaking of the pine tree tops. Dearest companion of my childhood, shall I never see you again? Scarcely older than you, I rocked you in your cradle; often we slept side by side. Ah, if only the same grave could hold us both one day! But no: I shall sleep alone beneath the icy marble of the resting place of those girls who have never loved.
> (pp. 222–3, ellipses Chateaubriand's)

This poignant note does not just communicate a passion René fails to understand until he has penetrated into the convent and heard it confessed from the ritual of the coffin; it also enacts Amélie's struggle to separate herself from the joint role of sister/mother/wife into which their love has cast her. An edenic mutuality has become her problem alone. Thus in the letter we see her efforts to pluralize her isolation, to a point where finally she can try (without success) to see the convent cell as the restored uterus of the mother.

29

Let us reconstruct the premise of the plot. No sooner was Amélie born than the male child usurped her place and killed her mother.[9] The enclosed cell in a building surrounded by water and peopled by women could be a true refuge, but within it her imagination will re-create a time when she and he together rediscovered the murmuring womb-sounds in a forest of pines. His usurpation made her both mother and wife; but as she remembers this impassioned twinship she loses the vision and finds herself already dead and buried with no one but virgin companions. In love with an infancy the brother both stole and represents, she is and is not a 'girl who never loved'. Although the other women, she knows, will have their own sad stories, she is separated from them by the unutterable taboo of her desire, which prescribes that this was not love at all; she is cut off from 'the society of women'.

René manages to enter the convent and, during the ceremony of Amélie's vows, to bring right up to its altar his refusal of a share in the 'criminal passion' for which she must perish. Already in her letter we can see how he violates that space in effigy, draining all life from the companionship of her future. In an effort to make an alternative both for him and for herself, Amélie puts her face back on the pillow in the image of the sisterly wife. But all that appears in the frame of her face are the beauties of René and a residual affection he will not admit as desire. When he departs for America, where he ends his life among the Indians, he crosses a sea identified with the sister by both metonymy and metaphor in an epithet – 'Amélie, stormy as the ocean' (p. 239) – that gives a new light to her character. All the rest we hear of her is imparted in the letter announcing her death which precipitates René's narration: loved for her kindness and devoutness, she has died of a disease contracted when nursing her fellow nuns. Thus perhaps eventually, in her actions at least, she has joined the group of her sex.

Like many *récits*, this one is bathed in the nostalgia of a time before birth. The man's sense of Romantic displacement is familiar enough; but occasionally, as here, we get a glimpse (male-mediated, of course, by narrators and author) of what the daughter's nostalgia might be. In *Adolphe* (1816), too, the woman imagines herself as another but only after her own death. Here again we find a world peopled by men in which the storm-tossed Ellénore struggles for a legitimate place. More faithful than a wife, more demanding than a mother, she is cast always in inauthentic roles. When finally her chance comes to inherit her father's estate, to be a society beauty or to make friends in her own country, Adolphe's contempt is there to render it valueless through his control of the narrative.

Adolphe is all about the triadic relation. Bound together by something other than love, Adolphe and Ellénore torment each other in a peculiarly inseparable way; Adolphe as narrator argues that only pity keeps him from leaving her, but his pity is remarkably cruel. There is, it seems, something so compulsive and so deadly in the ties of a heterosexuality identified almost from the first night as the image of a long-shared history (in other words, the ties of infancy, incest) that the two could not survive unpaired. Yet, though Ellénore is presented as pursuing Adolphe through the whole visible world with her desire, all moves made to separate or to change their life come from her, and it is she in the end who breaks the vicious circle in the only way possible, by more or less committing suicide. All through their blighted partnership, he inserts between them the certainty that he wishes himself out of it and cannot go.

Adolphe has been raised by a shy, cold, cynical father who controls him from a distance with a long rein. Implicitly, he has known no mother; in what we can call a screen memory, a clever, much older woman friend dies, leaving him with a melancholy cast of mind. He falls in love with Ellénore when it seems time for a youthful fling, and she holds off until he has hounded her beyond bearing. But almost immediately after she has agreed to sleep with him, he declares: 'she was no longer an aim, she had become a tie.'[10] So deeply embedded in the triadic logic of the motherless child, he is both compelled into a couple and unable to sustain any dyadic encounter; a distancing mechanism always intervenes. They settle uneasily on her estate in Poland, where his father's delegate, the baron de T***, regularly exhorts him to leave Ellénore, rephrasing the triadic argument in terms of the patriarchal world of adulthood: 'all routes are open to you, literature, the army, administration; you could aspire to the most brilliant alliances, you have it in you to succeed in any direction: but remember that between you and all these kinds of success there is one insurmountable obstacle, and that obstacle is Ellénore' (p. 100). Adolphe defends her with warmth; then he goes out and walks for hours through the landscape, dreaming of an imagined sweet-natured fiancée who would blend so naturally into the paternal space. At length, Ellénore's servant finds him and takes him home.

The morning after the nocturnal walk, Ellénore sends a woman friend to reason with him on her behalf. This manoeuvre fails just as Manon's does, because it allows Adolphe to structure a triad that he can use against her. Typically confident that he can read the motives that animate Ellénore, he puts his case to the friend in a way that immediately divides and rules. The friend sees his point; Ellénore breaks with her.

Ellénore collapses and begins to die when she is sent two letters by T*** which prove Adolphe's intention to leave her. Over the next few weeks, he respects her as he only did in the days of desire, for the relationship is now mediated by her certain death. At the close of the text Ellénore's voice echoes in the only form it can be allowed, the mediate, partial form of a quoted letter. In it we find a minimal version of plurality; berating Adolphe for 'a bizarre pity . . . both furious and feeble' (p. 144), Ellénore goes on to speak of herself in the third person:

> . . . Must I die then, Adolphe? Well, you shall be satisfied; she will die, the poor creature whom you have protected but strike with redoubled blows. She will die, that importunate Ellénore whom you cannot bear to have around you, whom you regard as an obstacle, for whom there is nowhere on earth you do not find tiresome [pour qui vous ne trouvez pas sur la terre une place qui ne vous fatigue] . . . You will come to know those men for whose indifference you are grateful today; and perhaps one day, crushed by their arid hearts, you will miss this heart which was yours to do what you liked with, which lived off your affection, which would have undergone a thousand dangers to defend you and which you reward with not even a glance. (p. 145)

In this letter, the pleas of passion are less striking perhaps than the lucidity with which Ellénore diagnoses Adolphe's paranoia: for him her desire, defined as unanswerable, overfills every space. The confusing ambiguity of 'pour qui vous ne trouvez . . .' shows very exactly how in believing her the pursuer he drives her off the earth, but will find the world without her empty. Into this imagined posthumous world she places a version of herself, an embodiment of her absence, able at the same time to observe a kind of revenge and to offer him a real pity. There are echoes here of the image of the other self presented in Amélie's letter to René, but with much less ability to hope: whereas Amélie condemned only herself, Ellénore condemns Adolphe and more tellingly damns the entirely masculine world that his triadic logic has desired.

In *La Confession d'un enfant du siècle* (1836), the woman is similarly isolated. While Octave is pursuing her, Brigitte is pictured surrounded, in her pastoral idyll, by roses, animals and country girls. A retiring widow, she tends a dying peasant woman (to whom Octave takes a vulgar dislike) and lives quietly with an aunt. But as soon as she gives in to his demands and speaks her desire, she becomes desexed. Her womanhood no longer under the sign of self-sacrifice, she is presented as both less female and wholly female in a negative sense. She passes off a piece of music of her own composition as the work of the male composer Stradella, and this awakens an obsessive jealousy in Octave that is as objectless as it is violent. During the tormented phase that follows, he hounds her with questions to which he seeks no exact answer, only the proof of her feminine duplicity. The few sunny moments occur when they take long walks through the countryside, he following contentedly as she strides ahead dressed in male clothing, reflecting that 'her little velvet cap set upon her mass of blond hair made her look so much like a determined little boy that I quite forgot she was a woman.'[11]

Brigitte resembles Ellénore in the gratuitous suffering inflicted on her and in the constantly stressed purity of her own feeling. Both of them must seem to love with a sort of saintly simplicity, in order to serve as mirrors of the men's tormented, over-scrupulous guilt. The only hints of ambivalence we get in the female characters are swiftly co-opted as hysteria: Ellénore's storminess, Brigitte's fits of wildness or gloominess.[12] There must be no justification for Octave's jealousy, until the final phase of the narrative when suddenly he ceases completely to suspect her just as she begins to emit the transparent signs of being in love with someone else. But even here, and right up to the moment when Octave 'gives her away' to his rival Smith, she is prepared to sacrifice all claim on her own desire for the sake of the bad boy.

Mother and father are doubled in this story by the first faithless mistress and Octave's corrupt friend Desgenais. The latter is thirty years old, rich, bald, thoroughly steeped in debauchery but dry and skeletal: 'his entrails are like those of sterile women' (p. 109). Desgenais himself offers Octave two portraits of the desiccating effect of debauchery on mothers. In return the protagonist attacks him with an image of mother–son incest:

> Nature herself feels her divine entrails withdrawing around you . . . you have played false with your mother's laws, you are no longer the brother of nurselings . . . Every woman you embrace takes a spark of your strength without giving you any of hers; you use yourself up on phantoms; where a drop of your sweat falls there grows a sinister graveyard plant. (pp. 133–4)

But while debauchery splits mother and son, leading to sterility precisely as it feminizes, it may have a different effect on mothers and daughters. Four women appear in this section of the text, forming a chain linking the radical reversals of the first mistress and Brigitte from saint to unregenerate. Each of them is a prostitute and for each the key relationship is with the mother.

The first befriends Octave in a Paris bar. Like Manon's surrogate she is 'very young and pretty' (p. 81), with clean clothes and sparkling teeth. While devouring the supper he buys her, she regularly wipes away his streaming tears with her handkerchief. She smiles a lot, always a suspect gesture in Musset; Octave finds in her an 'impudence . . . bizarrely allied to pity' which makes him 'at once revolted and charmed' (p. 82). The girl calls him a child and offers to take him home to his mother; at this point he identifies in her face 'the fatal image of my mistress' and the incarnation of the 'sickness of the age' (p. 82). He takes her to his room and uses her (like Des Grieux) to prove his beloved a whore. When he sleeps with her it is like being 'my own statue on my tomb' (p. 86).

The second girl is Desgenais's mistress. The exchange of women is starkly illustrated when Octave praises her loveliness and devotion: she is despatched to him, 'more pale than death' (p. 106), with a note exhorting him to do the same for his friend one day. But the protagonist recognizes in this apparent potlatch not so much a gift as a lesson: Desgenais is teaching him not to love. The girl weeps and begs Octave not to let Desgenais send her back to Paris, for 'her mother was poor and she could not let that happen' (p. 107). Octave reflects to himself on the nobility of this relation: 'a sublime, divine mystery was accomplished in the entrails that conceived her. Such a creature is made at the cost of nature's most patient and vigilant maternal care.' Here the turn from a patrilinear to a matrilinear structure is particularly clear. It is the relationship to the mother, which causes but also redeems the expedient of prostitution, that exposes the corruption of men.

The third girl is described tersely as 'one girl I had' (p. 118), but her story is exemplary. Young, poor and (familiarly) 'pretty', she takes up prostitution out of envy of the women she sees parading in dresses she has sewn, but also because her mother is sick. Full of wasted sparks of talent, she is judged 'another pitiful creature formed by nature, mutilated by society', so ashen that they call her Cinderella. And here again, the mother–daughter bond completes the explanation of an impulse not fully justified by desire, envy and boredom.

The fourth woman is the ambiguous Marco, desexed not just by her name but also by the description of her as metallic, supple, reptilian. 'The sight of this beautiful animal,' Octave comments tackily, 'set another animal roaring in my entrails' (p. 121) – his, at least, are not quite sterile. All evening he stares at her and she looks back with 'her black eye'

(p. 125) and laughs. But when she reclines before him in her apartment, all desire vanishes, he becomes 'as cold as death' (p. 126). As he dreams of boyhood days in the Bois de Boulogne with his brother and tutor, she falls asleep, resembling the livid statue on a tomb. He opens a letter recounting the death of a woman; who is it? 'My mother,' yawns Marco, 'she died yesterday; aren't you coming over here?' (p. 128). No Meursault, Octave commands her back to sleep, and leaves.

In all these portraits the question of birth and death hangs over the mother–daughter bond. But the life that links them is distorted by the slow murder of a masculine culture which separates desire from love and links it to economics. The corruption of women is not so much uncanny as necessitous. Marco proves the lowest rung for Octave: by her indifference she measures the last remaining scruples in himself – the two statues on tombs complete the circle of pessimism which forms the lengthy preamble of his love story.

In Bernanos's *Journal d'un curé de campagne* (1936), we find a hero for whom an artificial paternity is the problem. He is the opposite of an *enfant du siècle* in two senses: neither the Romantic youth Musset has in mind nor the child of the secular world he has chosen to leave behind.[13] His youth, ingenuousness, ineptitude are repeatedly stressed; but he must learn to become 'father' to a community that does not wish to be loved. What is at stake in the curé's desire for a fertile adulthood is not so different as it might appear from Octave's horror of the 'dead entrails' of the corrupt Desgenais. Here too, the other is always a woman, mother or whore, and the issue is how to love her without desire or contagion.

The curé is embedded in a masculine, exclusively patrilinear world; from within it, every testing encounter is with the feminine. Wherever he looks, the hard or disturbingly mobile gaze of women confronts him – in a series of early images, the parish, the village, truth, injustice and poverty are all likened to female figures with a dangerous or significant look. Four women in particular will mark his progress towards matrilinearity, and each, again, belongs in a significant mother–daughter structure.

His superior the curé de Torcy encourages his wish to nurture, likening the Church to a perfectly mirroring mother without whom 'a people will always be a people of bastards, of foundlings' (pp. 1045–6). But the protagonist knows that children and peasants (foundlings included) are not fresh and simple at all but on the contrary 'horribly complicated' (p. 1047), and that the foster relationship can be rooted not so much in compassion as in necessity. From his own infancy he remembers the figure of a mother marked by poverty, with 'that humble, furtive air, that pathetic smile of the destitute who bring up other people's children' (p. 1056). If prostitution is one end of the spectrum of patriarchy's exploitations of womanhood, such fostering is the other. Maternity distorted by the economic relation, the misloved infants of rich people neglected by wetnurses, or the foundlings raised for money on behalf of the state: these versions of nurturance have a corollary in the separation of the biological infant from its mother. His other abiding memory is of discovering vice and suffering during the two years spent fostered with an aunt, when, hidden behind the counter of a sordid bar, he observed the barmaid – another Cinderella, 'pitiful crippled girl with ashen skin' (p. 1127) – as the butt of men's drunken lust. Being fostered is presented as a kind of abandonment to the dangers of sexuality, a disconnection with the maternal gesture he has entered the Church to reproduce.

The other image of ecclesiastical maternity presented by the curé de Torcy is an image of the Virgin Mary as incarnating the coexistence of mother and daughter. Loved by this deity, the curé could be both father and son in a matrilinear structure absolved of desire: 'the Holy Virgin . . . is our mother, of course. She is the mother of the human race, the new Eve. But she is also its daughter . . . A little girl, this Queen of the Angels! . . . The Virgin's gaze is the only truly childlike gaze . . . [She is] at the same time as our Mother through grace, Mother of all graces, the youngest daughter of humanity' (pp. 1192–4). Here the maternal gaze is identified with the look of innocence which the curé both seeks and already possesses. In his encounters with real children, however, he at first meets nothing but duplicity and malice. Hoping to find acceptance and affection from the children of his catechism class, he singles out the cleverest, Séraphita Dumouchel, for special attention. It is only after a time that he realizes her gaze comes not from goodwill but from a kind of cruelty: to amuse the other girls, she teases him with the bait of piety, then assures him it is his beautiful eyes that interest her. Her premature sexuality recalling the bar-room horror of his youth, he finds himself the victim of an uncanny he should be able to control, the bird-tamer tamed. Séraphita not only acts as one of the girls, but is protected by a mother disgusted by the priest's accusation of a coquetry of which he should know nothing. As figure of 'the impurity of children' (p. 1106), Séraphita stands (at this stage) for the dangerous knowingness of women.

Also prematurely negatively feminine is the countess's daughter Chantal. Her mother describes her as never having been a child: 'at five years old, my daughter was what you see today' (p. 1148). Chantal is characterized by an avidity for experience identified as unseemly desire: 'everything, and all at once' (pp. 1148–9), 'I want everything, good and evil. I shall know everything' (p. 1226). The unloved daughter her parents want to abandon, she has a passion for her father which emerges as jealousy of both her mother and his mistresses. The curé is sympathetic when he represents her to her parents, but to her face he responds with uncharacteristic power, commanding her to her knees with violent sternness. She is materially privileged, neither dangerous nor tempting to him as an image of womanhood; and this political righteousness governs his relations with her mother too.

Mother and daughter resemble each other in their 'wilfulness', their gestures, their mutual hostility and their utter subordination to an incestuous patrilinearity. The same blighted passion as the daughter's for the father (for these passions are destined never to requite the desire that motivates them) marks the mother's unresolved mourning for a son who died at eighteen months. The curé reads her by a kind of overweening intuition, takes control and fills what turn out to be her last hours with a sublime reconciliation with God. A prototype of the patrilinear adulteresses we shall meet later – though she has always been a 'virtuous' wife – she is replaced in the patrilinear chain between God and her lost son by a gesture that makes the curé feel at last someone's father. In addressing her as 'my daughter' he becomes 'another child' (p. 1165) to her, and it is this that allows him strangely 'to understand the meaning of paternity' (p. 1170). At this point she has no more desires; she dies content.

With Chantal, then, the curé fails to bring grace, but confronts female power without fear; with her mother he enacts a complete conversion, performing without a stammer the mediating role with which he is charged. But this structure of patrilinearity is not the solution to his needs. Intervening to reinforce the incest structure even by defusing it, he has endorsed the mother–daughter split of a privileged class. It is among the race of poor women that he must find his own place:

> I know my weakness. But experience has also taught me that I get from my mother and no doubt from many other women of my race a kind of endurance that in time becomes almost irresistible, for it [elle] does not try to be a match for suffering, it glides into it, makes suffering little by little into a habit – that is our strength. How else could one explain the passionate survival of so many poor women whose terrible patience finally exhausts the ingratitude and injustice of husbands, children, relatives – O you foster-mothers [nourricières] of the wretched! (p. 1230)

37

Here, not long before his death, the curé has come to identify himself with his mother as one of a female group, the foster-mothers whom the paternal Church can never quite match. It is in their willingness to go beyond literal maternity by reason of their own wretchedness that he sites their sanctity: family and husband cannot fulfil but also cannot deplete their capacity to give. Here the avidity identified in rich women's desire is turned outward and allowed.

In the last pages of the book, a mother–daughter pair very similar to those in *La Confession d'un enfant du siècle* marks the culmination of this stage. Before that, the curé encounters the embodiment of his superior's image of the Virgin in the unexpected person of Séraphita, who rescues and supports him when he collapses in a ditch. In his delirium she appears as 'the sublime creature whose little hands cast forth thunder, her hands full of graces' (p. 1197), a precise answer to prayer. She tends him lovingly and a few days later explains the cause of her attraction to his eyes – their sadness: 'I think if I knew the reason why you are sad I would never be bad again' (p. 1206). The good bad girl as mother redeems the precocious nymphet. Correcting an over-enthusiastic tendency to mortification, the curé recognizes the clear face of saintly simplicity.

But the ultimate model is a city girl, the mistress of ex-priest Dufréty/ Dupréty, whom he meets on the visit to Lille during which he will die. She tends him as Séraphita has done, looks almost as young as she, but is more precisely characterized as martyr/whore by her status, her environment and the sublimity of her bond with her mother. She resembles the long-suffering mistresses of realist novels by Dostoevsky or Tolstoy, reviled, dedicated, tubercular like her companion but nursing his vanity along with his body. At the end she withdraws in order to return him to the Church, a bond between men that the text seems to judge valueless and deluded beside the 'irresistible endurance' of her race of woman. Before becoming an orderly at the sanatorium where she met Dufréty, she was a kitchen-maid in a children's hospital, her lost foster-motherhood nicely marked by the move from nourishing the child to servicing the man. 'Children, you know, there's nothing like them, they're like the good Lord himself' (p. 1251). But she claims to have caught her TB not from children or men but from her mother:

> 'She was married twice, both drunks, must have been jinxed. Dad was the worst, a widower with five boys, all of them devils. She got fat, you wouldn't believe it, all her blood turned into fat. She didn't care. "There's nothing lasts like a woman," she'd say, "a woman doesn't get down till she's ready to die." She suffered with

her chest, then her shoulder, then her arm, she couldn't hardly breathe. The last evening of her life, Dad came home plastered as usual. She was trying to put the coffee pot on, it fell out of her hands. "Damn idiot I am," she goes, "run to the neighbour's, borrow another one, and get back double-quick before your Dad wakes up." When I got back, she was practically gone, one side of her face kind of black and her tongue sticking out of her mouth, it was black too. "I'm going to have to lie down," she goes, "it's no good." Dad was snoring on the bed, she didn't dare wake him, she'd gone and sat down next to the fire. "You can put the lard in the soup now," she goes on, "it's starting to boil." Then she died.'
(p. 1253)

The implacable humility of this suffering passed down from mother to daughter is recognized by the curé as gratuitous, a sublime sacrifice treated as useful resignation by the violent men it supports. In the end her 'innocent revolt' (p. 1257) is nothing of the kind. But the text stops short of the critique of patriarchy or the patrilinear Church that this implies. If the gaze presiding over the curé's death is that of his feminized childhood, he still fails to exemplify the endurance he might, as a daughter, have inherited. Sons, he hints, are always foster-children, reclaimed by God, passionately loved but not able to live.

In the next two texts, *Dominique* (1863) and *La Porte étroite*, the unity and parallels between a pair of sisters suggest a fostering relation that, for a time at least, undermines the patrilinear exchange. Published half a century later and as nearly autobiographical as texts ever are, the second text was probably somewhat influenced by the first.[14] It is in the figures of the sisters that this influence is particularly felt, both in their names and in the versions of rivalry they are made to embody.

Dominique's beloved, the older sister, is named Madeleine after the regenerate whore of the New Testament.[15] Prostitute turned saint, she perfectly embodies the repression of unseemly desire in women. But this Madeleine follows the opposite trajectory: she begins so chaste as almost to be bodiless, and ends up throwing herself at Dominique with a passion that scares him away. In the meantime, her sister Julie's desire continues unexplained, unrequited and unquenchable.

Dominique is orphaned in infancy, displays no signs of mourning, but is suddenly and violently bereaved when he has to leave his family estate for the nearby small town of Ormesson. There he lives with an aunt of whom we see little except one spring day when, aged seventeen and suddenly susceptible to the burgeoning of suburban nature, Dominique first falls prey to desire. He returns home from a fevered walk, and she looks at him. 'With the gesture of an anxious mother, she drew me into the fire of her clear, deep eyes. They disturbed [troubler] me horribly: I could not bear either their gentle appraisal or the penetration of their tenderness; I was seized suddenly by a strange confusion, which made the vague questioning of that gaze unbearable to me' (p. 88). Now this penetrating gaze confounds Dominique not just because it seems to search out his unripe desire but because it bespeaks a knowledge on the part of a woman which suggests a different and larger, more focused order of desire. It is what is maternal in her look which does not mirror his own unformed feeling that makes him faceless. Throughout this text, the danger of women is embodied (exactly as in *Carmen*) in their uncanny gaze.

Dominique met Madeleine and Julie, through his schoolfriend Olivier, some years before the scene of the suburban walk. In his first description of them, both are presented negatively:

> One was a child named Julie; the other, about a year older than us, was named Madeleine and had just left convent-school . . . her white complexion had the chill of a life lived indoors and without any emotions, her eyes were half-shut as if she had scarcely woken up. She was neither tall nor short, thin nor fat, with an undefined figure that had still to develop its form; people said she was extremely pretty, and I repeated this opinion without taking notice or believing it. (p. 79)

The arbitrary nature of the incestuous object of desire is disingenuously described here; so is the familiar figure of the nun-saint. Madeleine's purity is possible only as a kind of anaesthesia; in this she disappears in a different but no less motivated way than her sister. Both are nothing, not so much because they are undesired as because they are not yet understood as having desire.

Madeleine goes away on a trip and returns transformed: 'her whole appearance had somehow diminished in volume while acquiring a more firm, more precise character . . . This was Madeleine beautified, transformed by independence and enjoyment . . . by the exercise of all her powers' (p. 106). All these phallic terms present the young woman as adult both in desire and in knowledge: experience has, familiarly, desexed her, making Dominique the more 'girlish' of the two. At the same time (and the two changes have an ambivalent causality) she has become engaged to a man described interestingly as 'Olivier aged thirty-five' (p. 119). Dominique stares in through a lighted window at the family into which this stranger has been admitted, and reflects bitterly: 'Madeleine is lost [perdue], and I love her!' (p. 120).

Madeleine's own attitude is of course not narrated, but when she speaks to Dominique it is of her plans for him and her sister: '"I have all sorts of ambitions for her, very similar to my hopes for you," she said, with an imperceptible blush. "No one understands Julie. She is still very reserved, she has not opened up yet, but *I* know her"' (p. 126). At the wedding ceremony, a strangely prominent place is given to Julie's reactions, as if these in some sense were representative of Dominique's. He feels 'a real physical pain' (p. 127), but she is shown 'pale as a dead woman, trembling with cold and emotion'. When the vows are pronounced, she is sobbing, though she tries to hide her feelings for the sake of her sister. Now nothing is ever said to account for this passionate mourning on Julie's part. It is as if the loss of her sister's virginity causes her an agony that can have nothing to do with fear or envy. So clouded by Dominique's more exact sense of separation, it is hard to make out what troubles her, unless we reread Madeleine's declaration to Dominique that this marriage will not change their closeness as being more accurately directed at her sister. The moment of exogamy seems to break Julie's heart. Madeleine's 'ambitions' and confidence of knowing her sister's needs seem a crude naivety beside the younger girl's knowledge that childhood is now cut off. This knowledge, it seems, goes beyond desire, even though her sorrow is presented by the narrator, through the image of the single eye, as a kind of avidity:

> What a strange child she was in those days! dark, slight, nervy, with the impenetrable air of a young sphinx, and her gaze, sometimes questioning, never answering, her absorbent eye! This eye, perhaps the finest and least seductive that I have ever seen, was the most striking feature in the physiognomy of this over-sensitive [ombrageux], suffering, proud little creature. Large, wide, with long lashes that never let a single bright point show through, veiled in a dark shade of blue that gave it the indefinable colour of summer nights, this enigmatic eye dilated without light, and all the rays of life were concentrated there, never again to spring forth. (pp. 127–8)

This remarkable description carries the full sexual anxiety of Dominique's reaction to Madeleine's marriage. The image of the eye as infinitely absorbent and ungiving focuses the phallus's fear of the female genital. Dark, shadowy, like the 'little creature' for which it is metonym, it is also large, wide, striking, it dilates like a penis, it mirrors the object it threatens. At the same time, it suggests a fear of fatherhood: the rays that do not emerge are the co-opted seed, alienated by the womb into a rival child. Both Julie and Madeleine will remain childless, as will the misloved Olivier. Only Dominique, in his 'mature' marriage of renunciation, will be vouchsafed a bland parenthood.

Julie and Dominique are fixed in their passions and implicitly for the same reason, which is the reason that prevents Olivier from loving his cousin: '"I've always known her. We more or less slept in the same cradle. Some people might find this sort of brother-and-sister relationship alluring. As far as I'm concerned, the very thought of marrying someone I knew as a little doll seems as ridiculous as the idea of joining together two toys"' (pp. 237–8). As endogamy repels Olivier, it attracts Dominique, who fantasizes a sibling-tie to Madeleine that he does everything to realize, and Julie, who lives out the tragedy of the incest taboo by turning her violent passion inwards. While Dominique lays siege to Madeleine, provoking her in a cumulative attack little different from simple sadism, and while Olivier experiences towards Julie a paranoia very close to Adolphe's – '"Julie has eyes that would find me even where I am not"' (p. 232) – Julie's expedient for survival turns inwards, typically masochistic: 'her excessively touchy [ombrageux] character grew daily more angular, her face wearing more impenetrable expressions . . . she spoke less and less; her eyes, rarely questioning now so as never to have to answer, seemed to have drawn back inward the one spark of life that had been a means of contact with other minds' (pp. 234–5).

Madeleine's attempt to marry Dominique and Julie founders on their common drive towards an endogamous union, but in one sense her own motive is the same. She wants to tie Dominique into a real kinship (believing perhaps that this will tame his desire), and as for her sister: 'she took Julie in her arms, as a mother would have done, kissed her tenderly for a long time and said to her: "Let us never leave each other, my darling little sister; if only we might never leave each other!"' (p. 233). Here we find the mother–daughter bond that could override desire. In Madeleine, who takes the mother's position, it is optimistic; but in Julie, for whom her sister's marriage was a trauma similar to the childbed death, it is now impossible, for desire has split her incestuous impulses along gender lines, and she is no longer free to love.

All Madeleine's plans are punished by failure. The men, who make the choices that make the rules – and this includes Dominique's arrogation of the right to adultery – decide in the end what shall become of the sisters. Madeleine is browbeaten by degrees (very much like Ellénore and Brigitte in the early stages of their stories) into admitting first her knowledge of Dominique's desire, then her own desire, until finally she reaches the point where Dominique can exult: 'Madeleine was lost [perdue] and all I had to do now was dare' (p. 250). The epithet 'perdue' has come full circle: the unavailability of the Madonna is transformed by attrition into the availability of her namesake the fallen woman ('fille perdue'). At this point Madeleine saves her sanity by sending Dominique away, and he travels, publishes, occupies himself with unsavoured successes for two years. Then Olivier writes that Julie is very ill and he goes to join the sisters at Madeleine's country house.

Julie is now recovering, but nearly died as the result of nursing a sick peasant child. Dominique observes her sleeping, her cadaverous form deceptively filled out by a garment 'which made her look like a woman' (p. 267). Feverish and agitated, all that is left of her are her 'cavernous eyes, wider and blacker than ever, in the obscurity of whose orbs there flamed a dark inextinguishable fire'. But she is not only occupied by the passion that simultaneously feeds and destroys her. She also, like Brigitte, nurtures plants, birds and animals, and has risked her life for the sake of a local baby. The image of the childbed death appears here by the side of a sisterly solidarity that also cannot cure.

While Julie languishes, Madeleine's desire for Dominique reaches fever pitch, represented in series of images of Carmen-like ferocity, riding like the wind, whip between her teeth, laughing uncannily. One night – after which he resolves to leave – Dominique prowls to her door, sees the key waiting in the outside, but collapses with his (and her) virtue still intact. The next morning, each is as haggard and exhausted as the other. Madeleine invites him to 'come and visit our sick' (p. 274):

> We went together to the village. The child that Julie had cared for, whom she had more or less adopted, had died the evening before. Madeleine asked to be shown the cradle in which the little corpse lay; she wanted to kiss it. Afterwards, on the way home, she wept a great deal, repeating the word 'child' in a tone of acute distress that told me much about a secret sorrow that was eating away at her life, and of which I was pitilessly jealous.

Two sick children are lost to Madeleine: the child she has never had, and the sister she is unable to mother. They are lost not just because of the 'secret sorrow' which devours her but also because of the envious destructiveness of heterosexuality, which, in the thematics of this text, everywhere sets out to undermine other kinds of love. Julie and Madeleine, left alone together and both (in the end) prey to the same pain of un-requited desire, are no less isolated for all their mutual sympathy than Amélie or Ellénore. Each is childless and has failed to foster. Dominique's extraordinary admission of pitiless jealousy signals that maternity is for-bidden to the object of the incestuous adulterous passion. So is sexual consummation – for it is when Madeleine starts kissing *him* that he casts her off 'as a beast might stop biting' (p. 276) – and so in the end is sisterhood.

La Porte étroite (1909) begins with the story of a mother and son and ends with a mother and daughter. Jérôme, the protagonist, describes on the first page how after his father's death his mother always wore mourn-ing. But one day she comes downstairs with a mauve ribbon on her bonnet. Her son cries out, "'Oh mama . . . that colour doesn't suit you at all!'" (Gide, *Romans*, p. 495), and the next day the black ribbon is back in place. Here we see a pattern that will be repeated throughout the text: acutely sensitive to the nuances of female vanity with its source in the legislating gaze of men, the 'ineffectual' Jérôme has chosen precisely the reproach which will keep his mother monogamous to the absent father. From here on we shall see him keep his cousin Alissa under a similar control. So stringently will he guard her chastity on behalf of a jealous *deus absconditus* that even his own apparently passionate desire goes unrewarded. This text is riddled with the agonies of a patrilinear religion – Protestant this time, but no less watchful of women's desire – in which, taken to its logical extreme, heterosexuality must be adultery because any couple is a triangle transgressive of the exclusive monogamy of the human soul with God. Moreover, in Alissa's mind, she enters as a woman disruptively into the superior male couple of God and Jérôme. Of course it is no coincidence that Gide's own sexuality was exclusively masculine, but this is not a story of desire heterosexual or homosexual but of the failure to desire. The protagonist's undesire is projected with deadly accuracy onto a daughter haunted by an adulterous mother, and there it transmits the effect of his presiding image of two kinds of women.

For there are two mothers, Jérôme's and Alissa's/Juliette's, and it is the protagonist who, in telling the story, sets the terms of their differ-ence. His mother wears black, the girls' mother wears white or scarlet, reads poetry, carries a significant little mirror at her waist. A beautiful Creole (the staple of the forbidden exotic of female sexuality in French), she entered the family like Heathcliff, fostered, disruptive, and married a mild-mannered cousin only to leave him cuckolded. The dangerous nature of her desire is told in a florid scene where she puts her hand down the boy's shirt-front: a precise reversal of the sartorial son–mother control in the scene of the ribbon. This unusually disturbing encounter (for seduction of children in Gide is generally homosexual and anodyne) contrasts sharply with the covertness of the sexual exchange in his relation to his own mother. The dangers and avidity of desire are all attributed to this uncanny figure. Her significance is less in the offence to a husband whom she lets her lover ridicule than in the sin of corrupting minors: Jérôme is particularly shocked to see her joking with her lover while the younger children play nearby. He finds Alissa weeping in her room, and calls God to witness that he will devote his life to 'protecting this child [two years his senior] against fear, against evil, against life' (p. 504). Thus the adulterous triangle centred on her mother is redirected to keep Alissa locked inside a pact that excludes her – for what else does 'life' mean here but female desire?

Like Dominique's, this love story begins with two sisters of whom one is a child, fit only for the deceptions of innocent play, and the other is not quite visible: 'that Alissa Bucolin was pretty I was not yet capable of realizing; what drew me to her side and kept me there was a charm quite other than that of mere beauty. She looked very much like her mother, no doubt, but her gaze had such a different expression that I did not discover this resemblance until later' (p. 501). Her striking features are two: 'the already almost sorrowful expression of her smile and the line of her eyebrows, set so extraordinarily high above her eyes, raised in a great circle . . . They gave her gaze, her whole being, a questioning look that was both anxious and trustful – yes, a look of passionate questioning. Everything about her was enquiry and expectancy [attente].'

We never find out when Jérôme first observes Alissa's resemblance to her mother. Both she and her father identify a much stronger similarity to Jérôme's mother, which no doubt presents him with a more worrying threat that it is convenient to cast off. But her look of expectancy is indeed significant. Like Julie's it suggests a readiness for dialogue which cannot be allowed. The protagonist immediately cuts off the questions: at the moment of his (not her) discovery of adultery he closes the dialogue by co-opting the subject position: 'this questioning took possession of me, became my life.' The term 'attente' is a key one in Gide's thematology of *disponibilité*, but only for young men: like her mother or the female characters of *Les Faux-monnayeurs*, Alissa's expectations must end in some trauma of sexuality, for her not fecundity but a sterile death.

Juliette is more attractive than her sister, but this is because (and in this she is the exact reverse of Julie) her 'joy and health' (p. 502) are all external, excessively visible. Throughout their relationship, Jérôme is insensitive to Juliette's talents as well as her desires. Placed both as mediator and as the subject of a mediate love, she enables an indirect communication between the lovers on which she can only feed with vicarious patience. In one sense the matrilinear triangle here initiated runs as a parallel to the 'deeper' one in which Alissa is the stake between Jérôme and God, masking it for the benefit of the conscious minds of all concerned (including the reader and probably the author); but it is also, in its failure, importantly symptomatic of the sisterly bonding the young man disrupts. It is to Juliette that Jérôme admits in a key scene that he has no urgent wish to marry Alissa or even to become engaged, for reasons very similar to Adolphe's: choosing one option for adulthood would narrow down his life. While he indulges in naive rhetoric, hoping Alissa may overhear, dramatic irony permits the two sisters to read the truth of each other's feelings across the garden hedge: Juliette realizes he will be the cause of her sister's suffering, Alissa recognizes her sister's desire in her envy of a honeymoon voyage which would be both expansion and consummation. While Jérôme keeps the narrative, we can only glimpse what ties the sisters to each other. Alissa's wish to marry her sister to her cousin is not simply a futile gesture of self-sacrifice born of her guilt at being preferred; it is also the attempt to evade a fate she knows Juliette could more fruitfully bear. Juliette's greater knowledge of the impending tragedy to them all is exemplified in her subversion of Alissa's self-sacrifice:

> 'Has Alissa spoken to you?' she asked me at once.
> 'Only a couple of words; I got in very late.'
> 'You know she wants me to marry before her?'
> 'Yes.'
> She gazed at me fixedly.
> 'And do you know whom she wants me to marry?'
> I did not reply.
> 'You!' she cried out.
> 'But that's madness!'
> 'Yes, isn't it!' Her voice was filled with a mixed triumph and despair. She got up, or rather flung herself back . . .
> 'Now I know what I have to do,' she added confusedly, then opened the garden door and shut it with a bang behind her. (p. 536, ellipses Gide's)

She accepts the offer of marriage from Teissières, the vulgar merchant whose repulsiveness is matched by his good nature. After she collapses, she is carried upstairs by Teissières, her aunt, Abel holding her head and Alissa 'holding her sister's feet and kissing them tenderly' (p. 540). But it seems to be Alissa's influence that Juliette most fears, for throughout her illness 'she kept an obstinate silence before her sister that nothing could overcome' (p. 542). The wedding is speedily celebrated and it is Juliette and Jérôme (though not together) who write from their travels while Alissa stays at home.

Juliette's marriage becomes a model for the sacrifices Alissa will later undertake in the name of sanctity: she gives up music and literature exactly as Alissa will later abandon the life of the intellect. But where Alissa makes herself increasingly isolated and narrow, chasing her reading and her writing into regions where Jérôme may not have preceded her, Juliette chooses expansion, pursuing her husband's interests, having babies. Where Juliette was once her sister's double, both in her desire and in her other interests, the split neither wished for has now been effected by Jérôme. At no point (even in the irony) is anything blamed but his stupidity and a passive position as their mutual beloved. But the two sisters are placed very precisely on the tracks provided for them by his caricatural images of the two mothers at the start: the one adored but saintly, the other loveless but fertile. Juliette's tragedy is turned into comedy; Alissa ends up withdrawing from her family to die in Paris in the anonymity of a nursing home. Her diary, everywhere couched in the second person of a last appeal to God, ends in the blank recognition that she is entirely alone.

Her sister's first child is a girl. Alissa is aptly made her godmother. As time goes by, she develops another fantasy of parenthood: '*for a long time now I have had a dream: he married, I the godmother of his first daughter, a little Alissa, to whom I would give [my amethyst cross] . . . Why have I never dared speak of this to him?*' (p. 592). When she finally does express the wish, it has become a posthumous one: the child will wear the cross '"in memory of me"' (p. 577). But the fantasy will only be fulfilled through the mediation of her sister's motherhood.

Alissa's death is announced in a letter from Juliette, in which she also sends Jérôme Alissa's diary, partially reproduced in the text. This journal is haunted by the intrusive image of the beloved, but it opens with the relation of the sisters. Alissa is disturbed to find herself ambivalent towards Juliette's success: '*I find myself feeling hurt to see this happiness, which I longed for so much, to the extent of offering to sacrifice my own happiness to it, achieved without trouble and so different from what she and I imagined together. How complicated this all is! . . . I seem to sense a horrible revival of selfishness which is offended that . . . she did not need my sacrifice in order*

to be happy' (p. 582). Her disappointment is not only, as she believes, a
scandalous wish for control but also a regret for the shared aspirations
and mutual concern that have been destroyed. In part it is the image of
her sister's satisfaction (and the wish not to locate blame where, it seems,
none can be suspected) that makes her, like Julie, choose to punish an
abused desire on her own body.

In the closing scene of the narrative, Jérôme visits Juliette ten years
after Alissa's death. She is now the exact image of her aunt, fussily intro-
ducing him to her sons, and showing him into a room she has preserved
as a shrine to Alissa. A year earlier she risked a painful pregnancy to give
birth to a sixth baby,[16] a little girl named after her sister and whom she
loves more than the rest; Jérôme agrees to be the child's godfather.
Juliette offers him a reason for his decision to remain single – '"If I
understand you right, you want to stay faithful to the memory of Alissa"'
(p. 596) – which he declines: '"perhaps I really want to be faithful to the
image she had of me."' The book ends on a couple haunted not only by
the dead Alissa but by all the failures of knowledge in Jérôme that have
come between them, Jérôme's refusal of any substitute reviving Juliette's
regrets both for herself and her sister. Through the darkness he sees her
face as a sort of ghost of herself and her sister at once: 'in all the furniture
Juliette had collected together here I saw Alissa's room once again. She
raised her face to me now, though in the darkness I could not make out
the features and could not see if her eyes were open or closed. She
looked very beautiful' (pp. 597–8). The domestic interior contains not
just the loss of love but also the failure of all Alissa's sacrificial choices:
the mother–daughter bond that gives the man a meagre godfatherhood
is no substitute for a doubling of sisters.

My last version of female bonding in the *récit* appears in *Sylvie* (1853)
and *Mademoiselle de Maupin*. I shall look at them in reverse chronologi-
cal order because the earlier text offers a fuller and more radical challenge
to the whole assumption of the Romantic confessional mode, finding in
and between women a sort of androgyny from which the man is excluded. In both these texts, a man's attempt to assign women to pairs
he may control turns against him as the women exceed his knowledge of
them.

There are three women in *Sylvie*, each presented as his other by the
retrospective protagonist: Aurélie the Paris actress, whom he gazes at
from the stalls, fixing her as unknown object of desire; Adrienne, now a
nun, who once kissed him when they were children; and the eponymous

Sylvie, a village girl, his image of 'sweet reality' (p. 624), who floors him by developing into a woman capable of speaking and reading. His project is to make pairs amongst the three, the uncanny pair of doubling and the reasonable pair of rivalry. In both attempts he is, in the end, defeated.

Parallels between the actress and the nun follow the familiar lines of their polarity to an uncanny image by which he declares himself haunted. What he is haunted by (like Jérôme and all the protagonists we have seen) is the reflected image of himself which this doubling allows; it scares and seduces him, offering the *femme fatale* effect of a kind of matriolatry. Both are seen singing, spotlighted, yet he is not simply the member of an audience. Of the actress, he notes in the opening line: '[in the theatre] I *appeared nightly* at the *front of the house* in the full *costume* of the *suitor*' (p. 589, my italics); all the terms I have marked suggest that he is the performer, she his viewer. In an image of prenatal symbiosis, he declares: 'I felt myself living in her and she lived for me alone' (p. 590). But the idealist has a keen sense of what money might buy: when he discovers he has come into a fortune, his first thought (rapidly dismissed) is that 'my beloved . . . was mine if I wanted' (p. 593).

Through a flash of involuntary memory, in which he recalls the encounter with aristocratic Adrienne, singing in her 'penetrating voice' (p. 595) in a circle of village girls, he realizes with a shock that his love for the actress is based on their physical similarity. But this opens up the uncanny: 'to love a nun in the form of an actress! . . . and what if they were the same person! – That way lies madness, a fatal pursuit of the unknown that flees like a will-o'-the-wisp across the rushes of a stagnant lake . . . Let's take a foothold again in the real' (p. 597, ellipses Nerval's). What is perhaps most dangerous in the uncanny pair is the implied pursuit of an original: hidden beyond the impossibility of origination in the love-object, each casting towards the other, is an absent mother desired as a deity. The protagonist turns away from this image to that of 'Sylvie, whom I loved so much . . . She exists, of course, good and pure of heart . . . she will still be waiting for me . . . Who would have married her? she is so poor!' (last ellipses Nerval's). The infinitely conserved Sylvie was one of that circle of peasant girls: simple, dark, humble, 'real', she is the reverse of the woman cloistered by class, wept when he preferred Adrienne, waits in Loisy till he shall choose to return.

If each pair functions to exclude and isolate a third woman, they also both work, we can see, on a similar basis of control. It is essential to his structure of the exchange of women that the two kinds of pairing – the uncanny and the canny – are perceived as exclusive; thus he can move both mentally and in the trajectories of plot from one option to the other. In each structure he decides what makes similarity and what makes difference, how the third is kept out and how the very parallel will divide the two. Like a juggler, he keeps his three objects in the air. Yet the images of theatre in his portrayal of Adrienne and the terms of deification in his description of Aurélie collapse into a common fixing of the woman available at a proper distance to the masculine gaze. And between the actress and the peasant the common means of policing is financial necessity. In the course of his adventure in memory, he comes to encounter in each woman the subject reality he fears.

He arrives at Loisy as the annual fête is ending at dawn and finds Sylvie dancing with a curly-haired youth. As they walk home together, she tells him she resigned herself to his abandonment, but adds:

> 'You told me once about *La Nouvelle Héloïse*, I have read it now; I got a shock when I saw the first line: "Any young girl who reads this book is damned [perdue]." But still I read on, trusting to my reason . . . in my mind you were Saint-Preux and I saw myself in Julie. Oh, why didn't you come back then! But they say you were in Italy. The girls there are much prettier than me, I'm sure!' 'There are none with your look and your pure features, Sylvie. You are a nymph of ancient times who[17] does not know herself.' (pp. 610–11)

We shall see more in the next chapter of the hazards of women's reading. Sylvie, however, has risked the condemnation of being 'perdue', by having confidence in her reason. The flattering fix by which she is made mythic and denied subjectivity is becoming less seductive. The next day he discovers further changes. Asked to sing a folk-song, she begins a tune from opera, and worst of all, 'she was *phrasing*!' (p. 617). Then he attempts to explain himself to her: 'I tried to talk of what was in my heart but, I don't know why, all I could find were common expressions, or even suddenly some pompous phrase from a novel – which Sylvie might have read!' This is surely the key moment in his education. Her knowledge trespassing on his space, he finds himself exposed as derivative, cheap. A moment later, he mentions Adrienne, as if to right the threatened structure: '"Oh you really are dreadful with your nun . . . Well . . . well, it all ended badly"' (p. 618, ellipses Nerval's) is all Sylvie will say.

The curly-haired rival for Sylvie's affections (whom she later marries) turns out to be the protagonist's 'milk-brother', the son of his wetnurse. A kind of twin, this double focuses rivalry with a special significance. For if the natural child creates the milk, the rich child would often be given more; some wetnurses even starved their own baby to death, mistakenly believing there would only be enough milk for one. The denaturing of maternity, a kind of prostitution over the freest of nourishment, is shadowed by the refusal of the rich child's own mother, who casts him out to be fostered. The characters amuse themselves remembering how the protagonist nearly drowned when his milk-brother assured him he could get across the river: culprit and saviour, he then rescued him from the water, as if in imitation of the double ambivalence of their relation to the mother. Thus as object of desire, Sylvie embodies a failure of motherhood and an original bereavement that has shaped the young man's fear of the female body.

Returning to Paris, the protagonist travels for a while and then meets and seduces the actress. But when he reveals to her his fantasy of doubling, she exposes its narcissistic motive: '"You do not love me! You expect me to tell you that the actress is the same as the nun; you are trying to create a drama, and the ending won't work. Go away, I don't believe you any more!"' Here then, for the second time, the difference and the literacy of the woman breaks down the pairings he has designed. Both Sylvie and Aurélie are 'too real'.

In the closing chapter of the text, the protagonist looks back as narrator to a past foolishness at which he can smile in a certain ignorance. He appeals to the like-minded reader for indulgence: 'I have tried to set down [my illusions] in no particular order, but many hearts will understand me. Delusions fall one after the other like the rind of a fruit, and the fruit is experience' (p. 624). But he has learned less than he thinks. Visiting Sylvie in Loisy, where she is married, cheerful and the mother of two children, he still invokes the 'unique star that shimmered for me with a double brightness [éclat] . . . It was Adrienne or Sylvie, the two halves of a single love. One was the sublime ideal, the other sweet reality.' The text ends:

> I forgot to mention that the day Aurélie's troupe put on a perform-
> ance at Dammartin, I took Sylvie to the play and asked her if she
> did not think the actress looked like somebody she knew. 'Who on
> earth do you mean?' 'Do you remember Adrienne?'
>   She gave a great burst [éclat] of laughter, adding: 'What a ridicu-
> lous idea!' Then, as if to reproach herself, she went on with a sigh:
> 'Poor Adrienne! She died at the Convent of Saint-S . . ., in 1832.'
> (pp. 625–6)

The 'éclat' of laughter destroys that of the star. In one gesture, Sylvie collapses both pairings: refusing to admit the resemblance between actress and nun, she also casts off the prescribed rivalry. In her sigh of sympathy for the dead Adrienne, she aligns herself with her in friendship. What happened to her? Sylvie's earlier reply shows that she knows how it 'ended badly', but the secret remains between the women. Even the date at the close, with its appearance of precision, tells us nothing, since it is the only date given in the text; thus the alliance between the narrator and his implied male reader is broken. What the men know, they do not know together, while the women form couples that cannot be policed.

Mademoiselle de Maupin (1835–6) is all about the uncertainty of gender. Both the protagonist and the eponymous woman aspire to exceed the boundaries of their sex. But she succeeds where he fails, and by loving the woman whom he misunderstands. The difference between them lies in their attitude towards knowledge: where all her actions are motivated by her desire to know, he flounders towards ignorance.

D'Albert has a clear idea of the woman he will love long before he has met her, down to her age, the colour of her eyes and the dress she will wear. In the meantime he languishes in a state of objectless passion, 'an undefined urge . . . a feverish irritation . . . I desire nothing, for I desire everything . . . I am waiting – for what? I do not know, but I am waiting . . . Nothing comes.'[18] In his fevered passivity, he seems in the position of a woman, not pursuing but hoping to magnetize. 'Is my existence trying to complete itself?' (p. 74), he wonders. But it is not simply that the desired woman is the phallus; he also has an abiding wish to become a woman himself:

> I have never wished for anything so much as to be like the seer Tiresias and meet those serpents on the mountain that cause a change of sex . . .
> At first I wanted to change into another man; then, realizing that in that state I would still be feeling things I could already predict, and not the surprise and change I wanted, I began to favour the idea of becoming a woman; that idea always came to me when I had a mistress who was not too ugly – for an ugly woman is a man to me: at the moment of pleasure I would have loved to change roles, for it is very annoying not to be aware of the effect one is having and only to be able to judge the ecstasy of the other by one's own. (p. 127)

In this fantasy of changing into his own object, d'Albert also desires to taste the *jouissance* of women. He has never experienced full pleasure because it seems something of the inside, a place he does not have, or rather a place that in him is haunted: 'as potent as it is, [pleasure] has never been able to touch me . . . my soul is the enemy-sister of my body' (p. 125); all he has known is a '*jouissance* of the skin' (p. 126).

The drama of this text is the difference between surface and depth. Beauty in Gautier's poetry always lodges on the surface and is most deliciously found in a texture that seems on the point of metamorphosis: garment and skin, marble and flesh, a colour poised between pink and white – in all these ambiguities, the transition between living and death marks desire as a kind of uncanny, a necrophilia. If d'Albert cannot imagine a beauty that is not incarnated as a woman, his narcissism can only imagine itself feminized: 'I have never asked anything of women except beauty . . . the one thing that cannot be acquired' (pp. 167–8), yet 'the only thing I have ever consistently envied is the gift of being beautiful' (p. 170). But to be desirable is to suggest a depth, an other inside which the surface aesthetic both covets and abhors. When he meets his ideal woman, he will be scandalized to find her surface is that of a man.

In a brief retrospect, he describes a childhood world of mother and sisters in which he felt an outsider: 'I do not belong to my family; I am not a branch of that noble tree but a poisonous fungus that grew [poussa] one wild and stormy night between its mossy roots' (p. 177). To this horrid primal scene he adds a vision of his gestation as a kind of murder: 'when I think that I was born of such a sweet and gentle mother, so resigned, so simple in her tastes and ways, I am amazed that I did not burst open her womb when she was carrying me' (p. 176). The childbed death is a fantasy here (for his mother is still alive and supporting him) but we can see how it shapes the split between surface and depth. Alien in a family of women, his entry and his exit are imagined as deadly.

In the meantime, he amuses himself with the brilliant Rosette, whom he has nicknamed after the pink colour of her dress. Witty, cynical, she seems to him not really a woman: 'she's a delicious companion [compagnon], a pretty comrade it's fun to sleep with, not a mistress' (p. 119). She dresses up, indulges his wildest fantasies, and he believes her totally in love: after one particularly exhausting orgy, 'she had never seemed so lovely as in that moment.[19] There was something so chaste, so maternal in her gaze' (p. 123). But he cannot 'descend into her heart' (p. 128); and this is in the end because he finds no image of himself there: 'Rosette's qualities are all in her, I have given her nothing' (p. 135). One day, staying at Rosette's château, he sees a young man arrive. He exactly resembles the object of desire; 'his only fault is that he is too beautiful . . . for a man' (p. 178).

At this point the text changes into the third person, and two chapters introduce Madeleine de Maupin, in her male disguise as 'Théodore' and in her ambivalent relations with other women. First we see her with her cross-dressed page Isnabel. Gazing at the latter, Madeleine's thoughts are as much maternal as sexual, and are reproduced in the masculine gender: 'truly I am jealous [jaloux] of your mother, I wish I were the one to have made you [t'avoir fait]' (p. 184). Though 'the master was as beautiful as a woman, the page as beautiful as a young girl' (p. 182), the narrative avoids a mother–daughter pairing: 'they seemed united by a greater affection than is usual between master and servant – could they have been two friends, or two brothers?' (p. 184). Then we witness a conversation between Madeleine and Rosette, who has long been in love with her in the guise of the handsome Théodore. To 'him', Rosette mocks the absurd d'Albert who, we discover, is serving her exactly as she serves him, as a second-best to the real passion.

Now what these two dialogues have in common, before we gain access to Madeleine's conscious motives, is to show what women say to each other when no man is present. But they are haunted by a masculinity contained in the surface – clothing, grammar – and essential to the eaves-dropping the reader is practising at the expense both of d'Albert and of the unknowing Rosette. And this conveys to the implied reader a signal that the secrecy of women is not (yet) unsafe. On the first occasion d'Albert met Rosette, at a somewhat *louche* salon, she entertained him by some trenchant gossip about all the other women. Here Madeleine uses a discourse very much like d'Albert's own, speaking the masculinity she professes, patronizing Rosette as she later will in her letters. Only finally, when they withdraw into the bedroom and are no longer overheard, does the speech between the two women become implicitly something so close as to be indistinguishable from lovemaking.

We return to d'Albert, who reluctantly voices the 'monstrous thought' (p. 218) that he finds himself in love with a man: 'what I feel for this young man is truly incredible; no woman has ever excited me so strangely' (p. 223). Théodore's presence is threatening: 'everything in me is upset and upside down; I no longer know who I am or what other people are, I don't know if I am a man or a woman, I loathe myself' (p. 220). This negative effect shapes all d'Albert's subsequent experience. For him the only solution will be a revelation of Madeleine's femaleness which will set his masculinity to rights; the realized test of the ambivalences of gender leave him split, confused and helpless.

In the figure of Madeleine de Maupin, we see the positive reverse of this. She reconstructs her motives in a letter to a woman friend: she has left home in men's clothing because, for all her efforts to know – 'I listened,

I watched' (p. 245) – her matriarchal education has left her incarcerated. Repelled by the discourse of gallantry, she wants to discover what language men speak when there are no women present. Like d'Albert, she views the home as 'a kind of vegetation, like that of mosses or plants' (p. 248), but she recognizes that it is men, not the mother, who really guard the prison. Her departure is a kind of suicide but also a project of adventure.

The friends take part in a private production of *As You Like It*. 'Théodore' appears as Rosalind, magnificently dressed as a woman. The men cheer, the women blush scarlet, Rosette turns white as a sheet and d'Albert crows with relief: 'I felt an enormous sense of well-being, as if a mountain or two [i.e. breasts?] had been lifted from my chest' (p. 294). We then return to Madeleine's story and discover how Rosette fell in love with her. The sister of a young nobleman 'Théodore' went to stay with, she tried every way to seduce her house-guest. In Madeleine this passion arouses something 'more than a woman's ordinary love for a woman' (p. 349), but so far she has evaded the exposure of the bedroom. Both Rosette and Madeleine are experiencing what in Gautier's terms is male desire: for the former it is 'innocent', for she does not know she is being turned on by a woman; for Madeleine it is a further adventure in knowledge. Though at times her voice most precisely echoes that of the men she has come to despise – 'to amuse myself a little, I found nothing better to do than pay court to my friend's sister' (p. 324) – she is moving towards an ideal state of androgyny. In a duel with Rosette's brother she proves herself as strong as any man: 'the most extraordinary thing . . . was that this wound had been opened by me, and that a girl of my age (I almost wrote, a man of my age, see how far I have entered into the spirit of my role) could have knocked a vigorous captain out cold on the floor' (p. 372). What she has not yet done is test out this strength in her own body:

> My dream would be to have both sexes by turns, in order to satisfy this double nature: today a man, tomorrow a woman, I would save for my lovers my languorous tendernesses, my submissive, devoted gestures, my most abandoned caresses, my melancholy little sighs, everything girlish, kittenish in my character; and with my mistresses, I would be enterprising, bold, passionate, with a triumphant air, my hat over one ear, and the swagger of a swashbuckler or an adventurer. Thus my whole nature would be brought forth and visible, and I should be perfectly happy, for it is true happiness to be able to develop oneself in every direction and to be all that one can be. (p. 394)

Evidence of the male author's fantasy obtrudes here: the female self is all naked languor and seduction, the male fully dressed and ready to go. But both images are focused on the sexual because 'this ignorance of the body . . . without the ignorance of the mind is the most miserable thing in the world' (p. 398). She has just a few things yet to know. D'Albert is appointed to relieve her of a burdensome virginity; as for Rosette, Madeleine sees in her the pure lover, entirely coherent in her desire: 'her soul is as fine as her body' (p. 348); she alone possesses 'the beauty of the soul' (p. 380). For by now (and we get no direct access to Rosette's thoughts) she alone knows what she wants and wants what she knows.

The final scene, back in the third person, is designed to gratify every-one. Madeleine undresses before d'Albert, he gazes his fill, then takes her to the bed. The narratee, in a brief parenthesis in which I think we can infer the real wink of man to man, becomes a woman: 'our charming reader would certainly refuse to have anything more to do with her lover if we revealed to her the formidable total that d'Albert's love reached, aided by Rosalind's curiosity' (p. 409). But however multiple, d'Albert's impressive virility is finally tired, and then Madeleine goes down to Rosette's room. At the door, the narrative stops: 'what she said there, what she did there, I have never been able to find out, though I have made the most conscientious researches' (p. 410).

Madeleine departs that night in self-possession. She leaves a letter for d'Albert closing with an exhortation to 'console poor Rosette as well as you can, for she must be at least as upset as you by my departure. Love each other in memory of me, whom you both loved, and whisper my name sometimes to each other in a kiss' (p. 416). The trace of the androgynous woman, then, is available to the man only in sex and speech with the woman she loved.

An examination of ten *récits* has revealed a variety of patterns in the woman's relations with other women. If, as I have suggested, she stands in every case for the mother, the taboos on her alliance with daughters and sisters are variously drawn. As the *femme fatale*, she is a deity more or less identified with the devil. Her attraction is always uncanny, she carries the investment of the young man's transgressions: most repressedly the impulse to incest, secondarily and more overtly, all his anti-social drives to crime, blasphemy, refusal of the masculine game. As long as she stands intact, he can play at rebellion, even invent a matriarchal religion. But she must be kept apart from other women. When Manon offers a surrogate, what she is extending is a suggestion so radical that it confounds her lover's deeper sense of propriety. The 'faithfulness of the heart' makes him exchangeable. So he types her one of a despised sex and from this moment allies himself irrevocably with the fathers who condemn her. In Carmen we find this uncanny more daringly projected, but again it is essential that she be seen as unique: if she is a woman among women, Don José will find himself a gypsy, tarred with her devilry, unable to escape. He murders her in order to evade the discourse she too exactly speaks.

Again in the texts most directly presenting incestuous desire, the woman's isolation is paradigmatic. Her desire is taboo, abhorrent but at the same time saintly: she is made to sacrifice everything to him, down to her virtue. Both Amélie and Ellénore are simultaneously devoted and 'stormy'. Their attempts to ally themselves with other women are destroyed by the disruptive image of the beloved, so that their only expedient before death is the fantasy of a posthumous doubling, the Echo that haunts.

In *La Confession d'un enfant du siècle* and *Journal d'un curé de campagne*, men are bonded by the extreme alliances of priesthood and vice. Both versions set up a chain that relies on an exchange of women whose bodies stand for their souls. Within that structure, the relations of parenthood are denatured, but the surviving, fostering couple is that of mother and daughter bound by a mutual sanctity of prostitution. In this image we find the logical conclusion of the deification of the *femme fatale* and the cloistering of the desired mother: sainthood for women is attainable only by virtue of what the patriarchy calls sin.

The alliance of sisters is strong but shortlived. The man breaks into it by his very position as object of exchange: focusing desire, he also defines its boundaries. Where Madeleine and Julie are at their most similar – in their impulse to endogamy or the power of their sexuality – they are differentiated as the desired and the undesired, their gaze equally dangerous, and abandoned to an anorexic sterility. Where Alissa and Juliette have similar aspirations, their wishes for each other are divided by Jérôme's definition of the two kinds of woman for whom they must stand. Again the one can only have what the other does not, though their solidarity, knowledge and sympathy survive in the shadow of his narcissism.

Finally, there are texts in which the women's knowledge confounds the man's efforts at control. Here alliance specifically crosses the lines of endogamy: it is by virtue of their differences that these women bond. Like Naomi and Ruth, they earn their solidarity by an exercise of choice, and the union that results is one that overrides the concept of sexuality as incest or of any 'natural' sympathy. It seems as if the strongest bonds must be those in which a structure is achieved by choice, undercutting the arrangements provided by 'nature'.

The motif of fostering has appeared in several of the texts, focusing the question of the natural. In *René* a sister becomes foster-mother to her scarcely younger brother. The accumulating crisis derives from the growing explicitness of the sexual flavour of their relationship, but not only from that. It is also clear that, just as René mortally disrupted the daughter's partnership with her mother, so he continues to exclude her from developing any maternal bond of her own, to the point where it is only in departing from the world, first to the convent then to death, that she attains any subjecthood. Both the dangers and the sublimity of fostering are repeated in other narratives. The only valid rival in *Sylvie* is a double not through similar situation but because he was the protagonist's milk-brother; though the implications of this twinship are repressed, we can infer its tensions, not least in the almost-murder by drowning that the characters recall. If the original childbed death is a premise for all these stories, we shall see in a moment how each beloved serves fatally as foster-mother to her male lover.

Several of the women have, until the lover appears or in an effort to keep his power at bay, a benign and coherent relation to people and creatures whom they nurture: Brigitte, Julie, Alissa move among animals and peasants in a way that is mutually protective. This version of fostering is a tenuous expedient, it seems; it is not allowed to replace the sexual relationship that centres the text. A more desperate version, that of the mothers and daughters who support each other by prostitution, becomes saintly as it both endures and is despised. Least justified, but equally benign, is the nurturing sympathy of a Sylvie for Adrienne or a Madeleine de Maupin for Isnabel or Rosette; these pairings are shrouded in secrecy, coloured by knowledge rather than nourishment, but hint at a similar closeness. The fostering relationship between females is presented as positive, whereas that between males is too sanctioned by law to offer a nurturing privacy: however kindly the baron de T*** or the curé de Torcy encourage their pupils, they speak for the system of what Ellénore calls the 'arid hearts'. And the foster-father relationship, presented each time as a version of 'God-fatherhood', is doomed to stand for something it does not know how to be.

The *récits* are, as I suggested before, sons' stories. But they are also, in most cases, novels of adultery. In each, literally in *Adolphe*, the woman is required to abandon her children. Madeleine and Alissa remain child-less (as of course did Gide's wife). Many of the fictional surrogates lack children that the originals had: Musset's George Sand, Constant's Madame de Staël, Fromentin's Jenny Chessé. And one meaning of the frequent recourse to the nunnery, literally or as reflected in the topos of sanctification, is to deny the women maternity. In the *femme fatale* narratives, there is no question of children; among the texts of greatest female solidarity, only Sylvie becomes a mother, and that is the sign of her emancipation from the protagonist's obsessions. In *Carmen* and *La Confession d'un enfant du siècle*, motherhood is specifically described as a disfigurement. All these themes suggest that the lover views his incestuous desire as threatened not chiefly by the rivalry of the husband – for none of the husbands or lovers or even God is the object of real hatred – but by the presence of other children. Dominique's 'pitiless jealousy' is merely the most explicit expression of this attitude.

I have argued elsewhere that the key transferential motive of aggression in these texts is directed not against the father but against the mother. No duels are fought, even in the head; on the contrary, once the woman is disposed of, the young man is a perfectly submissive if ineffectual son of patriarchy, never really a rebel. Or rather, what he is acting out is a separation which requires the murder of the mother as the body of desire; it is against her that he rebels. Her mossy, saintly world must be abandoned with a kind of shame, though he ends in an ignorance she refuses to relieve: in particular, he leaves behind the secret of her maternity, which he has grown up by destroying. In this view of the transference, I take issue with the analysis of 'triangular desire' proposed by René Girard and given a feminist turn by Eve Kosofsky Sedgwick.[20] Tempting as it is to see the triangle suggesting a more urgent relation to the mediator than to the object of desire, this is not precisely or always the case. To take one of Girard's own instances, I would disagree that jealous love in Proust is, as he argues, 'subordinated to . . . the presence of the rival' (p. 23). This is not to deny that Proustian desire is mediate (as, *pace* Lacan, it surely always is), but the motive of destructive epistemophilia is very directly focused on the 'beloved' woman; indeed, as long as the rival is conceived as a man, a kind of double for the protagonist, he is, like rival husbands generally in fiction, not treated as worth much grief. It is only when the rival is a woman, a double for the beloved, and the protagonist suspects the intimacy both sexual and verbal that we have seen at the climax of *Mademoiselle de Maupin*, that jealousy becomes really effective – though it is still pointed at the love-object, now pluralized and with her desire dangerously transformed. Here, like d'Albert, Marcel discovers a new focus of the uncertainty of self which he has diagnosed in so many other ways; for if the double proves a woman, what fixity can there be for him? Nothing in their embrace evokes an effigy of himself as a man; in the rival Andrée he finds the image of a feminized self which alone could love Albertine. What I am arguing is that the gender split is essential to the dynamics of triangular desire and that, taking the texts in question where the subject is always male and the object female (which, with the oedipal model at the head, is also the case for the most fully developed analyses of jealousy in Proust), we find the couple at the base of the triangle provoking a very different kind of response when they are both women from when they are the relatively innocuous heterosexual pair.[21] This has proved itself in the analysis of the *récit* and will continue to be explored in the next chapters, in which motherhood offers a particularly interesting variant on the couple structure because in it the woman is always (momentarily at least) the initiating and stronger partner. What different things happen when her child/other is a boy or a girl?

3

Patrilinear Mothers

*I*n this chapter I shall look mainly at four novels of adultery in which the woman is the mother of sons: Stendhal's *Le Rouge et le noir* (1831), Flaubert's *L'Education sentimentale* (1869), Tolstoy's *Anna Karenina* (1873) and Maupassant's *Pierre et Jean* (1887). Three of these novels are explicitly hominocentric – that is, told from the position of a man, the lover or the son. In the fourth, *Anna Karenina*, it is a matter of discussion whether a man or a woman is the central consciousness; I shall pursue this question later, as this text will reappear among those of the next chapter.

Since the two main studies of this genre, Judith Armstrong's *The Novel of Adultery* (1976) and Tony Tanner's *Adultery in the Novel* (1979), look in detail at several texts other than those that interest me – *La Nouvelle Héloïse, Die Wahlverwandtschaften, The Golden Bowl* – I should begin by defining and justifying my choice of material. With one exception, I am concerned with novels in which the woman alone is the married partner; in all cases she is a mother. It is not essential for my purpose for 'actual' adultery to have taken place (though it usually has); adulterous desire is enough. I am also not interested in fictions which trace the permutations in a structure of four, like the two last-mentioned above. What I shall examine is the nature of the patrilinear or matrilinear chain in which the woman is placed. My study does not pretend to do the same thing as either of these useful books, the first a history of marriage and its disruption in the world and in texts, the second an analysis of the way contracts and their transgressions inform the bourgeois novel.[1] I seek instead to trace the oedipal pattern of narratives in which women are contained and the politics of the structures in which they are placed.

But we must never forget that almost all the texts I refer to in Chapters 2, 3 and 4, even where they take up the woman's viewpoint, are evidence of men's imagination. If, as I shall argue more fully later, the metonymic relation of self to double is likely to be conceived differently by men and by women, I want now to pause and speculate what exactly is happening in the relation of author to his protagonist in the texts of this chapter, which offer the topos of the vulnerable son.

Author is to protagonist as self is to double; the double in phantasy or fiction plays the role for its creator of the automaton that kills, consummates, desires for him.[2] Doubles can be disseminated as it were laterally within the text (like the various brother-figures and father-figures who supply support to Des Grieux) and we can find other kinds of doubling in the relation of older to younger self in the protagonist, or the speaking of narrator to narratee. Another mode again exists in the doubling of implied author and implied reader, and of either of these with the protagonist. The implied author is the phantom a reader conjures of the owner of the name on the cover. The name both identifies a kind of historical reality and vouches for the absence of the author. Like God, like the father whose genealogy is always disputable, he both is and is not present in this thing he claims to have made. At the same time, the implied author is a phantom in the mind of the historical author. If all we know of the historical Flaubert now is the trace of his implied author, that is because (perhaps exceptionally clearly in his highly phantasmatic case) the latter is coextensive with the wish for him to exist. The implied author is a desire in act.

I want to suggest that for a male author the desire in act is made flesh in the protagonist, and that the relation of implied author to protagonist is, in the proper mode of masculine desire, that of the imagination to the phallus. The phallus cannot be possessed – yet an effigy of it is part of his body, reliable, unreliable, vulnerable. If the protagonist as double is desire made flesh (of course he is not really flesh, but in *that world* has a body, can love and die), then it is not surprising that the ambivalences of the author to his own desire and control come forth in the text via the implied author's voice which speaks to present the protagonist to the reader.

The *récit* is in the first person, the realist novel usually in the third person. Not confession but commentary is the latter's mode. The protagonist is *subject* in both mutually contradictory senses: the acting will and body of the story, but also held in by the voice that controls. So the narrative voice – worldly in Stendhal, cold in Flaubert, kind in Tolstoy, careful in Maupassant – always stands outside and above, legislating via a kind of irony on how this young man is to be read.

All realism is both idyllic and ironic: idyllic because it proposes an impossibly coherent world in which God's name is stamped on the cover and things must begin and end; ironic because, since there must be a 'relationship between the teller and the tale, and . . . the teller and the audience', there must always also be a disparity between them.[3] Such gaps are not just the wounds which make healing possible (even the joys of deconstruction may perhaps be reduced to this idyll), not just the graceful place of aporia but, on the contrary, the site of tightest control. In each of my texts, the relationship between the implied author and the protagonist, perceptible in the voice of the narrator, is a crucial instance of the paternal will to control.[4]

Le Rouge et le noir (1831) is the story of two levels of desire.[5] Conscious desire leads Julien Sorel 'onwards and upwards' into a public world of men – he grapples with a series of fathers, climbs the ladder of ambition – and unconscious desire leads him inwards to an enclosed world of women, nurturance and finally death. Students and critics alike are shocked by the attempted murder he commits precisely when, as he puts it, 'my novel is complete',[6] and he has achieved the change of name, the status, the military uniform he coveted; and students and critics alike identify the new self revealed in prison as the 'real' Julien, tamed by insight like any tragic hero before his death. Of course the crime must appear gratuitous: like Fabrice del Dongo and Meursault after him, Julien must choose an unnecessary and unjustified execution so that the very immobilization of the prison cell can seem to reveal a 'true self' masked by the earlier *divertissement* of desire. Julien has been in a state of perpetual motion, his eye on the next goal, his head aspin with what he thinks is firm ambition; but he never quite loses this 'boyish' quality ('with death two steps away, I am still a hypocrite': p. 481) and his genius has always been identified with it: 'what made Julien a superior being was precisely what prevented him from enjoying the happiness that was right in front of his eyes' (p. 82). The attempted murder of Mme de Rênal is no more unprepared than the still-point hero: both bring out the conscious/unconscious split that allows two kinds of desire to coexist and feed off each other. I want to argue that the shooting of the maternal figure whom he discovers he uniquely loves is essential to his engagement with her. At every turn, as he aims (he thinks) with classical oedipal motive to strike out against fathers, he has been directing a murderous desire towards a woman until, at the moment Mme de Rênal writes the letter saying so, he is so shocked as to turn on her and prove her right.

The book begins and ends with mothers and sons. Of its two women, Mme de Rênal, everywhere typed as mother, finishes up divided by scandal and then death from the sons she loves; while Mathilde de La Mole, parallel and opposite to the protagonist, never his complement, is the only survivor, his severed head in her arms, his 'son' still unborn in her womb. The baby whose sex seems such a certainty ends up as the potential mode of contact between these two women, hitherto kept in such dialectically distinct spaces, but it is not given the chance. Each of them is, instead, conserved in a deadly patrilinear chain.

Introduced to the small town of Verrières as if from the air, we are shown the marks that two men, the rich peasant Sorel and the aristocratic mayor Rênal, have made on the landscape. The latter appropriately dominates: he has had Sorel's factory moved down-river so that he can build walls in his grounds. Both these men have three sons. We first see the mayor walking with his wife and children along the parapet of his best wall, the Cours de la Fidélité. 'While listening to her husband, who was speaking in a serious tone, Mme de Rênal's eye was anxiously following the movements of three little boys' (p. 9). The eldest wants to climb, but 'a gentle voice uttered the name Adolphe, and the child abandoned his ambitious enterprise. Mme de Rênal seemed a woman of about thirty years, but still fairly pretty.' Thus we are introduced (before she or we meet the protagonist) to the text's central beloved. Her authority over the first child is both gentle and so absolute as to discourage the very ambition her lover will pride himself on. A few pages later, as she is making a suggestion that will anger her husband, 'she gave a cry. The second of her sons had just climbed up on the parapet of the terrace wall and was running along it . . . For fear of startling her son and making him fall, Mme de Rênal did not say a word. At last the child, laughing with pleasure at his daring, looked at his mother and, seeing how pale she was, jumped down on the walkway and ran to her. He was well scolded' (p. 12). The second son, though bolder and less attentive, values his mother's peace of mind above his own pleasure. Of the youngest child we see nothing on this occasion. But the mayor, noting the danger, remarks that the children are beginning to get too wild and he has decided to hire Sorel's son to teach them. His motive is less paternal than it seems: his political rival Valenod has just acquired some fine new horses and needs bringing down a peg or two.

Julien Sorel is not the first stake over which Valenod and Rênal have quarrelled; some years earlier they did battle over the woman:

> She was a tall woman with a fine figure, who had been the belle of the district, as they say in these mountains. She had a certain look of simplicity and her gait was youthful; in the eyes of a Parisian, this

ingenuous grace, full of lively innocence, might have provoked
thoughts of mild sensuality, but had Mme de Rênal realized the
nature of this success, she would have been very ashamed. For
neither coquetry nor affectation had ever come near her heart. The
wealthy M. Valenod, they say, had once paid court to her but
without success, and this had lent a special prestige to her virtue;
for the tall young man with his powerful build, high colour and
thick black sideburns was one of those vulgar, pushy and noisy
creatures who are considered very handsome in the provinces.

Mme de Rênal, very timid and apparently rather unstable in tem-
perament, had been shocked above all by the continual movement
and loud voice of M. Valenod. The dislike she showed for what
Verrières people call having a good time had gained her the reputation of being vain of her high birth. That never entered her head,
but she was not sorry to see people begin to call on her less . . . As
long as she was free to wander alone in her beautiful garden, she
never complained.

A simple, modest soul, she had never thought to sit in judgement
on her husband and never admitted to herself that he bored her.
She supposed, without ever thinking it aloud, that no husband and
wife had warmer relations. She felt fond of M. de Rênal above all
when he talked to her of his plans for their children, the first
destined for the army, the second for the law, the third for the
Church. In sum, she found M. de Rênal a great deal less boring
than the other men of her acquaintance. (pp. 13–14)

Mme de Rênal is defined negatively: the sexual gaze of the Parisian
misunderstands her, her fellow townspeople misread her motives, inter-
preting as snobbish pride an attitude more rooted in extreme ingenuousness. Highborn and beautiful, she does not perceive her advantages.
When two men haggle over her she passively accedes to the less offensive,
feeling that he cannot harm her as long as she has free access to her
children and a private Eden. There are many hints, though, that this
rounded innocence lives on unselfconsciousness, that she is unawakened
for all her years and that she will be vulnerable to precisely that combination of the boyish and the restless that Julien will represent. We have
seen her heart moved by the shouts and antics not of a hairy grown man
but of her own children; but the same maleness that makes her listen
with pleasure to her husband's plans for the boys will guarantee that they
belong (or soon will) not to her but to him.

Julien himself is the youngest of three sons; his father and elder brothers, after the manner of fairytale and the family romance, are all of a piece and entirely different from him. They work, he dreams; they are illiterate, he reads; they are brutal, he delicate. From here on, he and everyone else will indulge in the fantasy that he is a foundling, a changeling, a bastard son of noble blood. But there could be another plausible reason for his distinctiveness – the mother of whom mention is never made. Like the heroes of the *récit*, he is the baby of an all-male home, the probable result and perpetrator of a childbed death.

His habitual pallor made him as an infant seem too weak to survive, but he is as determined mentally as he is feeble physically. His longing to succeed takes the form of an elective hypocrisy: to get the status of a soldier he must rise through the priesthood, a parallel but more available homosocial hierarchy. Yet a pair of images hints that his motives are otherwise: he knows what he wants to leave – 'to make his fortune meant getting out of Verrières; he detested his birthplace [patrie]' (p. 23) – but what he desires is utterly vague: 'since his earliest childhood he had had moments of intense excitement in which, in a delicious vision, he saw himself being introduced to the pretty women of Paris and attracting their attention by some celebrated action.' What he wants to leave behind is a *father*land, what he seeks is a world of women and, most strikingly, the attention we have seen Mme de Rênal bestow on her sons. The two missing pieces of the game – his mother, her youngest son – are about to appear in effigy before each other.

When they do, he is armed with the aggression he carries around in the guise of class consciousness: his pupils' mother was after all 'raised in the enemy camp' (p. 90). Her anticipation is very different: she dreads the tutor she has no right to reject, imagining him as a ruffian who will beat her children. She is just coming out of the French windows 'with the lively grace which was natural to her when no man was watching' (p. 26), when she sees 'a young peasant lad, almost a child, who was very pale and had evidently just been crying' (p. 26). Her first thought is that he must be a girl in disguise; she addresses him as 'my child'. He turns round and is struck dumb by her beauty and refinement; nobody has spoken to him so kindly before. When she realizes this is the new tutor, her relief and delight partake of surprise to find herself 'standing so very close to this young man practically in his shirt-sleeves'. He is clearly a kind of man she has never known.

Both these people are distinct from everyone around them; they share a paleness that is occasional in her, permanent in him (though when he first gazes on her he blushes); both are proud and bored, though he alone knows it; both have an enabling innocence, though he would never own up to it. Julien wants to control by his gaze, but is as distracted as the boys on the parapet; Mme de Rênal flowers when she is not looked upon, but is awakened by his attention. On this first occasion, as on every other, he sets out to conquer but attains his goal by displaying vulnerability.

At first Mme de Rênal's reaction to Julien is mediated through his potential negative relation to her sons. It is only when he has promised not to beat them that she perceives in him a meaning of more interest to herself: 'once her anxiety for her children was completely dissipated, she was struck by Julien's extreme beauty. The almost feminine form of his features and his embarrassed expression did not seem ridiculous to a woman who was extremely shy herself. The masculine air commonly thought indispensable to the beauty of a man would have frightened her' (p. 28). In a sense what each of them is finding in their first encounter is a companionship of women, a mother–son transference that has shades of mothers and daughters.

Julien is very aware of how privileged his pupils are in contrast to himself, but in his very differences from them, he allows comparison. In his first encounter with them, he offers a kind of reciprocation: 'I will often ask you to recite your lessons, you make me recite mine now' (p. 31), and even the youngest, Stanislas-Xavier, lisps a cue-word for him to perform by. From this point on, the boys adore him unreservedly, even though he is strict with them and suspicious of their affection. Metonym of their mother, defining her innocence, they appear as mediators to the gathering affair, shadowing her fear of his departure (p. 73), serving as chaperones (p. 78), providing an excuse to switch seats (p. 80); they will be used, finally, as carriers of their mother's written plea for her assassin's life (p. 458). They also stand for a contrast between maternity and paternity:

> Though she would never have mentioned it to anyone, if one of her children ran a high temperature she suffered the same agonies as if he were dead. A vulgar laugh, a shrug of the shoulders accompanied by some trite maxim on the folly of women was all she had received when, driven by the need to confide, she had spoken to her husband of these worries in the early years of their marriage. Such pleasantries, especially when they were responses to the illnesses of her children, were like a knife in the heart of Mme de Rênal ... Too proud to speak of such troubles, even to her friend Mme Derville, she imagined that all men must be like her husband ...
> Hence the success of the young peasant Julien. (pp. 35–6)

Julien takes up the position of the kind husband and father Rênal fails to be. His sensitive frown at the sight of a dog run over by a cart is contrasted with the brutal laugh of the other man; thus the most and the least indifferent objects alike evoke warmer images in the stranger. At the same time, Rênal is not really the enemy. Absurd, easy to rout because his vanity is so susceptible, he arouses a hatred that 'has nothing personal in it' (p. 60), for he is 'well intentioned, honest at bottom' (p. 90). Even his wife, who is aware of his violence and coldness, is tempted to feel sorry for 'the very real suffering' (p. 128) his jealousy causes him.

The husband's cuckoldry is shown not so much by threatened interventions on the couple in love as by his outsiderhood to the unit formed by the mother, lover and sons. In the family's country house at Vergy, all five cavort as children together, playing in a careless Eden, chasing butterflies; this is where the love-affair begins. Though 'she would have given her life without hesitation to save her husband's' (p. 147), it is without him that Mme de Rênal fantasizes a perfect future in Paris with Julien and the boys. And in Verrières, he arrives to disrupt an idyllic scene of storytelling and laughter in which the sight of Julien with Stanislas on his knee has brought tears to the eyes of the mother.

This youngest child is the favourite. It is his caresses that console the tutor when his employer has humiliated him for, young enough still to be innocent, 'this one does not despise me yet' (p. 57). His mother kisses him twice as much as his brothers when she is about to go and imperil her future. As they part after two of the most tense and intimate scenes, he is the other the lovers mention (pp. 153 and 216): it is as 'the mother of Stanislas' that Julien commands Mme de Rênal to save herself from the risk of discovery. And the complexity of the patrilinear knot in which the mother finds herself is revealed when this child falls ill.

She has by this time been Julien's mistress for some weeks. Before she met him, simply pious, indifferent to her husband and absorbed in her children, 'their brief illnesses, their pains and little pleasures had preoccupied the whole sensibility of this soul that, in all her life, had adored only God' (p. 35). Seduced by the young man's helpless tears on the first night, grievously afraid she is too old for him, she loves him 'like her own child' (p. 92). The thought of adultery has touched her only briefly, dismissed by the pressing claims of a happiness shared reassuringly with the children; Eden seems free of the threat of the Father. Now, with Stanislas's illness, the latter returns.

Mme de Rênal was suddenly seized with dreadful remorse. For the first time, she was reproaching herself for her love in a coherent

way; as if by a miracle, she seemed to have understood what an
enormous sin she had let herself fall into . . .

Long ago, at her convent school, she had loved God with passion;
she feared him now just as fervently. The inward conflicts that tore
her apart were all the more terrible because they were beyond
reason. Julien saw that any argument maddened rather than calmed
her: it seemed to her the blandishments of the devil. Yet since
Julien himself loved little Stanislas dearly, he had the better right
to talk to her about the child's illness, which began to take a turn
for the worse. (p. 107)

His first reaction is to fear what her panic may make her do: habit and
guilt might induce her to confess to her husband. He begs her to confide
in no one but him for the sake of 'our Stanislas', but this is not yet the
moment for such an arrogation of the father's place. Instead he is, at this
stage, the dispensable third in her relation to the Father and the son:
'Mme de Rênal had got it into her head that if she wanted to appease
the wrath of God she must hate Julien or see her son die. It was because
she felt she could not hate her lover that she was so unhappy' (pp. 107–
8). He is deeply impressed by the nobility of this anguish, though what
still preoccupies him most is his own place in the drama. His rough
childhood seems to have found a new justification, he is amazed to see
himself preferred both to the tenderness of this infant and to the threat
of hell: 'she believes she is killing her son by loving me, and yet the poor
creature loves me more than her son . . . how could I have inspired such
a love – I who am so poor, so ill-bred, so ignorant, so crude sometimes
in my manners?' (p. 108).

At the height of the crisis, Rênal comes to see his son. His coldness
and obtuseness save the day:

The child, consumed by fever, was all flushed and did not recognize
his father. Suddenly Mme de Rênal flung herself at her husband's
feet. Julien saw that she was about to confess everything and all
would be lost for her.

Fortunately, her bizarre gesture annoyed M. de Rênal.

'Goodbye, goodbye,' he said, turning to go.

'No, no, listen to me,' cried his wife, on her knees before him,
desperate to stop him leaving. 'You must hear the truth. It is I who
am killing my son. I gave him life and now I am taking it from him.
Heaven is punishing me, in the eyes of God I am guilty of murder.
I must ruin myself, abase myself; perhaps my sacrifice will appease
the Lord.'

If M. de Rênal had been a man of imagination, he would have known everything.

'Romantic nonsense,' he cried, pushing his wife away as she tried to clasp his knees. 'What a lot of romantic nonsense; Julien, see the doctor is called at daybreak.'

And he went back to bed. Mme de Rênal sank to her knees half in a faint, and when Julien tried to help her she pushed him away with a convulsive gesture.

This image of adultery – the mother prostrate over the cradle of her child – increases the astonishment of Julien. Utterly atheistic, he is stirred by the possibility that the hypocritical priesthood might have touched on some truth of the human heart. But this is as near as the young abbé comes to a religious response; he is, instead, absorbed in the vision of his mistress entrapped by her belief.

As he gazes he becomes gradually less concerned with his own role – 'here is a woman of genius reduced to the utmost misery because she has known me' (p. 109) – and more interested in protecting her. Goaded by 'her automaton of a husband', she might go mad or even kill herself if he leaves, as she has demanded, and he is 'no longer here to take care of her'. The narrator does not point out Julien's unusual sincerity in this scene; his thoughts are simply followed by a speech that reproduces them. He holds out an offer of mutual parenthood: 'what would become of me, far away from you, knowing I have made you miserable? But let's not think about me; I will go, my love, since that is what you want. But if I go, if I am no longer here to take care of you, if I can't come between you and your husband, you'll tell him everything, you'll ruin yourself.' Ruin is what she wants, as the only price she imagines God demanding for the life of her son. At last Julien finds the right thing to offer: '"oh heaven! if only I could take Stanislas's illness upon myself!"' (p. 110).

The role of husband or protector/God is not one Julien can legitimately borrow yet; for all his tenderness, these are still 'the blandishments of the devil'. His position, as by the inspiration of sincerity he has discovered, is rather that of the youngest son. In wishing to suffer in the child's place, he breaks through the structure in which Mme de Rênal is caught between *her* son and *her* God. She recognizes his rightness by offering him the place of the child's father, who alone can legitimately be preferred to him:

'Oh, you love him, at least!' cried Mme de Rênal, rising and throwing herself into his arms.

A moment after, she flung him away in horror.

'I believe you, I believe you,' she went on, falling to her knees again. 'Oh my only friend, why are you not Stanislas's father? Then it would not be a horrible sin to love you better than your son.'

'Will you let me stay, and from now on I will love you as a brother? That is the only expiation that can appease the Most High.'

'And I,' she cried, standing up and taking Julien's head between her two hands, holding it a little away from her as she gazed at him, 'could I love you as a brother? Is it in my power to love you like a brother?'

Julien burst into tears.

The only innocence possible between them is in the image of mother–son incest, familiarly represented in Julien's tears. Two comments from the end of the text confirm the conclusion of this scene. First, the man's, contained in his defence speech, but sincere whether or not meant so: '"Mme de Rênal was a mother to me" . . . Before ending, Julien stressed once again . . . his repentance, his respect, the limitless and filial adoration he had for Mme de Rênal' (pp. 463–4). Then the woman's, at the point where she has effectively abandoned reputation and family for his sake: 'I feel for you what I should feel only for God, a mixture of respect, love and obedience' (p. 472). The son becomes God to the mother, just as, by the end of the narrative, images of Julien as Jesus multiply, only to be laid to rest in the cave of his burial. In this way we can see that the two key figures in the woman's patrilinear chain, child and deity, are both finally replaced in the person of the lover.

If everyone in this text, as Girard points out, loves mediately, Mme de Rênal is supposed to be the least derivative because her mediators are the unsophisticated clichés 'of "l'opinion publique" and of religious doctrine'.[7] Motherhood and literacy are, it seems here as elsewhere, incompatible. Worldly Parisians love according to fashionable fiction, country folk are more naive and slower. But there is some inconsistency. Julien who, in one place, is said to have 'read no novels' (p. 336), is able to impress Amanda Binet by quoting from *La Nouvelle Héloïse*; and even the good mother has read not so much 'no novels' (p. 76) as 'a very small number' (p. 42). Her innocence is supplemented by a 'somewhat romantic mind' (p. 26), allied to nobility (p. 147) but not entirely immune to the 'romantic nonsense' her husband accuses her of. In this and in other respects – not least her hard- headed intelligence which, as in all the other characters, coexists comfortably with stupidity – she is not wholly the opposite of the other beloved, Mathilde de La Mole.[8]

71

Mathilde is as obsessed with books as Julien, she creeps in secret into her father's library, which unsexes her as irrevocably as her wilful intelligence and her clipped upper-class voice. Her extreme passion, which awakens a similarly sado-masochistic desire in the hero, feeds off the visibility of her status and a boredom as explicit in her as it is unconscious in Mme de Rênal. If she is typed as the bad mother,[9] she is nevertheless vouchsafed the illegitimate maternity her rival desired. Her pregnancy fulfils the wish uttered by Mme de Rênal in her extremity and, pregnant still at the end of the narrative, she is left clasping the 'charming . . . poetic' (pp. 452, 487) head of Julien. But just as the head is now grotesquely separate from its body, Mathilde's maternity is presented everywhere as denatured – not on the basis of anything we see of her but because of Julien's proprietorial attitude towards 'his son'.[10]

Mathilde is disarmingly delighted to discover she is pregnant; without *arrière-pensée* she tells Julien at once, cites the child as 'guarantee' (p. 413) and repeats the vow she has made and will make many times that she is now his wife. Heroically for a woman in the first trimester, she rushes around without pause negotiating first with her father for Julien's ennoblement, then with the patriarchs of law and Church for his release. But nothing she does seems to make her lovable. Not only does Julien feel more moral concern for her father or suitors than for her, he is determined to marry her off after his death to one or other of the men she has rejected.[11] As if to punish not just her famous pride but above all her similarity to what he has been before they let him into the cell, as if to assign to her all the movement and noise he now feels ready to leave behind, a contempt he knows is unjustified drives him to contrast her cruelly with the incarnation of motherhood in whose embrace he nestles before death, and this contempt is focused on the unborn child.

Nothing of course proves that this child is male, but it is described as a son so often that, suggests Mossman, we must read it as 'a wish fulfilment . . . which permits Julien Sorel to father himself' (p. 152). That the baby is unborn when its father and the text come to an end is the only way to leave both suspended before separation: no birth means no loss, the son is permitted (perhaps) never to know the loss of the mother which is every exit from the womb. But if Mathilde is Medea, the Kleinian bad mother, the reading and knowing self who exceeds femininity, how can the text allow her body to be the final resting place?

Mossman's brilliant analysis of the desire of the mother in *Le Rouge et le noir* details the phantasy that marks every space as a womb, the churches, towers, cells and finally the cave where Julien is buried. But on occasion she observes that the mother, 'the most salient element, [is] missing' (p. 129), and she cites the '*in utero* ending' (p. 154) as restoring 'the missing mother' in the only possible kind of closure. I want to disagree with – or rather to amplify – this conclusion. For after all the baby is in the 'wrong' womb, left in the charge of the wild woman who will prefer to cradle the corpseless head she is kissing and putting to bed. The reason, I think, is that the mother whose body is the enclosing world cannot also be the woman you love (I shall return to this point in the Conclusion). Mathilde must be the perambulating body, the missing mother, because Mme de Rênal must be there in the cell with Julien. Similarly, though she has promised not to, the latter follows him involuntarily to the grave after an exact three days – for by doing so she has finally given him what he wants, proved her loyalty to him rather than to any of the children (for all she dies embracing her boys), either her own or his. If the text ends 'Mme de Rênal was true to her promise', that is because the real promise is to be faithful to Julien, to be with him inside a womb in which the mother must be absent in order to be good.

The protagonist of the realist novel is desire made flesh. Older brother of the narrator of the *récit*, he dwells less on a transition of adolescence than on the attempt to live out a *Bildungsroman*. For Julien Sorel, overt desire is truly patriarchal: he wishes to defeat (that is, to use) the system of homosocial patronage that will make a man of him. But meanwhile, determinedly sexual, his unconscious motive takes him towards the woman, the womb. The alternative of two women in this text seems to be that between two versions of heterosexual incest, with the mother and with the sister. It is as mothers and as readers that the two women are utterly split – the good mother must be illiterate. But the structure of men, for all Julien's concentration on the desired *Liebestod*, does not disappear. The topos of the sick son is crucial to it, and not only because of the mother's diminishment.

Masculinity is metonymic. If the whole of Freud's paean to masculinity is centred upon castration as a fear having the effective power of a certainty, that is surely because the boy, neurotic guardian of the penis that is never the phallus, jealously afraid of the father's magical equivalent, knows he must wish for separation from the thing he bears. Desire in its masculine form (in existentialism, in sublimation) is transcendence, the motion towards and away from. If will becomes flesh, it must be cast off. If there are, perhaps, two ways of conceiving the self as doubled in an other (internally and externally), then for transcendence the male imagination must pay the price of castration.

When the author incarnates his transcendence in a fictional desirer, he separates the latter from himself. *Le Rouge et le noir* is a fairytale. The third son, feeble as he looks, has the beauty that wins women and, to seduce men, his fairy godfather has given him the magical ability to repeat. But the idyll is lined with irony. If 'the perfect father . . . in Stendhal's fiction . . . is nothing more and nothing less than the narrator's voice',[12] that voice is one of worldly good-humour that allows the implied author to show he knows fairytale gifts are exactly what they must be, unreal. And the worldly irony repeatedly stresses one thing: that Julien is childish, foolish, that he believes in his own will precisely as the little boy puffing out his chest draws smiles from a doting grandmother: 'isn't he a real little man?' A little man is all he is, the smiles say: his imitation is seductive because it is absurd. Stendhal's narrator endows Julien with success in proportion as he is weak and foolish. In these moments, with the whisper over the shoulder, we as readers are to catch the hint, align ourselves with the smiling adults – and thus we may freely enjoy the enjoyment of the parody. In an autobiographical text written when he was over fifty, Stendhal notes:

> Loving [my mother] at the age of six years, in 1789, I showed absolutely the same characteristics as in 1828 when I was madly in love with Alberthe de Rubempré. My way of chasing after happiness had not undergone any fundamental change; there was just one exception to this: I was, as regards the physical side of love, just as Julius Caesar would be if he came back to earth and tried to use cannon and small arms. I would have learned very quickly, and it would not have made the slightest difference to my tactics.[13]

It is the very smallness of his weaponry that seems to give the boy-self his right to succeed. His feebleness is what shall 'conquer' the beloved mother.

Nothing is more obvious than the use of military imagery in matters of love in this text; it appears not just in Julien's reproduced thoughts but in the voice of the narrator – and obsessively in Stendhal's own marginalia. But Stendhal writes with equal urgency and expertise about impotence. What unites these two ideas is the figure of the oedipal boy. Castration is simply the putting-into-flight of this equation.

If the hero is the flying metonym for the author, the penis-phallus of which he is both proud and ashamed, then how is the hero to remain a man? Is he, like King Kong, to *be* and therefore never to *have* the idealized phallus? If this is so, he is merely a fetish, a female. So at the crux of the young man's story of success in failure there must be another small boy, enfeebled almost to death.

In comparing the four male-authored texts of this chapter, we shall see four different versions of this psychosexual drama of male autobiography. In none does the sick boy die; he must remain, as the last lost part of the man that the mother nurtures into life (though later, straining a number of themes from *Le Rouge* into a whole novel, Stendhal will base the whole fatality of *La Chartreuse de Parme* on the final death of a son). But the four boys fail to die in four different ways, and correspondingly we sense the author's control differently in each case. Stendhal is prepared to let Julien survive the crisis to his desire – he says the magic word and re-enters the woman's embrace. In the same vein, his implied author's irony exists to shore up indulgence. It recognizes the absurdity of the fairytale surrogate. It is worldly; the reader is expected to pick up the winks and enjoy what they permit.

Flaubert's implied author is quite different. In his texts, authorship is not worldly, but other-worldly. The author 'is' in his narrative (implied in the narrator) only negatively, as absence, sleight, divinity. 'The author in his work,' he famously wrote, 'is like God in the universe: everywhere present and nowhere visible.'[14] A general presence can exist only by a specific, perceptible absence. We shall have occasion to examine the politics of Flaubert's irony more fully later, but it is clear here that it rests on a divisive politics of *esse est percipi*. Such being belongs to characters: through a tireless series of devices of point of view, the author ranges them within the sights of every manner of critical gaze, and above or behind each new position of the protean narrator stands the gaze of the author, who (as Sartre so acutely observes) indulges in the divine privilege of 'hovering'.

If (as we shall see later) hovering is a frank idyll of the Romantic poets, a version of the 'indicible et mâle volupté' of free flight, for the novelist it is a state of knowledge. Flaubert's characters are utterly known; he their author is all around them and unknowable by them. For the char acteristic mark of the mortals in his universe is foolishness. Emma Bovary is foolish in a more complex way than Frédéric Moreau; for all (or rather, precisely because of) her other sex, she embodies her author's wish for linguistic transcendence with a special urgency. Frédéric looks superficially more like a direct surrogate, behaves up to a point as the classical double of rewritten desire, and there are many directly autobiographical motifs in the plot, but he has no impulse to action, he is all stupid passivity, the complete object. Above him, through the irony of his set of aborted wishes, the enlightened author invites the aspirant reader to know better. Emma's mistakes may be the world's, Frédéric's are all his own.

Foolishness in Flaubert can be saintly – either here and there, as in the blinkered Charles Bovary, or with rising consistency, as in the simple-hearted Félicité. But more often it has the airborne vulgarity of pretension. Frédéric's very desire is made unattractive, as if to punish the boyhood self by separating him even from his innocence. He is, as his author marks him, 'the man of every kind of weakness',[15] and if we take his part even for a moment, we are fools as great as he. Four women are grouped around the hero of *L'Education sentimentale* (1869). The youngest, Louise Roque, ginger-haired and gawky, has a freshness worthy of Julien Sorel, speaks and gazes, and never really enters the hero's desire. All the other three are presented as mothers, variously apt or denatured. They are also grouped (and perpetually regrouped by a dynamics of envy and 'contamination') around the stereotypical poles of womanhood, the *madone* and the *lorette*.[16]

The text opens *in medias res*, with the eighteen-year-old protagonist returning to his provincial home by boat. He watches a bluff middle-aged man flirting with a peasant girl, fondling the gold cross on her breast. The man winks, draws him into a bantering conversation about women, money, life; 'Frédéric felt a certain respect for him' (p. 5) and asks his name, which is Arnoux. Just then, a servant appears, asking him to come down because his daughter is crying; he hurries off.

A few minutes later, Frédéric catches sight of a woman:

> It was like an apparition:
> She was sitting, all alone, in the middle of the bench; or at least, he could make out no one else, in the dazzling light that shone at him out of her eyes. Just as he walked past, she raised her head: his shoulders bowed automatically; and, stopping a little way off on the same side of the boat, he looked at her.
> She wore a large-brimmed straw hat, with pink ribbons that trembled in the wind, behind her. The coils of her black hair, parted in the middle, were shaped above the arch of her wide eyebrows and hung down low, seeming to caress the oval of her face. Her light-coloured muslin dress, scattered with little spots, spread in numberless folds. She was busy with some embroidery; and her straight nose, her chin, her whole figure stood out against the background of the blue sky. (p. 6)

Nothing much in the description justifies the affect attached now and henceforth to this figure, but every detail of her body, like the things she possesses and the people close to her, is immediately charged with an arbitrary and total value. Frédéric gazes, and as he does so he already abdicates any directly sexual thought: 'the very desire of physical possession disappeared beneath a deeper wish, a painful curiosity that went beyond all limits' (p. 7).

In the inclusive shape she makes, a uterine containment bordered only by the fathomless matter of her dress and by the haze of a divine glow (her eyes generate this uncanny light, while she looks only at her needle-work, we presume) and in the limitless task of wishing to know her, she represents the mother. A moment later, we see her with her own child:

> A Negress wearing a scarf appeared, holding the hand of a little girl who was quite tall already. The child's eyes were full of tears, she had just woken up. She took her on her lap. 'Mademoiselle was a naughty girl, even though she was nearly seven; her mother wouldn't love her any more; she was given her own way far too much.' And Frédéric rejoiced to hear these things, as if he had made a discovery, an acquisition.

The lady's mauve-fringed shawl begins to fly away; Frédéric catches it; she thanks him. Then Arnoux arrives, addresses her as 'my wife', and the child jumps into his arms.

In these opening pages, the triangular scheme is set up. Frédéric stands outside a closed family circle – but in it, tensions of several kinds have already been sketched in. His respect for the silly husband, his abject and unphysical adoration of the wife place him clearly as the oedipal son – but the child in 'his' place is a girl, and her mother's toughness offers him no fear of difficult surrogacy. The daughter gets affection only from her promiscuous father; her mother excludes her from the embrace of infancy.

This opening is, more than anything else in the novel, based on a specific moment in the author's life: the meeting, when he was fourteen, with the twenty-eight-year-old Elisa Schlesinger at the seaside town of Trouville. About a year later, he wrote his first sentimental education, the autobiographical *Mémoires d'un fou*. The beloved here is given the real name of Elisa Schlesinger's daughter, Maria. This time, the fetish precedes the vision. The protagonist rescues a woman's 'charming red pelisse'[17] from the rising tide; the next day at lunch, she expresses her thanks:

> I turned round; it was a young woman sitting with her husband at the next table.
> 'Thank me for what?' I asked, distracted.

'For having picked up my cloak; wasn't it you?'
'Yes, Madame,' I said with embarrassment.
She looked at me.
I lowered my eyes, blushing. What a gaze! what an extraordinarily beautiful woman! I can still see this ardent eye beneath a black brow fixed upon me like a sun. She was tall, dark, with magnificent black hair tumbling in long tresses onto her shoulders; her nose was Greek, her eyes burning, her eyebrows high and admirably arched, her skin was ardent and velvety as if brushed with gold; she was slim and fine, one could see tiny azure veins writhing [serpenter] on her brown and crimson [pourpré] breast. Add to that a fine down darkening her upper lip and giving her face a virile, energetic expression that would reduce a blonde beauty to pallor. One could say she was a little too plump or reproach her for a certain artistic casualness. Thus women in general considered her lacking in taste. She spoke slowly; her voice was modulated, musical and sweet . . .
(pp. 25–6)

In this much earlier and more immediate transcription, the garment is scarlet, not mauve, and there is nothing pink or visionary about the woman's body, down to the slight moustache and the crimson breast. The adolescent's gaze is the very reverse of the older man's dazzled myopia: he perceives the faintest of veins on the breast, azure against purple, which he savours along with her somewhat *louche* reputation and the sweet-and-sour of a virile gaze set against a melodious voice.

Mme Arnoux also has visible veins, but they are transposed onto her hands: 'An irresistible daydream took hold of him and he remained gazing at some detail of her person . . . the blue veins of her hands.' Czyba, who quotes this phrase from one of the drafts, likens this 'epidermic preciosity' to other aspects of fetishism in the text,[18] but does not mention the original context for this gaze, which is a mother–daughter couple.

Maria had a child, a little girl; she was loved, kissed, petted and fussed over to the point of boredom. How I would have accepted a single one of those kisses cast in profusion, like pearls, on the head of that babe in arms!

Maria was feeding her herself, and one day I saw her uncover her bosom and offer the infant her breast.

It was a full, round bosom, with brown skin and azure veins which could be seen beneath that ardent flesh. I had never before seen a naked woman. Oh! into what strange ecstasy the sight of that breast threw me! how I devoured it with my eyes, how I longed just to touch those breasts! I felt as though, if I just placed my lips upon them, my teeth would have bitten them in fury, and my heart melted with delight, thinking of the pleasures of that kiss.

Oh! how long I have since contemplated that throbbing bosom, that long gracious neck, the head leaning, with the black hair in its curling-papers, over that suckling child, whom she rocked gently on her lap, humming an Italian air! (p. 29)

It is well established that the later bad relations between Mme Arnoux and her daughter are reasonably close to those of Mme Schlesinger, though the cause of the tension in the real-life family was more precise and socially based.[19] But the omission of the originating sensuality of the scene of breastfeeding is too marked to ignore. Within the novel of adultery, it seems, it is impermissible to portray such direct oedipal jealousy towards a female child. The mother cannot be seen to waste sensual love on a daughter.

The little girl appears only a few more times in the text. The next time Frédéric, by dint of weeks of searching, manages to track down the Arnouxs and eventually get invited to dinner, he is left alone for a moment with her. She stares, receives his compliments coquettishly, then slips away. (Years later she will still show that 'limpid, suspicious, virgin's gaze': p. 196.) Some months after this meeting, at Mme Arnoux's name-day party at their house in Saint-Cloud, the infidelities of the husband begin to be revealed. The wife accidentally intercepts a letter; on the journey back to Paris, she is preoccupied and irritable. In the carriage, Marthe lies across her mother's lap, with her head on Frédéric's.

It seemed to him that he communicated with her whole being across the body of this child stretched between them. He bent down over the little girl and, parting her pretty brown hair, kissed her softly on the forehead.

'How good you are!' said Mme Arnoux.

'Why?'

'Because you love children.'

'Not all children!'

He said nothing more, but put his left hand to one side, near her, leaving it lying open – thinking she might do the same and their hands might meet. Then he felt ashamed, and took it away.

Frédéric's interest in the child is an exact parallel to the gauche gesture of the casually placed hand. It is much less than the genuine affection of Julien Sorel especially for the youngest of his charges. We see no similar tenderheartedness (or even ambiguity) in the character of this protagonist. Frédéric's obsession is utterly fetishistic, metonymic: proximity, not consummation, is its code. In contrast to the frank sadism of the more sensual narrator of the *Mémoires d'un fou*, he wants to get no nearer than the aura around his beloved. But if every mediator (human or object-fetish) is an end as much as a means, it is also never anything more than an obstacle. There is, in this text, no place for desire to focus – for the image of the suckling breast has been occulted from its scenario. In its place is the foolishness of the man who wastes his whole life on desire but is incapable of properly conceiving it, and the jealous author who arrogates all the privileges of the reader's absented gaze.

If daughters in the novel of adultery exist only as irritants and distractions, it is the male child that provides a surrogate for the protagonist – but he must do it via the motif of sickness. Both Elisa Schlesinger and Mme Arnoux had younger sons. In the text, the boy is produced during the time Frédéric spends in the provinces, chafing but temporarily too poor to try and return to Paris. Flaubert, normally a stickler for research and accuracy, makes two striking errors in timing in this novel, and both have to do with the gestation of baby boys. Despite the fact that he has been away for only two years, the protagonist is introduced on his return to Paris to 'a little boy about three years old' (p. 109). Tossed high in the air by his proud father, this child reminds Frédéric irresistibly of the snotty-nosed brat in the restaurant where he has just wasted half the day. Mme Arnoux, in her new and less impressive home, 'seemed to have lost some quality, to be in some undefined way degraded, at all events to be different from before' (p. 110).

The mother of the son has lost something of her glamour: the child's existence coincides with an explicit souring of the marriage, and with economic and social decline. Frédéric becomes 'the parasite of the household . . . If anyone was unwell, he would come three times a day to enquire after them, visit the piano tuner, and devise endless little good turns; and without a frown he endured Mlle Marthe's sulks and the caresses of little Eugène, who was always wiping his dirty hands all over his face' (p. 171). Arnoux plays hide and seek with his son, then departs for other pleasures, and Frédéric is left to listen to the wife's complaints. It is a bitter confidence, however, for the children are in the way in two senses: chaperones for all they guarantee her presence, they ultimately prevent her ever leaving her husband.

After a series of tragi-comic peripeteias, Frédéric declares his love for Mme Arnoux. Horrified at first, she gradually gains confidence in his humility. They walk in the gardens at Auteuil. The children are now both absent: the girl sent away to a convent because of her ill-temper, the boy at school in the afternoons. The two of them discover common sentiments and interests; every banality is exchanged. Lustful when apart from her, he bathes in blissful undesire in her presence. But one day, things come to a head:

> One afternoon (around the middle of February), he found her very upset. Eugène was complaining of a sore throat. The doctor had said that it was nothing serious, a bad cold, a touch of influenza. Frédéric was surprised by the child's feverish air. However, he reassured his mother, citing many examples of little ones of his age who had had similar infections and soon got better.
> 'Truly?'
> 'Why yes, of course!'
> 'Oh, how good you are!'
> And she took his hand. He clasped it in his.
> 'Oh, don't!'
> 'What does it matter, you are holding the hand of your comforter! . . . You think me good enough for this sort of thing, yet you doubt me . . . when I speak to you of my love!'
> 'Oh no, my poor friend, I don't doubt you!' (p. 275, ellipses Flaubert's.)

Catching her in this mood, Frédéric asks for a simple proof: to meet him the following Tuesday on the corner of the rue Tronchet. Before she has time to reconsider, Mme Arnoux has agreed.

It is surely no coincidence that the threatened illness of her son causes just the right distraction in the beloved woman to make her 'weaken'. We have already seen Frédéric practising the comforter's role in the family, available in times of misfortune. He rents a small apartment, furnishes it with eager discretion, and takes up his post on Tuesday.

But his author has of course undercut him with a double *coup de théâtre*. That day is the precise outbreak of the revolution of 1848: heartless history, ever careless of private plans, fills the streets with other events. The young man waits till three, four, five, six o'clock. She does not appear.

Flaubert's early notes for this crisis read: 'it would be better not to let Mme Moreau [the original name for Mme Arnoux] get laid: chaste in her actions she would eat herself up with love. She would have her moment of weakness that the lover would never see and never take advantage of.'[20] Mme Arnoux's moment of weakness coincides with her son's near-death. It is narrated in one of the only two sections of the narrative to take a point of view other than the protagonist's. It begins with a dream.

> The previous night she dreamt that she had been standing for some time on the pavement of the rue Tronchet. She was waiting for something vague but extremely important and, without knowing why, she was afraid of being seen. But a horrible little dog, which had taken a dislike to her, was nibbling at the hem of her dress. He would not go away and barked louder and louder. Mme Arnoux woke up. The barking was still going on. She listened: it was coming from her son's bedroom. Barefoot, she rushed in. It was the child himself, coughing. His hands were burning, his face was scarlet and his voice curiously hoarse. His difficulty in breathing increased minute by minute. Until dawn she stayed there, bent over his coverlet, watching him. (p. 280)

This dream narrative fits Freud's first and simplest category of dreams precipitated by external stimuli. The sleeper wishes above all to go on sleeping, so the stimulus is integrated into the events of a dream. In this case, Mme Arnoux's agoraphobia allows her to street-walk at the price of not knowing who or what she is waiting for, and also at the price (here the author bends down over her as she will over her conscience incarnate) of the guilt rhythmically calling her to wakefulness. This is not the first importunate little dog in Flaubert. In an earlier novel by the same name, one of the two protagonists is ominously and uncannily pursued by a repulsive cur throughout an evening. By the end abusing, cursing and violently kicking it, he flees home and hides in his room. The nightmare seems over, but when he goes down to check, there the vile animal is, lying on the threshold.

Much ink has been spilt over this early episode. The chapter after the denouement begins with the words 'that was his last pathetic day; from that moment he was cured of his superstitious fears and no longer dreaded meeting mangy dogs in the countryside.'[21] How exactly the dog embodies pathos is unclear; but this later version seems a useful clue. Both the dogs and their waking counterpart, the sick son, represent the prohibition on desire. Here located in the imagination of the beloved, the man's failure to love to consummation is displaced onto her active conscience. In contrast to Julien, whose sublime gesture overrode immediate lust – but how much kinder his author, who gave him some weeks of pleasure first! – Frédéric has responded to the beginnings of the child's illness by exploiting the weakness it provoked in the mother. And she surrendered, as he started coughing, not to his demands but to those of his unsympathetic double. In the woman's one concession (innocent or not) she has sacrificed the virtue she must, for irony's sake, stupidly preserve. So, woken by the barking importunity of a man's disruptive desire, she spends the night before and the day after watching her son.

Arnoux is called out at eight in the morning to the *garde nationale*; he promises to call the doctor. By ten the latter has not come; Mme Arnoux sends her maid; he is away and his locum out on his rounds.

> Eugène held his head to one side of the bolster, he was frowning, his nostrils dilated; his poor little face was whiter than his sheets; and a whistling sound emerged from his larynx, shorter with each inward breath, dry and metallic. His cough was like the noise of the crude mechanism that makes toy dogs yap.
>
> Mme Arnoux was seized with horror. She flung herself on all the bells, calling in panic: 'A doctor! A doctor!' (pp. 280–1)

An elderly doctor visits, examines the patient and promises to return. His young locum offers no more help. The mother's devotion is tested to the utmost:

> The child began to tear at the bandages around his neck, as if trying to pull away the obstacle that was stifling him, and he scratched the wall, seized the curtains of his little bed, searching for something to hold in order to help himself breathe. His face was bluish now, and his whole body, drenched in cold sweat, seemed to be growing thinner. His eyes gazed in wild terror at his mother. He threw his arms around her neck, clinging to her in desperation. Choking back her sobs, she stammered out tender words:
>
> 'Yes, my love, my darling, my precious!'
>
> Some moments of calm followed.
>
> She fetched toys, a doll, a picture-book, and spread them out on his bed to distract him. She even tried to sing.
>
> She began a song that she used to sing him while rocking him and dressing him in his baby-clothes on the same little tapestry chair. But he shuddered in the whole length of his body, like a wave under a gust of wind; his eyeballs protruded; she thought he was going to die, and turned away so as not to see him. (pp. 281–2)

This description (and there is more) is reminiscent of the horrific pages of the death of Emma Bovary. Its tone could be called, with a small adjustment of viewpoint, ruthless or compassionate, Gothic or scientific. As striking as the appalling pathos, however, is the helpless foolishness of the mother in the face of the 'act of God' she confronts. Her efforts and gestures are inept (what else could they be?), even her endearments are without effect. Secondly, she is isolated: neither husband nor lover even witness this crisis. The doctors, one young, one old, come and go as helpless as she; their styles differ arbitrarily. Thirdly, though this scene uniquely espouses her viewpoint, it is entirely behaviourist in its technique. We see what she sees and does. Her thoughts or feelings are not described, as if she had none. The slow passage of time is (in another deflationary habit of Flaubert's) summed up in a cruel past historic: 'hours went by [se succédèrent], heavy, grim, interminable, heartbreaking.' Eventually, the child vomits up 'something strange, which looked like a tube of parchment'. Soon after, the locum arrives and pronounces him saved.

The strange object rendered by the child is the croupous membrane (Flaubert had been to watch a tracheotomy in hospital as part of his researches), a remote but not impossible spontaneous cure for croup. An act of God gives the pain, an act of God takes it away. It is not, I think, entirely coincidental that the 'parchment tube' resembles in grotesque parody the giving up of the phallus. The boy gives it back to the mother, his life is saved, and immediately she returns to her place in the legitimate chain.

> 'Saved! Can it be true!'
> Suddenly the image of Frédéric appeared to her, clearly and inexorably. This was a warning from Heaven. But the Lord, in his infinite mercy, had chosen not to punish her altogether. What an expiation would have been due later, if she had persisted in this love! Her son would have been insulted on her account; and Mme Arnoux saw him as a young man, wounded in a duel, brought home on a stretcher, dying. Jumping to her feet, she flung herself on the little chair; and with all her strength, casting her soul up to the heights, she offered up to God as a holocaust the sacrifice of her first passion, her only weakness. (p. 282)

This scene is genuinely pathetic, but it has none of the willing complexity of the half-mad conflicts of Mme de Rênal or Anna Karenina. There is here somehow and deliberately no psychological dimension. We must remember also that in this encounter between the love-object, death and conventional morality, what prevents tragedy is above all the function of the scene: a bit of dramatic irony, the routing of Frédéric's devious plans, a comic misunderstanding coming in the way of love. The topos is being hollowed out, reduced to just another coincidence. To be a madonna, the woman must pass through this crisis; but, madonna, she is obliged to refuse adultery out of pious superstition and because of children who never rise above the status of occasions.

The children are the mediation of marriage: when they are out of the way, hope springs eternal; when they almost die, a chance is missed. Mme Arnoux is anchored to her husband both because he is a good father and because he neglects his family's greater good; his philandering preserves the two classes of women between whom he mediates, and also keeps Frédéric attached to the same route from *madone* to *lorette* and back, telling the same warmed-over lies. For when the passion is unconsummated, as by the author's unkindness it is here, then it is not so much the husband as the lover who is a fool. In the end, all the characters lack sublimity, as Flaubert's first note attests: 'the husband, the wife, the lover, all in love, all cowards'.[22]

If the worst coward is the lover, however, the woman, simple and mindless, comes out the best of the three. The most a character can hope for in Flaubert is to attain *sancta simplicitas*: in her rocking and crooning, perhaps, Mme Arnoux touches that here. We see this more clearly when we compare two more scenes in the text that circle the same motif, the one frankly satirical, the other full of ambivalences.

When the hypocritical Mme Dambreuse – cold fosterer of a niece who turns out to be her husband's bastard, plans to marry her lover and inherits the family fortune in a denouement worthy of Balzac – discovers that she has been left nothing, she is described in these words: 'a mother in mourning beside an empty cradle is not more piteous than Mme Dambreuse in front of the gaping strongboxes' (p. 386). At the same moment, Frédéric's mistress Rosanette (whom he meets through her lover Arnoux, whom he brings to the love-nest prepared for Mme Arnoux), the whimsical and sprightly 'Marshal', has been transformed by maternity.

The tart with all the skills, she has of course always longed for a little home, a faithful man, a baby. When she discovers she is pregnant by Frédéric, she informs him with bravado and joy. He goes off into a reverie: what if this were Mme Arnoux's child, a little girl, 'dark-haired and white-skinned, with black eyes, arched eyebrows, a pink ribbon in her curly hair! (Oh, how he would have loved her!)' (p. 362). Rosanette has plans for a boy: 'they would call him Frédéric. She must start getting his layette.' All through her pregnancy (which, by another of Flaubert's slips, lasts twenty-five months) the expectant father works on his relationship with Mme Dambreuse. Rosanette is delivered of a son. Frédéric peeps behind the curtains of the crib:

> He saw, in the midst of the bed-clothes, something yellowish red, extremely wrinkled, which smelt horrible and was wailing.
> 'Kiss him!'
> He replied, to cover his repulsion:
> 'But I'm afraid I might hurt him?'
> 'No, no!'
> So, with distended lips, he kissed his child.
> 'Isn't he like you!'
> And, with her frail arms, she clung around his neck, in an effusion of feeling that he had never seen before. (p. 388)

Again, maternal love is presented as both genuine and grotesque: paternity is nothing but the latter. Looking at the infant, Frédéric imagines him growing up 'a fool, an unfortunate' (p. 389), saddled with the disadvantages of the bastard: 'better if he had not been born at all' (p. 390).

A short while later, the father's fantasy comes true. Rosanette brings the baby home from the wetnurse. Terribly thin, his lips are covered in white spots. The doctor has said he has thrush. As once before, Frédéric assures her automatically that it is nothing serious. By the evening, the white marks look more like 'patches of mould, as if the life was already abandoning the poor little body, leaving nothing but dead matter on which vegetation had started to grow' (p. 402). His hands are cold and he cannot feed.

> Rosanette was on her feet all night.
> In the morning, she went to fetch Frédéric.
> 'Come and look at him. He's not moving.'
> Indeed, he was dead. She picked him up, shook him, embraced him, calling him by every pet-name, covered him with kisses and sobs; then she turned upon herself in despair, screaming and tearing her hair; – and she dropped down onto the divan, where she sat, mouth open, a flood of tears pouring from her staring eyes. Then a torpor overtook her, and everything became quiet in the apartment. Some pieces of furniture had been knocked over. Two or three nappies were lying on the floor. The clock struck six. The night-light went out.

Frédéric, observing all this, felt as if he were dreaming. His heart contracted with fear. It was as if this death was only a beginning, and behind it a more terrible misfortune was on its way. (pp. 402–3)

This time horror completely replaces pathos. The child's unwilling father witnesses its death, a death he has wished for. The mother's stupid devotion resembles madness. Both parents seem to know that Rosanette is a mere usurper in the role of joyful mother. As if to seal the repulsion required of this bereavement, Flaubert has Rosanette's distraught vulgarity commission a portrait of the beloved corpse. The picture is a derisory patchwork of primary colours. The baby, laid out in a bed of camellia petals, looks like an altar-piece.

> Every quarter of an hour or so, Rosanette parted the curtains and gazed at her child. She saw him, a few months from now, taking his first steps, then at school, playing prisoner's base in the playground; then aged twenty, a young man already; and all these images that she created were like so many sons that she had lost. The excess of her grief multiplied her maternity. (p. 408)

This, if you like, is the underside of the sacrifice required of Mme Arnoux. Flaubert the jealous God seems almost shocked at the fierceness of the punishment he has meted out to the desiring woman. Doubly killed – 'a true "still life"' (p. 404) – always already its own effigy, this son of the son is self-hatred incarnate, to the point where both his ugliness and his piteousness multiply out into an uncanny space. The doom that Frédéric anticipates is enacted in the definitive ruin of the Arnouxs. He watches his beloved's lacy underthings – so many infants to his fetishism – sold off like *disjecta membra*. This is, in *L'Education sentimentale*, the true meaning of the illness of the beloved's son. Appendages paraded, desire displaced, sour smalls offered to the highest bidder, all signify the woman utterly lost.

Both mothers end the text accompanied by sons. Mme Arnoux, now a widow, visits Frédéric and they share a poignant moment; later we hear she is 'living in Rome with her son, a cavalry lieutenant' (p. 425). Rosanette has the ambiguous privilege of fostering: 'I ran into the dear old Marshal in a shop the other day, holding the hand of a little boy she's adopted. She is the widow of a certain M. Oudry, and very fat nowadays, enormous' (p. 426). Thus we see the pair who were 'saved', mother and son, survive in alienation: Mme Arnoux, now white-haired, tries to offer herself; Frédéric discreetly refuses. Rosanette, on the other hand, ugly now but enjoying the material comforts she earned, is pictured as forming by choice rather than accident the mother–son couple she once fantasized.

As for Frédéric, he is reminiscing with his friend Deslauriers. They have had their ups and downs, but now at last they are still playing together. They smile over a silly moment of their youth, when they took a bunch of flowers to the local prostitutes, and then ran away. Their lives equal failures, they agree 'that was the best time of our lives' (p. 428).

Two bachelors nodding over a winter fire, appreciating their moment of non-consummation: the text ends in comic mode, anticipating the late Flaubert of *Bouvard et Pécuchet*.[23] What do bachelors end up doing? Why, copying – the obverse of reproduction, the inverse of creation. To copy is to aspire to the exact representation of the same, a cloning that exists here and there in nature (only in the feminine of course) but everywhere masculine in the fantasy of patriarchy. Flaubert's last product, the *Dictionnaire des idées reçues*, is the perfect piece of irony: every word in it is parodistic, every joke a trap for the stupid. The implied author hovers on high, nowhere in the narratorless text, implied readers flap nearby guffawing at the bourgeois they almost are. We should remember that the adolescent comic invention of Flaubert and his friends, *le Garçon*, was a figure they both mocked at and took it in turns to play. *Garçon* means fellow (here) but also both bachelor and boy. A sort of eunuch, his buffoonery holds up a hideous portrait both to the uncreative reader who thinks himself better and to the sorry sterility of the author whose style is his only offspring. In the end, the sick son, coughing up his tubular gut, denying the crudity of direct desire, incarnates the project of loveless control over the ironic text.

In a crucial essay, Lionel Trilling analyses the extraordinary comfort readers take from the narrative tone of *Anna Karenina* (1873). A sense of delighted recognition is rooted, he argues, not (as it never is) in a measurable gift of accuracy to the reader's material world, but because, just as 'Flaubert's objectivity is charged with irritability . . . Tolstoi's [is charged with] affection. For Tolstoi everyone and everything has a saving grace.'[24] This apparent love of the characters by the author, this moral optimism, is in the interests of the reader as much as of the writer: 'we so happily give our assent to what Tolstoi shows us and so willingly call it reality because we have something to gain from its being reality' (p. 61). Here is the perfect form of the realist idyll: a world controlled by love, a God both reliable and utterly benign. He is still entirely a God: he, like Flaubert, leans down to gaze and hides his face, but with a smile rather than a frown. But this is not to suggest that he does not judge. On the contrary, Tolstoy's implied author is as pitiless in his condemnation of the adulterous mother as any of our other authors – and this is consistent with his seductive espousal of what Trilling calls 'life in its normal actuality' (p. 63). Normality is of course a political structure; Trilling's examples (leaning on biography no doubt: Tolstoy was nothing if not a father) are a significant litany. 'In Tolstoi the family is an actuality; parenthood is a real and not a symbolic condition . . . the biological continuity is a fact, not as in James Joyce's touchingly schematic affirmations, but simply and inescapably.' Parenthood, 'the biological continuity', the very thing that adultery adulterates, in its sweet disguise as nature rather than culture, is the moral medium of this good father. The poignancy of Anna's decline begins with her early appearance as the perfect sister, sister-in-law: her incomparable charm cannot be separated from her position in families. It is no chance, either, that the first encounter between Vronsky and her is mediated, in a railway carriage, as the delightful recognition of two mothers of sons.

This is, of all the texts in this chapter, the furthest away from a *récit*. As I suggested earlier, it is curiously difficult to locate a central point of quest or desire in this text; least of all is it (as are all the other patrilinear novels) the lover's story. Though occasionally his viewpoint is taken, but always with a fundamental casualness, Vronsky is not the angle from which Anna is seen. In this respect, precisely as Trilling rightly describes Tolstoy as 'the most *central* of novelists' (p. 60), the narrative is the most uncentred in all the novels of adultery. This happens in two key ways. Firstly, the desire of Anna, Anna's desirability, is located in no lover's adulterous designs; it cannot stand or fall by the childishness of a Julien or the stupidity of a Frédéric. Vronsky is strangely irrelevant to Anna's adultery. She 'is as she is perceived', because no one less than the implied author is perceiving her. His invisibility vouches absolutely. Secondly, and connectedly, there is something not universal but very everyday after all in her desirability. Levin, who is not allowed to desire her, is the completely straight male centre of the novel. His touching belief in marriage endorses what we see in the very first sight of Anna in her only possible place: marriage and parenthood are the modest and overweening values of the textual world. These good-smelling things – the weaving of relationships, living and letting live, that mark Anna as everyone's fairy godmother – manifest themselves, from the very instant of her 'surrender', with horrific immediacy, in a total condemnation that demands her suicide. Anna's position as agent of this plot, its active charm, requires her to end it. From the moment she makes love outside marriage, for all the kindly gaze of her author, she is on the tracks and must end on the tracks.

In splitting up my analysis of *Anna Karenina* between this and the next chapter, I am aware of a dislocation that cannot seem just; but it may prove useful. I want to take two distinct looks at the same story: a reading of Anna's place first as the mother of a son and in the structure of men (including the implied author as a figure of desire), and then as the mother of a daughter in the structure of women (which strangely will turn out to be the key way in which the author prepares desire). The awkwardness of splitting the argument in this way is obvious, but it will also allow two separately gendered considerations of the admitted mystery of this text's moral and sexual power.

Anna's love for her legitimate son Seriozha is the cornerstone of her moral condemnation. Little wonder that Lawrence got so angry with Tolstoy for not letting her cut the tie with serene rebellion; his own is the classic fantasy of mothers leaving children for the sake of passion, breaking the deadly chains of a Paul Morel reincarnated as adult lover. When Tolstoy headed the text with the epigraph 'Vengeance is mine; I will repay', taken from Romans 12:19 via Schopenhauer, he omitted the closing phrase 'saith the Lord', leaving the action and its judgement as unattributed as is everything else under his special kind of realism. But moral certainty, if it is found anywhere, is found in the question of the Karenin boy. He never falls ill – that happens twice if incompletely to his sister, once very centrally to his mother – but his position in the argument is to be the embodiment and object of the loss of love.

The opening sentence of the text, 'All happy families are alike but an unhappy family is unhappy after its own fashion',[25] was an addition to a book begun in the excitement of an *in medias res* narrative: the author, we are told, impressed by Pushkin's way of presenting his characters already assembled at a social gathering, intended to do the same. Precisely, though, in the development of 'the family idea' as central compensation for the dangers of Anna's story,[26] he added a sententious opening that one critic terms the 'only digression' in the book.[27] The aphorism is, of course, not even true; and that becomes increasingly obvious the longer we try and work out which the happy and unhappy families are in this text. Things do not look all that rosy for the Levins: their living happily ever after in the implicit style of the opening is exactly what Tolstoy has avoided showing. No other happy families are portrayed at more than a few lines' length. Or do we think of the Oblonskys who will, after all, continue to rub along and stay married by dint of an expedient combination of sentimentality on one side and tolerance and graft on the other? Or – can it be? – the Karenins before the irruption of sexuality, a family in which the early Anna has after all lived what she calls her 'nice, everyday life' (p. 114)? In all these cases, happiness relies on the sort of invisibility from within and without that could well make the incurious see them as all alike. Perception begins at the moment when apparently happy families are revealed as unhappy ones: when desire, or what is here and there termed 'the demon', begins to adulterate them.

What Anna discovers when she returns to the everyday world from the trip that has taken her severally away from normality is that a bit of ice has got into her eye and she can see what has always been wrong. Her visit to her brother made her almost simultaneously both angel and devil: sister, sister-in-law, friend, aunt and redeemer, she has never before gone away from her son's side, nor ever it seems looked an attractive man straight in the eye (though, with her honest directness of gaze, we find this hard to believe – but let's leave this for later). All the moments of the visit, with Vronsky's mother, with him, with Kitty, Dolly and with the children, have been pleasures or, more precisely, gifts of herself that Anna has seen delightedly received, and then the wild journey home realizes her dream-life by bringing her the impossible declaration. From this she steps out of a carriage to see her husband's prominent ears, arrives home to an annoying dressmaker and a child not quite as lovely as she had remembered.

Families are two things: vertical but also horizontal. Extending laterally they consist of siblings who succour, torment or teach one another. Of the four lovers in the book, Anna is the only one who has no same-sex siblings. To Dolly, she denies the parallel with Stiva that the whole text's structure forces back on us; as two adulterers they are indeed very different. But it is important to see right from the start that her essential sisterhood does not offer her an other from whom to learn; as a family member she belongs among males. In this sense she is as isolated as she is connected. Her charm is similarly both like Stiva's and different. His is perhaps primarily the ability to form relations so much like blood-relations with everybody that he is everywhere safe. Both as guest and as host, he makes links and provides enabling currents. She enchants everyone but not with safety. She is a kind of sister, a kind of mother, but in a way that leaves her strangely cut off.

Anna's charm is crucial to her initial effect. We never forget her initial effect – the meeting between her and Levin, belated and through a cloud of intoxication and unease, functions as a momentary restoration of that charm, framed as the portrait which is all she can now be, no longer acting to any familial effect – because it is a peculiar mixture of the objecthood that makes her visible and her function as agent in other people's family life. In a cruel aside, Camus's cynic Clamence defines charm as 'a way of making people say yes without ever asking a direct question'.[28] It is the object position of a pure unspecific subject: in other words, the mother's place. Anna enters the text as a mother to everyone, yet her relation to her son is disauthenticated in several ways. She is separated from him by choice and by, momentarily at least, preferring to him her brother, her nieces and nephews and the potential lover. She arrives home a day early to his delighted 'I knew!' (p. 122),[29] but less for his sake than for his rival's. And the viewpoint from which she is perceptible as maternal is anyone's but his: those who have said yes to her unvoiced question are those to whom she gives but does not owe nurturance. She is always already fostering. If the charm is not exactly desire, it is also not exactly what it is. How Anna's function as mother is displaced into a world that will soon be filled with desire takes up the whole opening section and remains fixed as the role she is irrevocably in. When critics suggest her author is in love with her – and the development of the character from a fat devilish matron to the enigma that centres the text endorses this *cristallisation* – this is surely what they mean. We all want her just as we all want Mrs Ramsay; and though she dies to the text before her suicide in a way Mrs Ramsay never does (and the ambivalent gender of our looking is the difference), we never forget this image. It remains now to see how the mother in Anna is denatured and made to cause her disaster.

We have met almost every other central character before we see her, but the problem posed on page one awaits her as its hoped-for reply. When she emerges from the carriage it is after sharing a journey with her future lover's dubious mother. Between Vronsky and this adulteress relations are formal but risky; she is the one who pronounces the last, unjust judgement on the dead Anna, taking over charge of her son just as she did on the day of the suicide; indeed this parody of herself, it is hinted, is the one who really drove Anna to it. Like my other texts, this one also closes on two mother–son icons: while Kitty is fulfilled in her bond with her developing child, Anna's fate is reproduced in the final parting of the two Vronskys.

'"I should have known you,"' she says to him endearingly, '"your mother and I seem to have talked of nothing but you the whole journey"' (p. 76), but it is Seriozha she thought she was talking about and of him that the other mother said '"don't fret . . . you cannot expect never to be parted."' At this first meeting, Anna's smile is fresh but serious, just as the energy of her walk and animation of her look are tempered by being directed somehow not at the young man; when her remark seems coquetry and he replies in kind, she refuses to pick up the tone. Similarly, when Vronsky acts on her concern for the wife of the guard who has been killed, his charity seems misplaced; Anna is embarrassed, not gratified. Desire, it is clear from these merest touches, is disruptive in a place where giving and receiving (money, warmth, speech) are ordered by familial structures. Anna is lavish where she might be dutiful: her being in those structures is always in excess of the necessary, but those are her structures, and at their first meeting she can only accept Vronsky as a Seriozha.

' "How I should like to know the whole romance of her life!" ' (p. 87), Kitty thinks when she first meets Anna, but neither she nor we ever discover it. This romance, it seems, can only begin now, as is proven by the ball at which the thirtyish matron steals the little princess's beau. We like Kitty find it impossible to associate such a woman with 'the unromantic exterior of Anna's husband'. Tolstoy is cheating us here. Anna must spring fully grown from his brain, beginning as an adult and only later degenerating into a fractious girl because, as we have already observed, she starts as the absolute mother and can never have become one.[30] When, later on, she gives birth it is towards death and falsehood, not a beginning of life. We never learn how she came by either Karenin or Seriozha; they are what is there – but there only as the absences from the scene in which she appears to us.

Anna was betrothed by an aunt, orphan to orphan, to an embarrassed older man. The Oblonsky children, like the Karenins and the Vronskys but unlike the Levins and Shcherbatskys, are highest aristocracy but weak links in a chain. Married young for the sake of security and fortune, she has it seems never lived out the beauty and gaiety in her demeanour. But however suppressed the animation may be, it is not just *disponible* but visible in the opening scenes. Again, we sense a difficulty on the author's part in wishing to make her both entirely virtuous and unawakened and also utterly open, blazing already though yet unburnt. Only incest can properly be understood as the motive for this: as sexed as unsexed, the mother's appeal is both focused and arbitrary.

Anna can't keep her mind off 'her curly-headed Seriozha' (p. 89); as she goes to find her album, she sees Vronsky below in the Oblonskys' hall and 'a strange sensation of pleasure mixed with apprehension suddenly stirred in her heart' (p. 90); they catch eyes and he leaves. Later she will know he has won when she uses his photograph to push her son's out of the same album.

At the ball Kitty watches Anna's charm come into focus: Vronsky's perception is perceptible as an expression of slavish submission; she becomes all the more animated. Her power, that '"strange, diabolical, and enchanting"' (p. 97) quality, emanates from her yet does not make her agent, but what she has half-passively done to Vronsky and Kitty already makes her guilty, because her beauty has begun to function beyond its assigned place. She leaves early but only after her 'uncontrollable radiance' (p. 98) has 'set Vronsky on fire'. The next day she has lost the love of Kitty and Dolly's children; her remorse is mixed with pleasure in proportions of control and uncontrol. Anna is an utterly good woman. Her whole fate is bound up with scruples she can gradually no more control than she can control desire. Or rather, her desire fills the place of unspent narcissism at first and later that of the wasted remorse no one will any more accept – and that is because not adults but a child is the focus of remorse.

Dog-like, slavish, reverential, Vronsky follows Anna not so much to capture her as to be caught. Despite his declaring as much (and his 'feeling like a king, not because he believed that he had made an impression on Anna – he did not believe that yet – but because the impression she had made on him filled him with happiness and pride': p. 120) the text also offers us images of sadism in the scene of first lovemaking, the horse-race and in Anna's angry fantasy-life at the end of the text. He is excessively healthy, enjoying the *samodovolnost* of gratified narcissism that Tolstoy portrays in his favourite characters and worlds;[31] he desires and is given what he desires; but if he has motive he never seems to have agency. Imagined by a male writer as the exact fit to a lovely woman's need (the folly to which she will stoop) he is not a hero: handsome but not sexy, wrong for her, object of her desire but never her equal, he is even less than Julien and Frédéric. Rather, like Karenin and Seriozha, he is simply there, taking over temporally and spatially from her unjustified past. Familiarly, where his assumption of Karenin's place moves no serious furniture around, the double he makes for Seriozha is never less than grievous.

Karenin is ugly; Anna sees it; has she really never seen it before? We know only the perception that arises after the meeting with Vronsky. She asks after her son; he is all right, says his father, '"sorry to disappoint you"' (p. 122). But Seriozha, healthy and lovely, is disappointing. Anna 'had to descend to reality in order to enjoy him as he was' (p. 123); what he is not is a man. Because she is good, she prefers what she has; in this restored everyday, she 'felt an almost physical pleasure in his nearness to her, in his caresses, and it was a moral solace to meet his artless, trusting, loving gaze and listen to his naive questions.' She honestly says he is '"nicer than anyone in the world"' to her, and he knows this to be true. Spending a quiet evening with him, her guilt is allayed: nothing has happened, after all. Steadying for her now, he acts as just recompense for what still waits to be spent. Karenin returns, criticizes Stiva's adultery, calls Anna to bed with a creepy 'special smile' (p. 127) but, in the mood of restoration, Anna accepts him, defending him in her mind from an attack implicitly Vronsky's as well as her own. The opening ends, in the tentative restoration of good habits.

Anna next meets Vronsky at the *louche* circle of Betsy Tverskoy, cousin to both of them. Chided by her, he observes 'a new spiritual beauty in her face' (p. 155). Her gaze speaks love, her words are maternal but she 'listens rapturously' (p. 157) to his ardour. The same glow, as she lies beside Karenin that night, continues to emanate from her 'wide-open eyes, the brightness of which she almost fancied she could see herself in the darkness' (p. 164). This light is the incarnation of a desire enclosed in Anna's narcissism; her husband alone cannot see it. A page later, Anna has slept with Vronsky and is broken. To the lover is attributed the cruelty which manifests itself in her as shame; he is described as her murderer, his kisses so many more blows. In this bitter scene, anticipating the divine vengeance he has co-opted, the author declares his unforgiving reading of pleasure that is not, even briefly, allowed to give gratification. Anna is condemned, from now on, to be a consciousness that has no outlet but guilt. 'Shame, rapture and horror' (p. 166) attend her 'new life'. She dreams of a false solution, both Alexeis making love to her together, the child excluded from a transgressive embrace.

We transfer again to Levin, whose loveless home has everything but a sexual centre to legitimate it. His dog, his prize cow and his faithful housekeeper surround him with a comical femaleness. He is busy as Anna is never properly busy; the masculine role of attendance is never wasted in time or space; he breeds, shoots, breeds. Vronsky too has not yet lost his occupation; his mother and brother disapprove but 'most of the younger men' in his regiment (p. 191) envy him his liaison. For him too a female animal provides justification; it is only at the last minute that he breaks the back of the mare he loves. Visiting Anna before the race, he dismisses her suffering as a function only of the false situation that keeps her married to a repulsive husband. But what he meets first at her house is the thought of her son. This is the only scene at which son and lover are simultaneously present – not in actuality but via the lover's and then the child's thoughts.

Seriozha is 'the most painful side of his relations with her – her son with his (as he fancied) questioning, hostile eyes'. With deadly effectiveness, the text offers us a child's uncertainties as the balance to the others' shifting motives:

> When he was present, neither Vronsky nor Anna would allow themselves to speak of anything – or even refer by hints to anything – the boy would not have understood. They had made no agreement about this: it had come about of itself. They would have considered it unworthy of themselves to deceive the child. In his presence they talked like acquaintances. Yet, in spite of their caution, Vronsky often noticed the child's attentive, bewildered gaze fixed upon him and a strange timidity and uncertainty in the boy's manner to him – at one time affectionate, at another cold and reserved. It was as if the child felt that between this man and his mother there was some important bond which he could not understand.
>
> The child did in fact feel that he could not understand this relation; and he tried but could not make out what feeling he ought to have for this man. With a child's sensitiveness to feelings in others, he saw distinctly that his father, his governess, and his nurse all not only disliked Vronsky but regarded him with aversion, while his mother looked on him as her greatest friend.
>
> 'What does it mean? Who is he? How ought I to love him? If I don't know, it's my fault: it means I am a silly boy, or a bad boy,' thought the child. And this was what caused his scrutinizing, inquiring, and to some extent hostile expression and the shyness and uncertainty which so embarrassed Vronsky. The child's presence invariably called up in Vronsky that strange feeling of inexplicable revulsion which he had experienced of late. The child's presence called up both in Vronsky and in Anna a feeling akin to that of a sailor who can see by the compass that the direction in which he is swiftly sailing is wide of the proper course, but is powerless to stop. Every moment takes him farther and farther astray, and to admit to himself that he is off his course is the same as admitting final disaster.
>
> This child, with his innocent outlook upon life, was the compass which showed them the degree to which they had departed from what they knew but did not want to know. (pp. 203–4)

Seriozha is the only one of the textual sons (so far) whose consciousness we enter. His confusion, so tenderly represented, and protected instinctively by the couple, is in fact nurtured by nobody. As his innocent knowingness was the gauge of his right to maternal love, so his wish to know and behave rightly – the same scruple that his mother will die of – is the symptom of the unity between the two that breaks into the family. Anna cannot speak of her son to Vronsky. The latter's glimpse at the child's significance is never allowed to repeat itself, for he is something they cannot share. In this Tolstoy chooses differently from Stendhal and Flaubert; more always than a fetish, the boy is not once a connective factor in the real love between two adults. He has, indeed, always been an interceptor of love: we never see his mother and father love him equally, let alone together. Thus his knowledge, always embedded in invidious choice, has only one direction, and Anna is no longer available for anyone to know.

As she hears Seriozha return, we see Anna rise and, in carefully ambiguous wording, put her lover in her child's place:

> She heard the sound of her son's voice coming towards them and, glancing quickly round the terrace, she rose hurriedly to her feet. Her eyes lit up with the light he knew so well; with a swift movement she raised her lovely hands, covered with rings, took his head, gave him a long look, and putting her face near his, with parted, smiling lips, quickly kissed his mouth and both eyes, and pushed him away. (pp. 208–9)

The same day, she receives a visit from her husband. Karenin's coldness and banter towards his wife has been extended lately to his son. '"Aha, young man!" was the greeting with which he addressed him' (p. 219). The child's isolation, as we see him in both parents' presence, is painful.

> Had Karenin cared to, he might have noticed the timid, lost look which the child cast first at his father and then at his mother. But he was unwilling to see anything, and so saw nothing.
> 'Aha, young man! He has grown. Really, he's getting quite a man. How do you do, young man?'
> And he held out his hand to the scared boy.
> Seriozha had always been shy of his father and now, ever since Karenin had taken to calling him 'young man' and since he had begun to worry over the problem whether Vronsky were friend or enemy, he shrank from his father. He looked round at his mother, as if seeking protection. Only with his mother did he feel at ease. Karenin, meanwhile, was talking to the governess with his hand on his son's shoulder, and Seriozha was so miserably uncomfortable that Anna could see he was on the verge of tears.

> Anna, who had flushed a little when the boy came in, noticing
> that Seriozha was wretched, got up hurriedly, lifted Karenin's hand
> off her son's shoulder, kissed the boy as she led him out on to the
> terrace and came back at once. (p. 224)

What we see in this brief scene is the necessity of Anna as maternal
mediator. When she leaves the child behind she abandons her duty to
protect. Later, when Seriozha adjusts himself, life without his mother is
not wholly painful: we see that his days pass in a bearable continuum of
lessons and play; but his first reference-point is gone. Nothing available
in desire replaces this for Anna; and when, a page later, we read that 'two
man, her husband and her lover, were the two centres of her existence'
(p. 225) we know it is not true. That Tolstoy keeps Anna entirely a
patrilinear woman is clear; in the next chapter we shall see how far this
takes her. Positioned between men, her nurturance, which is moral responsibility tuned as love, has no place.

When Anna blurts out the truth, Karenin withdraws with relief from
both wife and son. She decides, remembering suddenly 'the partly sincere, though greatly exaggerated role of the mother living for her child,
which she had assumed during the last few years' (p. 311 – and is this
her knowledge or only the author's?), to leave with Seriozha, her only
'support'. With this term, the author signals his disapproval of Anna's
maternity: such need has no hint of duty. Her plan is intercepted by
Karenin's coldly formal injunction; he threatens to part her from Seriozha
if she does not comply. The only alternative left – 'the shameful one of
a woman who has deserted husband and child to join her lover' (p. 316)
– is still more unthinkable; she bows to the patriarchal law and ceases to
think.

'"Women are all more materialistic than men"' (p. 335), Vronsky's
successful friend Serpuhovskoy tells him, '"We make something immense
out of love, but they are always *terre-à-terre*."' What keeps Anna *à terre*
is her child. From the moment she is airborne into a commitment without
anchor, she cannot return to the ground. This is the reverse of the
relation of Antaeus to his mother; she can only gain strength from her
son. Tolstoy's morality, 'the family idea', damns Anna out of perceptibility. From the point where she loses the chance to hold fast to Seriozha,
she lives in a nightmare of consciousness, for the son's gaze is no longer
hers.

After the seductive interim following birth and illness, when lover and
husband seem the equal issues in her life and momentarily swap places,
Anna returns to life and runs off to Italy with Vronsky. She is temporarily

'unpardonably happy and full of the joy of life' (p. 489), but every index shows them living inauthentically. Vronsky is less blissful: no longer a soldier, he cannot seriously be an artist. Anna is twice painted, socializes as best she can; then they come back to Petersburg because she wants to see her son.

He has, in the meantime, been taken over by Lydia Ivanovna, who has promised to 'apply to [Karenin] only in the last extremity' (p. 538). She refers to him as 'our angel' (p. 545) and has told him his mother is dead. On her advice, Karenin refuses Anna permission to visit. Seriozha is not unhappy, but he does not believe his mother is dead; he looks out for her on his daily walks, rehearsing the joy of their reconciliation. His father takes him through his Bible lessons, speaking to him always 'as if he were addressing some imaginary boy out of a book, utterly unlike himself. And when he was with his father, Seriozha always tried to be that boy out of a book' (p. 553). He is surviving as well as he can, but his authenticity is in his mother's hands: yet her reality, which he still 'knows', can henceforth only be in the night-time world of imagination.

For Anna too, who has plotted her entry without thought of what exactly she will say to her son, the first sight of him early on his birthday morning is a shock; she has remembered him 'as he was at four years old, the age at which she had loved him most' (p. 562). Thinner, longer, older, he opens his eyes and gazes at her, then topples forward into her arms. As he does so, he becomes again the soft infant:

'Seriozha, my darling boy!' she murmured, catching her breath and putting her arms around his chubby little body.

'Mama!' he whispered, wriggling about in her arms so as to touch them with different parts of him.

Smiling sleepily, with eyes still shut, he moved his plump little hands from behind him, flinging his arms round her shoulders and leaning against her, enveloping her with that sweet fragrance of warmth and sleepiness peculiar to children, and began rubbing his face against her neck and shoulder.

'I knew,' he said, opening his eyes. 'To-day is my birthday. I knew you'd come. I'll get up now . . .' And as he spoke he began to doze off again.

This is the most sensual passage in the whole book. Physical love is at its calmest and sweetest, though at the price of happening, for the lover, more or less in a dream. To Anna, the feel of his chubbiness is counter-poised with the sight and knowledge of what has been lost. Her 'hungry eyes' see as much change as restoration. She stops herself crying, helps him get up; he pulls off her hat, takes her hand from his hair, 'pressed the palm to his mouth and covered it with kisses' (p. 563).

The servants respect the icon, leaving them together; when the nurse enters, she too embraces Anna. But the father is the disruptor for both, morally as well as physically:

> How many times afterwards did she think of all the things she might have said! But now she did not know what to say, and was unable to speak. But Seriozha understood all she wanted to say to him. He understood that she was unhappy, and that she loved him. He had caught the words 'regularly at nine o'clock', and he understood that they referred to his father, and that his mother and father must not meet. All this he understood, but one thing he could not understand: why there should be a look of dread and shame on her face. She could not have done anything wrong, but she was afraid and ashamed of something. He wanted to ask a question that would set his doubts at rest, but he did not dare: he saw that she was suffering, and he felt for her. He clung to her in silence and whispered, 'Don't go away. He won't come just yet.'
>
> His mother held him away from her a little, to look into his face and see whether he understood the meaning of what he was saying, and by his frightened expression she read not only that he was speaking of his father but was, as it were, asking her what he ought to think about his father.
>
> 'Seriozha, my darling,' she said, 'You must love him. He's better and kinder than I am, and I have been wicked to him. When you are grown up you will understand.'
>
> 'No one is better than you!' he cried in despair through his tears, and, clutching her by the shoulders, he hugged her with all his might, his arms trembling with the effort.
>
> 'My precious, my little one!' murmured Anna and burst into tears, crying in the same thin childlike way as he did. (pp. 565–6)

In this scene, interrupted a moment later by Karenin's entry and brief bow and Anna's hurried exit, we see most clearly (however blurred by poignancy) Tolstoy's use of the child's perspective. In none of our other texts is such space allowed to the justness of the maternal bond. But where the boy's knowledge exceeds, in its insight into the moral difference between Anna and Karenin, any other male viewpoint in the text, he must indeed grow up, is growing already, and the best that can be

hoped for him is that he will learn to love the patriarch. Anna's anger at
the father's hold over the child she loves better is not all she leaves with.
She also recognizes that Seriozha, unlike her baby daughter, is there to
judge as well as love her. 'And she was for ever separated from him, not
physically only but spiritually, and there was no help for it' (p. 567).

As the photo of Vronsky, which she uses to get her son's photograph
out of the album, falls into her gaze, she reflects that she 'had not
thought of him all the morning. But now, coming all at once upon that
manly, noble face, so familiar and so dear to her, she felt an unexpected
surge of love for him' (p. 568). As once before, and again painfully, she
realizes that he is all she has left to love; but this love, denatured already
by jealousy and the resentment of his freer movement in their city, is
henceforth a ruined substitute. Vronsky's familiarity does not make him
family. For all his assiduous efforts to create a home for her later and to
protect her from humiliation while they are in Petersburg, his adulthood
and sexuality make him less hers than the child of the man she has left.
From this point on, his unstinting loyalty (for Anna's jealousy must not
be justified if she is to die by the internalized judgement of the vengeful
deity) is tinged with impatience. What she has not told him of her
suffering is the key thing in their increasing dissonance, for all it cannot
be separated from the practicalities of his greater social independence and
their incompatible versions of *désœuvrement*. She later expresses this
suffering to Dolly:

> My son? They will never let me have him. And so he will grow up
> despising me, in the house of his father, whom I have abandoned.
> Do you see, I love . . . equally, I think, but both more than myself,
> two beings – Seriozha and Alexei.
> . . . I love these two beings only, and the one excludes the other.
> I cannot have them both; yet that is my one need. And since I can't
> have that, I don't care about the rest. Nothing matters; nothing,
> nothing! And it will end one way or another, and so I can't – I
> don't like to talk of it. (pp. 671–2)

This is not the whole of Anna's problem, but it is the centre. Her choice
to have no more children is, essentially, the decision to deny Vronsky
a son; for he, conscientious and concerned for what he sees as Anna's
happiness (as Dolly's reliable view vouches) is also looking to his own
genealogy in his wish to marry her: '"some day we may have a son . . . my
son, and by law he would be a Karenin"' (p. 658). Anna has no wish to
obviate this paradox; her refusal of a divorce is a double insurance against

replacing Seriozha. Her suspension in the impossible patrilinear choice between lover and son has to be preserved because it captures as no more purely social considerations can the dilemma of two incompatible kinds of love. The sexual mother is, for Tolstoy more than for the other more truly hominocentric authors, as much a horror as a delight.

Seriozha is last glimpsed, through Stiva's viewpoint, playing dangerously the 'railway game' he has learned at school. Refusing to remember Anna, his eyes ('so like his mother's – they had lost their childish look of innocence now': p. 760) shut out not only her but any direct contact with the rest of the world. On the day of her suicide, Anna's stream-of-consciousness once again conflates son and lover: '"how dreary it is, how wretched . . . The boulevard and the children. Three boys running about playing at horses. Seriozha! And I shall lose everything and never get him back. Yes, everything will be lost if he doesn't return. Perhaps he missed the train and is back by now"' (p. 790). The replacement implicit in this phrasing takes over directly later, in a moment of cruel insight: '"Seriozha? . . . I thought, too, that I loved him, and used to be moved by my own tenderness for him. Yet here I have lived without him. I exchanged him for another love, and did not complain as long as that other love satisfied me"' (p. 797). As she jumps under the wheels of the train, it is her own childhood she recalls, not his.

Returning to this text in the next chapter, we shall see the female relationships which fail to sustain the patrilinear Anna Karenina from this choice among men. But while the adulteress perishes, the good mother receives better. After Anna's near-fatal birth of a daughter we watch, through the nervous husband's eyes, Kitty's happy struggle to produce her deserved son. Levin, like Frédéric, is initially shocked at the ugliness of the newborn: 'the strange, wriggling red creature . . . only inspired him with a feeling of disgust and pity, which was not in the least what he had anticipated' (p. 751); rather, he finds a new burden of responsibility and apprehension that does nothing to allay his suicidal impulses. Kitty, fully occupied at last, feeds and bathes her baby as Anna never does hers. And the complete patrilinear significance of this child is seen in the closing pages. Kitty, who can feel the child's hunger in her breasts before he even begins to cry, gazes down at him and wishes him no better future than to '"try to be like your father"' (p. 820); Levin reacknowledges, via an encounter with a peasant, 'those spiritual truths that he had imbibed with his mother's milk' (p. 832); he finds the two of them, soaked through but safe after a rainstorm in the woods; and the baby, lifted out of his bath, shows his father with smiles and gurgles how he can recognize his mother. This above all, it is suggested, is that banality that makes happy families all alike. The mutual regard of one son and mother is the seal upon the doom of the other pair, smiling and together no longer.

Maupassant's *Pierre et Jean* (1888) is a story of retrospective discovery, told from the viewpoint of the legitimate son. The mother's adultery is his drama; like Hamlet, he discovers her sexuality though she is long since a virtuous wife again and purely maternal in function. What he also learns, in a crisis that finishes with his semi-voluntary exile from the family circle, is that it is he, not the illegitimate brother, who stands apart and excluded. Questions of similarity and separation are the structuring pattern that shapes this otherwise entirely internal drama.

There are two sons in the Roland family, the dark, nervous Pierre and the blond hirsute Jean: from infancy a semi-benign rivalry has shaped their relations. Their father is a brash ex-jeweller, retired to Le Havre to indulge his passion for the sea, their mother economical and mild-mannered, young looking at forty-eight. Both brothers have qualified at the same time, the elder after several stormy career changes as a doctor, the younger as a lawyer. A neighbour, the pretty Mme Rosémilly, a wealthy widow, hovers on the edge of the family circle, poised to marry one or the other. Then an old family friend dies, leaving his fortune to Jean.

Maréchal had entertained the two brothers often in his apartment when they were students in Paris. Open-handed, he embraced both equally. Now, when asked how he came to know their parents, the mother recollects:

'It was in '58, I think, dear. Pierre was three years old. I'm sure I'm not mistaken because that's the year the child had scarlet fever, and Maréchal, whom we didn't know well yet, was such a help to us.'

Roland cried: 'That's right, that's right, he really was wonderful! Your mother was worn out and I was busy in the shop, so he would go to the chemist to get your medicine. He was a fine chap and no mistake! And when you were better, you've no idea how pleased he was, hugging and kissing you. It's really after that that we became great friends.'

And a sudden, violent thought tore like a bullet into Pierre's soul: 'If he knew me first and was so devoted to me, if he loved me and kissed me so much and I was the cause of his great friendship with my parents, how come he left his whole fortune to my brother and nothing to me?'[32]

This is not just jealousy or envy but more precisely the trauma of legitimacy. The infant son, part of the charm of the lovely unloved woman whose devotion lies in her maternity, receives as proxy the earliest caresses of her lover: Maréchal was vouchsafed the role of a Julien Sorel (for all Maupassant's apprenticeship at the hand of the family friend Flaubert), not a Frédéric Moreau or a Vronsky. Like Julien, he displayed his love via a child-mediator, showing the skills of the helpmate meanwhile. When the child fell ill he fetched medicine, and thirty years later Pierre is a doctor. Another medical intervention followed after five years. At the birth of the second son, Maréchal rushed off to get the doctor's assistance, grabbing Roland's hat in his haste; the latter, ever the ignorant quoter of his own disadvantage, suggests: '"We had a good laugh about that afterwards. He probably remembered that detail when he was dying and as he had no heir he said to himself: 'You know, I contributed in a small way to the birth of that child, why don't I leave him my fortune?'"' (p. 52).

Recapping a bit further, Pierre gradually disinters the likely beginning of the affair. The aptly-named Léon Maréchal entered a jeweller's shop one day:

> So this Maréchal, young, free, rich, all ready for a tender love affair, walked quite by chance one day into a shop, perhaps because he had noticed the pretty assistant. He bought something, came back, got chatting, a little more familiar every day, and by frequent purchases bought himself the right to sit in this house, smile at the young wife and clasp the hand of the husband.
>
> And then what . . . oh my God . . . then what?
>
> He had loved and caressed the first child, the jeweller's child, until the other was born, then he had remained secretive until his death, and then, his grave closed up, his flesh decomposed, his name wiped out from the names of the living, his whole being gone for ever, with nothing more to be careful of, to fear or to hide, he gave his whole fortune to that second child. Why? This man was intelligent . . . He must have realized and foreseen that he might, that he was bound to make people think that child was his. – So he compromised the honour of a woman? Why would he have done that if Jean was not his son? (p. 105, all ellipses Maupassant's)

Contributing to the saving of one child, he gets to contribute to the next one's birth and seals the gift by contributing everything to him at his own death. By the end of the text, when Pierre departs for the life of a ship's doctor, interned in a tiny cabin in a huge unmaternal vessel, Jean has taken his place as the legitimated son by reason of his inheritance. With the money, he is able to win two things Pierre desired in order to establish himself as a man: a flashy apartment with rooms to receive clients, and the pretty widow next door. As he makes his unromantic proposal, is accepted without blushes – all to the accompaniment of a shell-fishing trip, slipping among rock-pools – Jean is sealed in to the family structure of a continued line, however redirected via desire, and it is he who delights both his parents, while Pierre growls to his mother on observing the betrothal scene: ' "I'm watching and learning: so that's how a man prepares to be cuckolded" ' (p. 150).

Critical gossip has it, on the grounds of a surely conventional address as 'mon fils', that Maupassant may have been Flaubert's son;[33] hence his fascination in story and novel for adulterous women and every permutation of the situation of the 'natural child'. Some point out that he was himself, as profligate as irresponsible sexually, the father of three known and possibly more unknown children. But the point of the theme in *Pierre et Jean* is surely the very reverse of this.

In Freud's family romance, bastardy is every child's fantasy: fancying itself born of finer, richer and nicer parents, merely fostered by those who take care of it with normal imperfection, it (or, more especially, he) then moves on to the neater expedient of imagining itself a bastard, thus casting discredit on both parents at once.[34] We have seen this theme exemplified in Julien Sorel, and eagerly endorsed by characters and implied author alike; in our own century, Gide and Sartre continue to play with the theme. Romantic fiction is, if you like, always the psychodrama of the bastard-fantasy, whose most famous exemplar is Jesus, merely if kindly fostered by a kind of adulteress and a sort of cuckold. But *Pierre et Jean* overturns Romanticism in a very precise way. It shows how the real cuckoo in the nest is the child born of marriage, not love. In the same moment that the mother's desire is discovered as exogamic and scandalous, the legitimate son discovers himself to be extraneous to everybody's plans. It is because the cuckold is irrelevant to such wishful narratives that his genetic offspring has no place. Through the expedient of the obsessively genealogical thinking of Maupassant's characters, via the new genetics of money – inheritance down the line of love, not blood – the family is restructured. And if Roland remains in typical ignorance of the whole arrangement that disempowers him, Pierre agonizes into knowledge.

This is why the sick son must grow up to be a doctor. Pierre wields a nasty scalpel not only against his own sore heart but also against the closed wound of the mother's past losses (here labelled sins, of course –

sins less against a husband's rights and purity than against the sons'), but it is to Jean that she 'confesses', by him that she is 'pardoned' and given the passionate caresses Pierre has forever lost the right to offer.[35] The desire of the mother can, *pace* Shakespeare, only go via a contempt phrased as forgiveness. This belongs to the blond son, for Pierre is dark-haired like his bumbling father.

Most critics start by following the antithesis in the first scene of the text and taking the fraternal-feud theme as a nicely structuring referent. Others observe that Jean, for all his fairness, is more like Père Roland in his complacency, conventionality and tendency to take life easy, preferring ignorance to discomfort; in various ways he has always been held up to Pierre, like an elder sibling, as an example of how to behave. They note that Pierre has the makings of a Romantic poet-type like Maréchal, with his restlessness, masochistic self-examination and bitter sense of exclusion. None point out that his bitterness resides precisely – and what spinner of the family romance's does not? – in the shock of *not* being given the badge of the outsider at birth. Instead, he learns exclusion as he perceives that money smoothly replaces other modes of genealogy and that out-siderhood is sordid, circular and unenlightening, exactly like his thoughts. Nobody in Pierre's world can forgive the fruits of conjugal boredom.

Thus the physician cannot heal himself: the sick son is condemned to wield his investigative skills, read the symptoms and fail to care, both for his love-object and for himself. As we last glimpsed Seriozha playing at railway accidents, Pierre, once he has discovered (he is never told, but his assumption runs easily ahead of knowledge) that his mother is an adul-teress, takes upon himself the task of her punishment, tormenting and goading her. In this, he plays the magistrate more surely than his brother who, endowed with everything a good son could want, embraces and reinserts the mother into her threatened place. The final scene of the story shows them all at sea again, the parental and the young couple together in the little family boat and Pierre, from his ship, waving fran-tically at his mother in a farewell that is both permanent and provisional – for the ship will soon be back but he will never forgive.

That forgiveness is necessary is an unshakeable premise of the text and all its readers. Few do more than glance at the fact that pardon is the prerogative of son not husband, for it seems so eminently right. Mme Roland's story, as she tells it to Jean, is the nearest justification an adulteress can get:

'If we are to go on living together and embrace one another, my little Jean, you must tell yourself that if I was the mistress of your father, I was even more truly his wife, his real wife, that deep in my heart I don't feel ashamed, I regret nothing, that I love him still even though he is dead, I'll always love him, I never loved anyone but him, he was my whole life, my joy, all my hope, my consolation, everything, everything to me, for so long! Listen, my darling: before God who hears me, I would have had no happiness in life if I hadn't met him, nothing at all, no tenderness, no sweetness, not one of those moments that make us regret growing old, nothing! I owe him everything! He is all I had in the world, he and then the two of you, your brother and you. Without you all it would have been empty, black and empty as night.' (p. 171)

If it is an afterthought that the sons are as much the love-objects as the lover, the husband is nowhere in sight, except as that darkness from which passion and maternity emerge as light. But we can see that, even though Jean hears these words (Pierre has gone and his position as narrative viewpoint has been pointedly appropriated here), the mother makes no distinction between her love for the legitimate and the illegitimate sons. As a patrilinear mother, she is devoted not just to both but to an idyll of equality between them – until the moment, that is, when Pierre becomes her tormentor and exiles himself from a circle he cannot re-enter.

Money and desire equally centre the family in this text, as elsewhere in Maupassant. Family fathers (and Roland belongs in Molière or even Feydeau rather than tragedy, as Cogny points out)[36] are the occasion for the placing of a group and no more. All parents, here the three of them, not just the married pair, seek the equality, even similarity of the children – that is until the one act that opens up the past. But this text is as Freudian as it is Shakespearean because it is quite literally the son's story and most directly tells the tale of disallowed desire via the lover *as child*. Maupassant has taken up the drama of the sick son to retell the homino-centric novel of adultery more frankly than we have seen before: here are Julien, Frédéric and Vronsky reincarnated as the real loser. Pierre wants his mother both sexual and 'pure', the whole object of young-man's desire. He ends by taking on himself a version of the death the other three protagonists avoided and passed on to the woman. Properly patri-linear, Mme Roland is allowed to keep the lover intact in the son who resembles his image (the portrait Pierre hunted out and gazed on) but also preserves the pleasures of her after-all conventional soul. Before love, now and since, the 'economically-minded, rather sentimental bourgeoise, gifted with a tender shopkeeper's heart' (p. 29), she has long since

passed her Romantic phase, and finds a consoling future in the continuation of her double line in the one remaining boy.

As for the author's strategy, we see in the sick son reinvented as doctor
a version of distancing distinct from the other texts. In the so-called
'Preface' to *Pierre et Jean*, published with the novel for editorial reasons,
Maupassant begins by disavowing any connection between the fiction
and the argument, even though the latter defends diversity in novels'
forms and styles. It also most famously defends a behaviourist mode of
representation that will scrupulously 'observe' external symptoms rather
than presenting feelings as felt. The book, of course, does just the opposite, dwelling inside the protagonist's head in a merciless exposé of his
accession to knowledge. Pierre's ignorance and passion is the whole story
of this narrative and what makes its externally comic elements into something more like tragedy. By contrast to Stendhal's use of the protagonist
as desirer, Flaubert's stance of ironic repulsion, Tolstoy's most carefully
distributed omniscience, Maupassant agonizes with his character about
what can legitimately be discovered. It is as both revealer and revealed
that the son is most an outsider.

I want to end this chapter by offering in brief four more recent examples
of the motif of the sick son. In each of these, the son is invoked, familiarly,
as the criterion by which a woman's badness, her disloyalty to legitimate
family life, is measured. Her adultery, real or potential, is always with a
younger, single man who in one way or another is implicitly compared
with the child.

The first of these texts is the only one in my book by a woman author.
In her writing, the motif of the sick son is used satirically, as the focus
of the husband's reproach that a mother's desires (not yet adulterous,
merely a wish for some free time) are disruptive of her duties. In Kate
Chopin's *The Awakening* (1899), the protagonist Edna Pontellier is a
twenty-eight-year-old mother whose slow sexual awakening accompanies
a need to shake off domestic responsibilities that have never really suited
her. The family is staying at the resort of Grand Isle; the husband returns
late from an evening out, 'in an excellent humour, in high spirits and
very talkative',[37] and wakes his wife, chattering while she, 'overcome with
sleep, . . . answered him with little half utterances'.

> Mr. Pontellier had forgotten the bonbons and peanuts for the boys.
> Notwithstanding he loved them very much, and went into the ad-
> joining room where they slept to take a look at them and make sure

they were resting comfortably. The result of his investigation was far from satisfactory. He turned and shifted the youngsters about in bed. One of them began to kick and talk about a basket full of crabs.

Mr. Pontellier returned to his wife with the information that Raoul had a high fever and needed looking after. Then he lit a cigar and went and sat near the open door to smoke it.

Mrs. Pontellier was quite sure Raoul had no fever. He had gone to bed perfectly well, she said, and nothing had ailed him all day. Mr. Pontellier was too well acquainted with fever symptoms to be mistaken. He assured her the child was consuming at that moment in the next room.

He reproached his wife with her inattention, her habitual neglect of the children. If it was not a mother's place to look after her children, whose on earth was it? He himself had his hands full with his brokerage business. He could not be in two places at once; making a living for his family on the street, and staying at home to see that no harm befell them. He talked in a monotonous, insistent way.

Mrs. Pontellier sprang out of bed and went into the next room. She soon came back and sat on the edge of the bed, leaning her head down on the pillow. She said nothing, and refused to answer her husband when he questioned her. When his cigar was smoked out he went to bed, and in half a minute he was fast asleep. (pp. 12–13)

No further sign is given that the boy, 'tumbling about' (p. 15) cheerfully with his brother the next day, has been ill. Edna's rightness is expended in a bitter-sweet crying session that night and a subsequent gradual separation from the family and its demands, culminating in moving out of their New Orleans house to a small home of her own nearby, taking up painting and, much later, starting an affair with a man she does not love. Robert, the one she does care for, a young neighbour on Grand Isle, returning finally from a self-imposed journey to Mexico, reluctantly reveals he loves her but leaves after the beginnings of seduction.

Edna's need for independence and self-development, perceived by her menfolk as caprice, is presented in a contrast to her friend Adèle Ratignolle who, unlike her, is a 'mother-woman'. Deliciously beautiful, empty-headed but for maternal and domestic concerns, she argues with Edna about what a mother's commitment entails. Edna swears 'that she would never sacrifice herself for her children, or for any one . . . "I would give up the unessential; I would give up my money, I would give up my life for my children; but I wouldn't give myself. I can't make it more clear; it's only something which I am beginning to comprehend, which is revealing itself to me"' (pp. 79–80).

On the evening of the sexual encounter with Robert, Edna is called out to assist at the birth of Adèle's fourth child; at the end of this 'scene of torture' (p. 182), the latter's whispered imprecation '"think of the children!"' remains in her mind when she returns to find the young man gone. The next day she goes to Grand Isle and walks into the sea, thinking as she does so:

> 'Today it is Arobin; tomorrow it will be someone else. It makes no difference to me, it doesn't matter about Léonce Pontellier – but Raoul and Etienne!' . . .
>
> There was no one thing in the world that she desired. There was no human being whom she wanted near her except Robert; and she even realized that the day would come when he, too, and the thought of him would melt out of her existence, leaving her alone. The children appeared before her like antagonists who had overcome her, who had overpowered and sought to drag her into the soul's slavery for the rest of her days. But she knew a way to elude them. (pp. 188–9)

Her suicide in the sea represents a rebirth (drowning naked, recollections of girlhood) but it is the only reply to the conflict between maternity and autonomy. The romantic pessimism of this text chimes in with all the other suicidal adulteries – except that here the child is never sick and the woman's health is more explicitly ruined for the sake of an unnecessary duty. Loss of both lover and sons, innocently but not exclusively loved, is the punishment of a simple wish for separate activity, just as desire here is a mere outreach of that motive of independence, not its source.

In Evelyn Waugh's light, grim *A Handful of Dust* (1934), we have that rare thing, the cuckold's story. Less cruel, the author is as ironic as Flaubert in his treatment of a society of butterflies, its nearest victim left finally trapped in an Amazonian jungle condemned interminably to read Dickens out loud to a madman. Here the wife's lover and son have the same name; the scene of her damnation is a black comedy of misunderstanding. The boy, briefly drawn as naive and lonely, has been killed in a riding accident. A family friend hurries to London to break the news to Brenda. Her lover meanwhile has taken a plane to France and '"she's been worrying all day thinking he's had an accident."'[38]

'Jock Grant-Menzies wants to see you downstairs.'
'Jock? How very extraordinary. It isn't anything awful, is it?'
'You'd better go and see him.'
Suddenly Brenda became frightened by the strange air of the room and the unfamiliar expression in her friends' faces. She ran downstairs to the room where Jock was waiting.
'What is it, Jock? Tell me quickly, I'm scared. It's nothing awful, is it?'
'I'm afraid it is. There's been a very serious accident.'
'John?'
'Yes.'
'Dead?'
He nodded.
She sat down on a hard little Empire chair against the wall, perfectly still with her hands folded in her lap, like a small well-brought-up child introduced into a room full of grown-ups. She said, 'Tell me what happened. Why do you know about it first?'
'I've been down at Hetton since the week-end.'
'Hetton?'
'Don't you remember? John was going hunting to-day.'
She frowned, not at once taking in what he was saying. 'John . . . John Andrew . . . I . . . oh, thank God . . .' Then she burst into tears. (pp. 117–18)

In this tiny scene everything of the sick-son topos is dramatized. No reader can fail to be shocked by the farce of misreading and the blurted climax of 'thank God' – the boy is of course the only appealing figure of the text, learning painfully the snobbish graces his elders live and breathe – which makes the adulteress unforgiveable. The story continues an indigestible comedy in which desire is never allowed to be more than curiously desultory, even when it destroys innocents. Authorial disgust has a kind of voyeuristic disdain for the sexuality that motivates bored people. The line of the Lasts (no naming is casual in this book) is doubly buried alive.

My other two examples are both films. Vittorio De Sica's *I bambini ci guardano* (*The Children Are Watching Us*) (1942) depicts a mother's adultery through the gaze of her small son. She leaves home with her lover, but when the child falls ill, returns to see him, arriving behatted like Anna Karenina, leaning tenderly over his bed. Temporarily she comes back resolved to fidelity but later meets the lover again at a holiday resort; the ignored boy runs away and is found by policemen; her transgression visible to the clacking crowds, she departs again. The father takes him to a Catholic boarding school and commits suicide. When the mother comes to reclaim him, he looks at her, refuses her embrace and walks away to bury his loss in the skirts of a teacher-priest. The bleakness of this closing bereavement is sealed by the enclosing of the child into a masculine world of celibate protectiveness, a loveless but safely institutional incarceration. Once again, the sin of temptation and fall is written in the terms of a patrilinear exchange: fatherhood can legitimately be transferred, motherhood never.

The topos lives on. There must be more instances still than I have found, but my final one is from 1988, David Hare's film *Paris by Night*. In the text, the writer's introduction cites 'one of the two or three American actresses whose participation would have made the film an instant "go"'.[39]

> 'I like the script,' she said, 'but I couldn't possibly play Clara Paige.' Reluctantly, I asked why not. 'Because she is so neglectful of her child.' I asked if this was something which, as an actress, she could not simulate. 'No way,' she said, showing me a lot of famous leg. 'You must understand, David, one day I'm hoping to have children myself.'

The author's sexy surprise is disingenuous. Clara is a thoroughly bad lot – a Tory MP whose adultery is mixed up with her impulsive murder of a former business associate who she thinks has followed her to Paris, when he has really arrived there by mistake with his likeable daughter – and her cold-heartedness is underlined by her exploitation of the drunken husband and long-suffering sister who take care of her son in her place. Working mothers may find the point irritating, for Clara is affectionate in her moments but hurried and distracted by professional timekeeping like the rest of us. When she abandons a conversation about the clock-work train he has just made in order to tell her sister of the latest 'enabling legislation' (p. 8), every viewer, raised up on sick sons, registers that the gooey chocolates from Fortnums are a bribe and Mum will be off again in a moment.

Her lover is of course young and helpful. But when young Simon gets acute appendicitis and the husband and sister telephone her hotel in vain, she is with him by reason less of adulterous passion than of panic at the gratuitous act of murder. Both the other children in the film are girls: the lover's niece whose warm place in the home sets Clara to envying other people's lives, and her victim's daughter whose presence in Paris is part of her reason for not being able to come home. This girl reveals the truth about the unnecessary crime, reminds her of a happier past, displays her lame leg and storms out of a restaurant. Meanwhile, the sick son waits in hospital in London. The cuckold puts in a claim from both menfolk:

INT. HOSPITAL. EVENING.
A nurse goes by, carrying flowers. GERALD *smiles at her absently, turns away, because what he is about to say is so intimate and sincere.*
GERALD: Clara, I've been a bloody fool. You know that. [*He looks down the ward to the distant, sleeping figure of the* BOY.] When you see this little boy, you realize. I love him. I love you. We've both been beastly and careless of each other. Me as well as you. You forget why you first married. And the whole purpose of your life. When something like this happens you realize we must make an effort. Please come back to me. I want to see you tonight.

INT. EMBASSY. EVENING.
CLARA *has tears in her eyes now, from* GERALD*'s tone on the telephone.*
CLARA: Look I . . . you know I want to . . . For some time I've wanted to . . . settle things down. It's just . . . [*She looks across. The* GIRL *is putting her tea down on the seat next to her and is picking up her things as if to go.*]
I can't leave Paris right now. (p. 47)

It is left to the lover to pronounce judgement on Clara's moral turpitude, once he has learned that not simply desire of him (shocking enough) but also an unfollowed murder kept Clara in Paris the night her son was ill. Vaguely socialist, he lets us share his disgust at having once slept with such a poor creature as her. Her ethical level is illustrated by the combination of crimes and mischances, but it is her absence at the sick son's bedside that is most unpardonable – and most unmediatedly adulterous, whatever the local excuses. 'I'll say what sort of mother you were' (p. 65), threatens Gerald as they talk divorce. 'You didn't come home when he was in hospital. [*He looks at her*]. Well, did you? It doesn't look good . . . If you've got a man, I'd like to know.' As Wallace elicits her confession, the son is reintroduced: 'I'm not a killer. I won't kill again. I made an honest mistake. For which I'm always going to suffer . . . The whole thing is over. I have a son. Think what would happen to him if I went to prison' (p. 75). 'You're corrupt,' he retorts, 'You have no character. That's your real curse. Words come out, but there's nothing in you.'

Thus the woman is condemned by her failure and her use of maternity. Her Conservatism – 'People are crying out to be led. [*She pauses a second, a little overwhelmed.*]' (p. 71) – is a parody of motherly sacrifice, the '[*glint of mad excitement in her eye*]' a lust for power not the body. The husband is vouchsafed the final act: he bundles the boy in a blanket, drops him at the kindly sister's, awaits Clara's arrival and then surprises us by shooting not himself but her. But the last frames belong, in order, to the son, the lover and again the son: ['SIMON *wakes up. Sits up. Listens.*]' (p. 83). The sick son, as ever, survives.

In sum, the topos of the sick son is used to keep both mother and lover enclosed within a form from which neither is ready to escape. Desire is legitimated by its safely marginal position to a surviving structure, just as the child is only briefly at risk from the wrath of a paternal author who cannot quite support unmarried desire. We have only to contrast the icon of the Madonna and Child with that of Venus and Cupid to see where the son-topos can be made to go. The virgin mother sits with a boy presented forward in her arms: here the larger, the bodily maker, is the less, the infantile the divine. In the always erotic Venus-pair, however, the male child serves an entirely different role: moving within the frame for the unrepresentable phallus of the viewer's (and painter's) gaze outsie it, he leads the way in to the woman's available body. Playing protagonist to the author/reader, or rival to the protagonist of filial sexuality, he is, as always in desire, *nearly* in place. The son's position is always, quite precisely, nearly there.

4
Matrilinear Mothers

*I*n male-authored texts, bad women have daughters. Unfit for either icon, they are outlawed from either Mary's or Venus's story, left instead to grapple with the distasteful mystery (to patriarchy, the absurdity) of a female self-reproduction. Why double the unique, except to make more useful things – thus mother–daughter pairs have a kind of bleak justification if they produce and support each other by prostitution; we have seen this picture framed here by the masculinity of an orgiastic Paris, there by a rural priesthood's involuted fraternities. If however the female genealogy reaches out further (back, forward or laterally), it must above all be enclosed. Occulted by both exclusion and incarceration, the mother–daughter pair is what the mother–son pair fails to be, *always there*. Wherever 'there' might be, it does not bear looking at. The male author of the matrilinear text makes what he cannot make. Like lesbianism in Proust, this is the place where authorship halts.

I have four main texts again to examine in this chapter, but I shall transgress chronology in one instance, taking them in the following order: *Madame Bovary* (1857), *Anna Karenina* (1873), *The Scarlet Letter* (1850) and *Effi Briest* (1895). My first two texts offer a (at least immediately) negative view of the mother–daughter pair as disappointment. The other two, one as light of touch as the other is heavy, represent the structure as punishment, certainly, but also as potential knowledge. In each text, again, I seek the phantasy of authorship that places characters, readers and structures in a motivation of desire.

The anecdotal origins of *Madame Bovary*, Flaubert's first published novel, tell us that he was advised by his friends Bouilhet and Du Camp, who hated the byzantine *Tentation de Saint Antoine*, to look for a subject a bit closer to the ground. In a letter written four years later, he comments:

> What is natural to me is what is unnatural for others, the extraordinary, the fantastical, a metaphysical and mythological bellowing. *Saint Antoine* did not cost me a quarter of the intellectual tension that *Bovary* demands. It was an outlet; I had nothing but pleasure in the writing, and the eighteen months I spent in writing its 500 pages were the most deeply voluptuous of my whole life. Consider then, every minute I am having to get under *skins* that are antipathetic to me.[1]

The sexual terms in which this author expresses the pleasures and agonies of writing are not unusual for him and invite a more fundamentally gendered reading of this text than we have seen before. Flaubert is a figure in his fiction more than other writers for the very reason of his avoidance of appearing there. The tension of non-consummation is precisely what makes his aesthetic personal: if the saint's pained continence lets him pour forth, this novel of adultery is repressive exactly as it represents the entry into the woman. Everything in *Madame Bovary* is a sexual-political relation: the author refuses the very entry he desires.

There is, essentially, only one woman in the text: with her, the author enacts a perpetual distancing act by reason of his ambivalence towards the identification that tempts him. His position (in Joyce's words) as 'God of the creation, . . . within or behind or beyond or above his handiwork, invisible, refined out of existence, indifferent, paring his fingernails',[2] is an extreme choice of refusing the body which must be that of a female, a fool, a reader. Not only Emma but all the merely human characters occupy this space, and the reader has nowhere to be but there with them. For if a man is a man by not being a woman,[3] an author is an author – that is, a deity – by removing himself from the space of reading into some unbodied 'above' in which alone creation can take place. This supremely modernistic phantasy informs such writings as those of Joyce or Gide, such dead seriously ludic 'experiments' as the *nouveau roman*, the frantic wish of Sartre's Roquentin to create something in which authorship can only be intuited posthumously by the reader as a reproach. It is always again a question of masculinity as that divine quality, the disincarnated everything.

It was again between *Saint Antoine* and *Madame Bovary* that Flaubert made his already quoted remark: 'the author in his work must be like God in the universe: everywhere present and nowhere visible.' As we observed earlier, this is no abandonment of power but the refusal to be that merely perceptible thing, an idol: in Flaubert's fictional real, everything is woefully visible, every speech in double quotation marks,[4] every object mercilessly lit, with the sole exception of the author who, even as narrator, knows how to dart and metamorphose out of our sight. We then have the choice: to fail to equal the state of the always-too-clever author or to stay on earth and be, like Emma, redeemable as beautiful perhaps but interminably hopeful, stupid – a reader.

This is the politics of irony. Emma must not escape or enjoy, in order that the pleasure and free play of the text (deplored by the art-for-art's-sake author, but really the ultimate buzz of abstinence) remain in the author's pallid hands. All that makes him perceptible is the famous 'style' – a thing that is no-thing, that readers must sigh after, that the text must somehow not contain: 'what would be beautiful to me, what I should like to make, is a book about nothing, a book with no external attachment, which would stand up by itself by the internal force of its style.'[5] The book that could self-erect and need nobody and nothing: that is the author's desire. Meanwhile, since body there must be, his fictional matter shall be dull, debased, disappointing, following a spiral-arc of risible desire, so that where it is he is not. The body of these desiring disappointments can only belong to a woman.

The irony of *Madame Bovary* is much more radical than that of *L'Education sentimentale*, for here the author goes extraordinarily beyond the embodiment (albeit ridiculed) of his male wishes in a text. That the feminocentric text preceded the more directly confessional one serves only to stress (as Sartre knew) that Flaubert's desiring phantasy has more of the shock of feminization than the transcendent fun of the boy's story.[6] Emma Bovary is less what than how he desires. Thus she must repeatedly be punished, not least in the birth of a daughter whom she, more irredeemably than any of our other female protagonists, can never love.

To illustrate this politics, and before looking more closely at the question of maternity in the novel, I want to examine the clearest instance of the irony, which is Flaubert's use of the technique of *style indirect libre*. It is not his invention, and is not universally used ironically; indeed, even with regard to Flaubert's usage, critics have (falling into the fool's place, of course) suggested that it shows a certain sympathy. But he uses it to *tease* sympathy, to appear and withdraw in the same motion, to get under those skins and not be there.

The technique works thus: grammatically consistent with the narrative thread (that is, continuing in a third person and past tense, and without any introductory verb of saying or thinking) the words on the page somehow seem to represent thoughts or feelings of a character – yet they are never wholly in that character's voice, always carrying a hint that the implied author is making them as they are. 'The author,' as Alison Fairlie puts it, 'can move almost imperceptibly between their semi-articulate conceptions and his own more exact and heightened expression of them.'[7] 'Emma couldn't,' she goes on, have given her dreams these phrases, this tone. Thus the touchingly stupid thoughts are hers, the fine exactitude his, or sometimes the revelatory quality of cliché is hers, the sensitive exposure his; it does not much matter who supplies what, as long as we recognize the difference between high and low, his and hers. And how we measure the portion of Emma among the 'Flaubert' (for he is a fiction too, of course, of which more in a moment) is the coefficient of foolish to wise, and above all his status as writer, hers as merely reader.

Emma is a consumer doomed never to give forth. Like Don Quixote, like Joyce's Gerty MacDowell or Eveline, she is immature, unmasculine and touchingly stupid in so far as she thinks and feels in derivative language. She has fed on clichés. Her dreams of transcendence are braked not only by her secondary position, fated to rely on men to let her (or fail to let her) fly, but also by the body and mind that are made up out of others' rubbish, the stuff that women read. The writer, both masculine and unbodied like God, is that which makes good language.[8] Indeed, as a debate over certain locutions in Joyce's 'Eveline' shows, the never-definable portion of the implied author in *style indirect libre* (since *pater semper incertus est*) is gauged purely by the 'level' we intuit at work. Emma and Eveline breathe uncritical jargon: Flaubert and Joyce know and parody. This is how Seymour Chatman discusses it in a footnote:

> For example, a recent article misreads 'Eveline' by confusing character's point of view and narrator's voice (Clive Hart, 'Eveline', in *James Joyce's Dubliners: Critical Essays*, London, 1969, p. 51). The author argues that Eveline is shallow and incapable of love – which may be true – but supports his argument with questionable evidence: 'She over-dramatizes her association with Frank, calls it an "affair" and him her "lover"; she thinks of herself in pulp-literature terms as "unspeakably" weary. But most obvious of all is the strong note of falsity in the language of the passage in which she reasserts her choice to leave: "As she mused the pitiful vision of her mother's life laid its spell on the very quick of her being..." Dublin has so paralysed Eveline's emotions that she is unable to love, can think of herself and her situation only by means of a series of tawdry clichés.' Surely the objectionable words are not Eveline's but the narrator's. It is he who is parodying pulp-literature sentimentality in tawdry clichés (as does the narrator of the 'Nausicaa' section of

Ulysses). Eveline may indeed feel maudlin sentiments, but 'mused', 'pitiful vision', 'very quick of her being' are not in her vocabulary.[9]

There is a lot of confusion here. Precisely, if Joyce is parodying (and how crassly) her clichéd mentality, these words *are* in her vocabulary – and are in it pure and fully endowed with feeling, as Emma's most hackneyed love-terms avowedly are; it is rather the implied author who is speaking them with the tips of his fingers, as it were, and it is simply the distaste of his speaking that we are asked to respect, so that the girl's unconscious quotation is condemned in the name of his conscious one. Yet how does Chatman, Hart, Fairlie or any other reader know with such certainty what such young women 'would' say? It is the same prurient entry under the woman's skin that formulated Flaubert's aesthetic of divine disgust. It is a laughable but dangerous sureness, born of the preference of irony over the body – that is, of the paternal to the maternal mode of knowledge, as Freud compares them.[10]

Chatman is confused also in attributing what is not Eveline's to 'the narrator'. It is rather the implied author who is at stake here. We are inferring, when we read *style indirect libre*, that 'Flaubert' or 'Joyce' is too good for these words, recognizing here that 'narrator' is a poor fictional term for the protean wit of the textual stream of our author. The impossibility of a narrator is these authors' trademark (the only one, they hope). On the contrary, the real fiction at work here is the figure of 'Flaubert' or 'Joyce', and the most phantasmatic fiction of all. It is the implied author they set out, when they write, to engender in us. To be him in the making and again in our reading is the true *volupté* of such creators.

No wonder this pleasure is painful: it is above all a *coitus interruptus*. Neither Emma nor I may reliably be the body in whom the author is carried. He must after all be simultaneously father and son. And again, it must be the phantasy of deification on the Judaeo-Christian model. The Jewish God is incarnated only in a text: in all else he is bodiless, sexless, non-carnal, plural in noun and masculine singular only in the dependent verb – but here of course ineluctably gendered, because his real motivation is the regendering of the qualities that belong, visibly, in the female body: creation and providence. In the Christian God the redrawn stake is after all genealogy and after all it turns out that he has, if he is to engender something both human and divine, to descend to the material/maternal, if embarrassedly and just for an instant. This phantasy is Flaubert's *Madame Bovary*, the text wherein he briefly enters that body as shamefully as any Gabriel, and leaves the husk for us to read him in.

Flaubert loathed paternity, driving Louise Colet mad (presumably) in a series of letters panicking at the lateness of her periods. But literary paternity, in the divine mode, is his unashamed wish – and by it we all become Bovarys, reading him and exhaling him through the clichés he dares us to disavow. Whatever we do, we will be stupid. To read is to be stupid. Whatever we do, we will be women.

Let us now look a little more closely at this phantasy of literary paternity and measure it against other forms of self-reproduction. Flaubert was Hugh Selwyn Mauberley's 'true Penelope', not his Ulysses.[11] Weaver-unweaver – a motif tied up with femininity in this text, and to which we shall return – he performs the woman's mode of making, not the man's. For all he protests that making a book resembles the building of a pyramid rather than the gestation of a child, sexual generation returns in the image of the impregnation that is the grown man's way of proving he is not just playing about. Here to Louis Bouilhet he offers a comparison between aesthetic virtuosity and the *real thing*: 'We're good at sucking, we tongue a lot, we pet for hours, but can we really fuck? can we discharge and make a child?'[12]

If style for its own sake is like petting, the book is the child. But what sex is it to be? When Flaubert wrote of Colet's possible pregnancy, it was the terror of having a son that got to him: 'Me – a son! Oh no, no, sooner be knocked down by a bus and die in the gutter . . . The mere possibility of transmitting life to someone makes me roar, from the depths of my heart, with infernal rage.'[13]

The horror of reproduction is directed quite explicitly at a same-sex generation. To make another himself would necessarily be to make a son; this 'transmission' is not conceivable across gender boundaries. But, precisely, it is the blurring of gender boundaries that is at stake in the created text.[14] In an exact parallel, Emma Bovary's horror of life, her inability to escape from a circular weaving-unweaving visited on her by her author, is in the production of a daughter.

Critics vie with each other to debate the valuation of Emma Bovary's gender. There is for many something so disturbing in even wryly endorsing Flaubert's indirect avowal 'Madame Bovary, c'est moi' that the woman's masculinity must at all costs be proved.[15] But if we examine the finest of these arguments, in Baudelaire's review of October 1857, we can see what manner of masculinity is being invoked:

> One thing remained for the author to complete the whole *tour de force*: to strip himself (as far as is possible) of his sex and to make himself into a woman. The result is a marvel: despite all his actor's

talent, he could not help infusing virile blood into his creature's veins and Mme Bovary, for all her most energetic and ambitious and also her most dreamy qualities, has remained a man. Like armed Pallas born out of the brain of Zeus, this bizarre androgyne has preserved all the seductions of a virile soul in a charming woman's body.

. . . this is the poet as hysteric.

Hysteria! Why should it not form the depth and tuff of a literary work, this physiological mystery unsolved by the Academy of Medicine, which, expressed in women in the form of a lump [boule] that rises up and asphyxiates the victim (I refer only to the main symptom), is translated in men of sensitive nerves into every kind of impotence and an aptitude for every kind of excess?[16]

This appreciation of Mme Bovary, then, far from reversing her sex by way of a compliment to her author, rather locates her androgyny in his: if she is the 'poet as hysteric', the wandering womb is Flaubert's. What Baudelaire is doing here, with the seductive virile qualities he describes as the focus of her charm, is defining the ambivalence of gender that he, like Gautier before him, found the most tasty irritant of the creative mind.

It is no surprise then that, for the many critics who declare her un-femininely bold, others find her pathologically passive, destined towards suicide by the habitual logic of the involution of female aggression.[17] Emma is the portrait of the artist as a brain trapped inside a female digestive system. What is essential about gender in Flaubert is precisely this – that the body is also verbal: pleasure for Emma is inextricably tied to words, just as it is for her author; for both, taking in and giving forth are a matter of language.

Womb, belly: Emma eats up words and brings forth only a girl-child. If Berthe is the only thing she makes, the latter functions not simply as her failure of lovingness but also as the condemnation of a compulsive repetition whose very innocence is that she does not recognize it. For Jean-Pierre Richard, the daughter is of a single substance with her mother,[18] exactly as Flaubert's characters, when he does not condemn them utterly, blur and blend slightly nauseously with himself.

We come back to the politics of self-reproduction. Flaubert, here as elsewhere, is the useful limiting case of an author concerned to disguise the reproduction of the creative act. In going underground to portray the artist as hysterical, stupid woman, he reveals himself – but not simply with horror, as in the bodily production of another male. *Madame Bovary* is neither a roaring of the entrails nor a metaphysical bellow. As we saw in the last chapter, to double the self as male is for Flaubert essentially to copy. From the protean *Garçon* to the old codgers, the *deux bonshommes* in the author let him transmute the terror of an intergenerational relation into a finally compulsive portrayal of equivalence which is purely spatial, two men on either side of the fire. In the *Dictionnaire des idées reçues*, the author is at last nowhere at all: taxonomy and other people's foolishness fill up every space. But *Madame Bovary* is a daring book because it follows through the consequences of literary making: the author creates the character as his 'other self', the poet as hysteric.

'If Madame Bovary had had a television, would she have succumbed?' ponders a writer in *Le Monde* of 1953;[19] we can leave the answer to our own private thoughts. But it is significant indeed that Emma has no women friends. In this regard, the text is more closely related to the *récit* than to the novels we shall look at in the rest of this chapter; in fact it goes further than these in isolating her in the position of the unique female, though she is viewed too intimately for a *femme fatale*.[20] But if her position is that of the mythical mother, reviled as sexual while elevated out of comparison, she is represented to us always rather as a daughter. Emma cannot mature, for her progression in life does not proceed by knowledge (this, as I remarked earlier, is both her innocence and her doom). She also cannot be a mother; when she reproduces herself it is by way of copying, not development.

She is the sole daughter of a practical father who sheds tears more easily for his son-in-law than for her and to whom she does not think of turning in her mortal crisis. Her mother and brother have died in quick succession a few years before she enters the text as a bored teenager, housekeeping for want of another occupation. Unlike Charles and Léon, she is given no other maternal relationship than a bereavement in which she rehearses inauthenticity. Interestingly, in a preparatory *scénario*, Flaubert meant Charles to meet Emma while treating her mother for breast cancer: this image presumably coming dangerously close to the old icon of the *Mémoires d'un fou*, he abandoned it for the innocuous father and his broken leg.[21]

From her convent days and the social ambitions they gave rise to, Emma retains no friendships that might have brought her, like other restless heroines, to big-city experiences. Her relations with her mother-in-law are always bitter, and the other women of Tostes and Yonville exist as lumpish contrasts or dangerous gossips. Madame Lefrançois, towards whom the author seems to have an attitude of some respect, barely speaks to Emma at all. The protagonist is, then, viewed in significant contact with only two females: her daughter Berthe and the latter's wetnurse.

As far as Emma's relations with men are concerned, they are always triangular and mediate: if momentarily with Rodolphe she is allowed the pleasures of that body which constitutes her universal charm, in all other cases sexuality is far less her motive than the wish to depart. But the masculine idyll of free flight is available to her only in vicarious imagination; she never gets beyond the hopes of the hitch-hiker. If there is any sense in which Emma is 'masculine' it is simply in this conventional way: she wants what (it seems) men have got, in order to go where they seem to go.

If even in the convent she has had no friends, that must be because she focused, via the female mediators, on the sensual image of a God who could transport her. In her last moments, she returns to this proposition, offering 'the body of the Man-God . . . with all her dying strength the greatest kiss of love that she had ever given'.[22] He at least, or the promise of the effigy, will now arrive to carry her off. Hitherto, each man she has wanted, in whatever different way, has been asked to take her 'anywhere out of the world'. She is a Romantic. The body is the mediation of a mediation, always deceptive.

So when she gives birth it is a boy she wants, and like the pseudonymous Eliot and Sand she will name the boy George:

> She wished for a son; he would be strong and dark and she would call him Georges; and the idea of having a male child was like an anticipated revenge for all her past impotences. A man, at least, is free; he has the run of loves and lands, crosses obstacles, bites into the most distant delights. A woman is continually held back. At once inert and pliable, she is confronted by the frailties of the flesh and the dependencies of the law. Her will, like the veil of her bonnet held on by a cord, flutters in every wind; at every moment some desire pulls and some propriety restrains.
>
> She gave birth on a Sunday, towards six o'clock, as the sun was rising.
>
> 'It's a girl!' said Charles.
>
> She turned her head and fainted. (p. 91)

This is Flaubert's famous proto-feminist passage, and its sympathy is eloquent but swiftly punished – for Emma has impudently believed in a vicariousness nearer to desire than sexuality could ever bring her. This son would be a being, not a having, of the body. But this would be to insert her into an icon she must not deserve. Her author cannot countenance this hallowed version of cross-gender reproduction, for his own is more perverse and more important. Emma must be condemned to the copying he will thereby escape.

The birth strikes dead certain hopes in both parents. Emma has looked to the baby for an exciting new experience and for the fetishistic joys of a nice layette, Charles anticipates the bourgeois pleasures of family life. She is thus the child of two stupidities. Not existent enough to be freakish, she will act the familiar role of pretext in the adulterous arrangements, but without the enthusiasm or danger embodied in the sons of my last chapter. For Charles the companion of his unknown victimization, for Emma she will be the occasional fetish of a gesture. She occupies the early weeks in the search for a name, opting finally for the interestingly Romantic 'Berthe'. Emma not so much is a bad mother as puts her child in the charge of a bad mother, Mme Rolet, the pimp-messenger whose perversion of bonding (someone else's milk) becomes a binding (she links by weaving). In the rest of this section, I shall examine the scenes where Berthe and her nurse feature, marking out the limits of Emma's will to escape.

In an earlier version, Flaubert intended the first stage of the Léon affair to founder partly on the presence of Emma's child – 'she has her daughter (very much tied up with this first passion) whom Léon loves' – a set-up he later transferred in its specificity to *L'Education sentimentale*.[23] In the final version, Berthe is less an obstacle than the occasion of their encounters. Not six weeks after the birth, on a blazing hot day, Emma sets out on impulse to see her baby, and invites Léon to accompany her. The landscape is idyllic, he measures his pace by her fatigue, gossipy tongues begin to clack. When they arrive, the child is asleep in a wicker cradle; Emma takes her out to dandle and she is sick on her mother's smart collar. The elegant lady (Léon's view) in the shabby cottage, the hasty lifting-up and putting-back, and the figure of Mme Rolet demanding first soap, then coffee, then brandy – these are tangential features of the opening moves in the abortive seduction between two sentimental people.

Vomiting, as Collas points out, is characteristic of Emma's own desperate attitude to an indigestible world, 'a consequence of being deprived of love' (p. 40). What the child throws up is not her mother's milk. The wetnurse stands of course for Emma's refusal to nurture. Unmothered (for all the text tells us), Emma must be unmothering: between herself and her child she sets a caricature of maternal neglect and a distance that can only be crossed for sexual reasons. The nickname-epithet of *mère*

Rolet is redolent with the ironies of maternal failure: where selfless nurturance should be, there is erotic desire, itself mediate in motive and always disappointing.

Berthe is brought home when Emma, confused by Léon's slowness, is playing the virtuous wife and mother. She embraces her with hyperbolic enthusiasm. But the child here, along with Charles digesting in his carpet-slippers, is part of a picture held up to repel and to seduce Léon. Like Frédéric, he is both repelled and seduced, and does nothing. Emma eats herself up with rage, desire and boredom. Frustrated, she is full of an energy turned inwards, in which the last person to receive anything from her would be her daughter. We see her at this point at the extreme of her femininity, accepting her passive position along with its iconography as hollow, decorative, without issue. Desperately depressed, she appeals for spiritual help to the burly priest Bournisien for whom every ailment is gastric. On arriving home, she throws herself in a chair. There follows the most extended encounter between mother and child:

> Between the window and the work-table was little Berthe, staggering towards her mother in her woollen bootees, trying to grab hold of the ends of her apron-strings.
>
> 'Leave me alone!' said Emma, pushing her away with one hand.
>
> A moment later the little girl was back at her knee; leaning with both hands, she gazed up at her mother out of huge blue eyes, while a dribble of pure saliva ran from her lip down her silk bib.
>
> 'Leave me alone!' repeated the young woman impatiently.
>
> Her expression frightened the child, who started to cry.
>
> 'Oh just leave me alone!' she said, pushing her roughly away with her elbow.
>
> Berthe stumbled away and fell against a brass fitting at the foot of the cupboard; she cut her cheek and it began to bleed. Mme Bovary darted over to pick her up, broke the bell-rope, calling the maid at the top of her voice; she was beginning to curse herself when Charles appeared. He had just arrived home for dinner. (p. 118)

Charles reassures her and she stays upstairs to keep an eye on the child.

> Watching her sleep, the last of her anxiety gradually disappeared, and she thought how soft-hearted and silly she had been to get upset just now for so small a cause. Berthe had, indeed, stopped sobbing; the cotton coverlet rose and fell imperceptibly with her

breathing. Big tears stood at the corners of her half-closed eyes, and between the lashes two pale, deep-set irises were visible; the sticking-plaster on her cheek pulled the taut skin to one side.

'Strange,' Emma was thinking, 'how ugly this child is!' (pp. 118–19)

The narrative exposes Emma in her irritable neglect, not without giving ample cause – frustration at the hands of three men to whom she variously tries to appeal and a physiological and psychical exhaustion well spelled out – nor omitting to show her short- and longer-term remorse for a violence she has not directly committed. But it guarantees that we will blame her for her failure of tenderness over the sleeping cradle. After refusing with a triple denial the tireless repetitiousness of a baby's demands, she is first sorry and then thoughtful; but her contemplation is askew. It is her aesthetic scruple that seems out of place. This is the reverse of the maternal mirror: in her infantile reflection she finds nothing to feed her narcissism.

Berthe is introduced next on the day of Léon's farewell; her entry separates two moments of trembling, platitudinous embarrassment. The child, dragging a toy windmill upside down on a string, is lifted and kissed passionately on the neck, then quickly passed back to Emma who hands her to the maid. The nearest, then, that the first love-affair – all set about with feverish inexperience – can come to consummation is the substitute affection of a child-proxy. For Léon, Berthe is as much a piece of Emma as she is for Charles; for her mother she has proved a false excuse. In the Rodolphe affair, she will feature similarly tangentially.

For the small-town Rhett Butler, a child is no more or less than a stupid husband, the problem of an introduction or the anticipation of a parting, all of which pass before his eyes at the moment of tactical planning: the 'brat always hanging around' (p. 134) turns out to come, surrogate for the obliging cuckold, to wave the wife off on the adulterous horse-ride. On Emma's return and in the first months of her affair, the mirror-image she sees of herself as a member of 'the lyrical legion of adulterous women' (p. 167), the fulfilment of 'the long reverie of her girlhood', is all the reflection she could desire. Temporarily, her body is satisfied and offers an adequate counterweight to the verbal hunger Rodolphe will never quite slake. But there are two stages to this affair, like the other. By the sixth month, it has settled into habit, when a letter comes from Emma's father, ending with some tender words for his granddaughter. Emma muses on her past hopes and wonders why she is so unhappy:

A ray of April sun played on the china crockery on the dresser; the fire was burning; she felt the softness of the rug under her slippers; it was a bright, warm day and she could hear the laughter of her child outside.

The little girl was busy tumbling about among the hay being dried out. She was lying on her stomach on the top of a rick. Her maid was holding her by the skirt. Lestiboudois was close by, raking, and every time he came near, she leaned down, beating the air with both arms.

'Bring her to me!' said her mother, running to embrace her. 'How I love you, my poor child! how I love you!'

Then, observing that her earlobes were a bit dirty, she called quickly for some hot water and cleaned her up, changed her underwear, socks and shoes, asked a thousand questions about her health, as if she had just arrived back from a voyage, and finally, kissing her again and shedding a few tears, handed her back to the servant, who was standing there dumbfounded at this excess of affection.

That evening, Rodolphe found her more serious than usual.

'It'll pass,' he reckoned, 'it's just a mood.'

And he missed three rendezvous one after the other. When he returned, she was cold, almost disdainful.

'Oh, you're wasting your time, my pet . . .'

He pretended not to notice her sighs, her melancholy or the handkerchief she drew out.

It was then that Emma repented! (pp. 177–8)

The hiatus in the affair, prompted by boredom, sentimentality and Rodolphe's overplayed manipulations, returns Emma to the family-self she had tried on in the first-stage Léon affair – but it ends as swiftly with the fiasco of the club-foot operation, a restored horror of Charles and a more complex erotic appetite.

During the period before her anticipated departure with Rodolphe, Emma is at her most beautiful: seductive, languorous and energetic at the same time, 'she bloomed at last in the fullness of her nature' (p. 199). Charles admires her more than ever and, as she lies awake silently anticipating escape, he fantasizes a domestic future centred upon the daughter as her double. Like the bereaved Rosanette, he sees the years proliferate girls and hopes, and makes practical plans for her financial needs,

because Berthe must be nicely educated, develop accomplishments, learn the piano. Oh how pretty she would be, later, fifteen years old

127

and the image of her mother: in summer she would wear big straw hats just like her! from a distance, people would take them for two sisters. He saw her in his mind's eye sitting beside them sewing in the lamplight; she would embroider slippers for him; she would take care of the home; the whole house would be filled with her sweetness and gaiety. Finally, they would have to consider her future: a fine young man with a good situation would be found for her; he would make her happy; it would last for ever. (pp. 200–1)

While Charles drifts off into these future specificities, Emma is being transported in a four-horse carriage through vague tinted landscapes, all plurals and imperfect tenses. Each is equally seduced by the impossible, hers transcendent (as far as it goes), his a delightful immanence. For Charles more of the same is supremely imaginable: the child is a multiplication of the woman, down to her education, her straw hat and her happy-ever-after. The modestly introduced 'fine young man' is himself reproduced to make a second Emma happy. In this so obviously ironized version of mother–daughter doubling, the author further marks maternity as a destructive absence. This is one of those moments in which many readers identify a gender reversal among Flaubert's characters; in Charles nurturant and Emma chafing we might rather see a simple difference of desire, one looking to the everyday, the other to the exotic for satisfaction. But both imaginings are equally pictorial, equally second-hand and equally deluded. The goodness of Charles and the badness of Emma both use the child as a part of something else.

Berthe's coughing, like Charles's snoring, interrupts Emma's half-awake dreams. The child interrupts them a second and fatal time when Rodolphe cites her as one reason for letting his lover down. '"After all,"' he argues to himself, gesticulating, '"I really can't go into exile, and take on a child! . . . no, it would be too stupid!"' (p. 205). Writing, he uses Berthe again: '"Preserve the memory of a wretch who has lost you. Teach my name to your child, let her remember me in her prayers"' (p. 208).[24]

In the trauma of abandonment, Emma contemplates suicide, is saved by Charles's voice, then faints on seeing Rodolphe's blue tilbury cross the square outside. At everyone's outcry, Homais rushes over with a vial of aromatic vinegar and she opens her eyes.

'Speak to us!' Charles was crying, 'speak to us! Everything's all right. It's me, your Charles, who loves you! Don't you recognize me? Look, here's your little girl, give her a kiss!'

128

The child stretched her arms out to clasp her mother round the neck. But, turning her head away, Emma said in a sharp voice:
'No, no – no one!'
She fainted away again. (p. 213)

This second turning and fainting echoes the disappointment of the birth. Again, via the child's domesticated femaleness, Emma experiences the failure of her hopes of vicarious freedom.

She is ill for many months; during this time, Berthe is sent back to mère Rolet. When she returns, Emma is going through her religious phase and teaches the child to read with unruffled patience. Resigned, indulgent and 'full of expressions of the ideal' (p. 221), she enquires all the time: ' "Is your colic quite gone, my angel?" ' This is the brief period in which Emma keeps the company of other women: her mother-in-law (who 'found nothing to reproach her for'), the other ladies of Yonville, and 'regularly from two to five every afternoon, the excellent Madame Homais, who for one had never believed all that gossip about her neighbour'. With their mother come the four Homais children – from this point on, presented as a counterpoint to the gradually declining Berthe – and Justin, who leans on the door and gazes at the lady's luxuriant hair.

When Emma recovers some of her former energy, she first dismisses mère Rolet, who has acquired the habit of hanging around the kitchen with her greedy charges, next the Homais family, then her other visitors, and finally she stops going to church. From the visit to the Rouen opera a few weeks later to the end of the Léon affair and of her life, Emma will pay no further attention to Berthe, whose place as mediator is essentially taken by her former wetnurse.

After the *fiacre* ride, Emma returns to village life irritated by every distraction: the family merely forms an alien presence whose thoughts constrain hers. By contrast, Mme Rolet now becomes the enabler of the affair: her house marking the outer edge of Yonville is the nearest point of contact between urban adultery and local ennui. Letters delivered through her come wrapped in a double envelope, a touch of sophistication on Emma's part that Léon observes with innocent respect.

Twice before, this house has been the stopping-point of deception, though each time only in part. First when Emma and Léon walked there together, plotting idylls they could not yet arrange; second when in panicky excuse, caught in a dawn run to Rodolphe's mansion, she claimed to Binet to be on her way to visit Berthe. In this third instance, with sexual disorder taken to its highest power, leading to financial chaos and ultimate suicide, and at the tangential edge of the urban space which so surely for Emma signifies realization, the wetnurse comes into her own.

Elisabeth Badinter has illustrated in gruelling detail the consequences in child deformation and mortality of putting infants out to nurses and foster-mothers in eighteenth- and nineteenth-century France.[25] The wetnurse, as we saw in my discussion of *Sylvie*, represents not only a choice of maternal-parental neglect but also a particularly poignant version of women's prostitution. Nurses often let their own children starve, valuing the sustenance for which they were paid over the 'free gift' of the maternal relation; for the fostered infant, this privilege cannot altogether have compensated for the loss of an immediate relation to the real mother. In the suppressed rivalry of the protagonist and his milk-brother, Nerval thus suggests a complex of relations in which, long before the *pis-aller* of sexuality, two sons argue class and desire over the absence/presence of two mothers' bodies. In *Madame Bovary*, the prostitution of the wetnurse is more directly conveyed: slatternly, ungiving, she collects her dues from Emma's guilt at every stage; and if she, the mother and the daughter form a triangle of mediations, it is she alone who benefits.

In Collas's reading of the tragedy, bad mothers abound in Yonville. Homais and Lheureux especially feed Emma the poisons she ends by choking on. It is true that, other than her designation, we see nothing of mère Rolet that suggests nourishment, even in poisoning; rather, she is glimpsed only in consumption. The cottage in which Berthe survives the first months is a vulgarization of Emma's home, with the makeshift decor of the truly bereft. Yet, as the denouement takes its course, this place and its guardian will be the only site of feminized refuge.

Emma's weekly trips to Rouen begin to shape her doom. In place of the piano lessons which would enable her to teach her daughter, there are assignations in an overheated, overdecorated hotel room (where in erotic accents she calls Léon 'Child': p. 271) followed by a journey home haunted by the leer of the blind beggar, and arrivals where 'she scarcely stopped to kiss the little girl' (p. 274). Berthe reappears only to ballast a lie when Emma swears 'on the head of her daughter' (p. 275) that in her one past love-affair *'nothing happened'*. On the evening that Emma fails to return in the *Hirondelle* we hear the piercing sobs of the child 'who refused to go to bed without her mama' (p. 282).

As Lheureux homes in, chaos enters the domestic space, replacing desire as Emma's current obsession. Debt covers debt. Everything becomes confused.

Home was not a happy place these days. Tradesmen came and went with angry faces. Handkerchiefs lay about on the stoves; and little Berthe, to the horror of Mme Homais, had holes in her stockings. If Charles hazarded a timid comment, she replied roughly that it was no good blaming her!

Why these outbursts? He put it all down to her old nervous illness; and, reproaching himself for treating an infirmity as if it were a fault, blamed his own self-centredness and wanted to give her a good hug.

'Better not,' he said to himself, 'she'll only get annoyed!'

And he held back.

After dinner, he would go for solitary walks in the garden; or, taking little Berthe on his knee, unfold his medical journal and try to teach her to read. The child, who never had any lessons, soon opened great sad eyes and began to cry. Then he would do everything to cheer her up, fetching water in the watering-can to make rivers in the sand, or breaking off privet-branches to plant little trees in the borders. This did not harm the garden, which was all overgrown with long weeds; they owed so many days' work to Lestiboudois! Then the child would get cold and demand her mother.

'Call your maid,' Charles would say, 'You know, darling, that Mama doesn't like to be disturbed.' (p. 294)

Meantime, Emma lolls in her bedroom, half-dressed, reading books full of sex and violence. In Rouen, 'she was finding in adultery all the same platitudes as in marriage' (p. 296). One night, travestied in male clothing, she goes to a masked ball, dances all night, and discovers herself in the morning to be among clerks and students, and 'as for the women, Emma quickly realized from the tone of their voices that they must almost all be of the very lowest class' (p. 297). She faints again, then comes round thinking of 'Berthe, asleep out there in her maid's room' (p. 298) and longs to 'escape like a bird, flying far away to find renewed youth in the immaculate skies'. Images of innocence are here both masculine and feminine: for a split second, the little girl serves Emma as a good double, taking her out of a prostitutes' world into one more like that of infancy or the convent.

The final act begins. Emma runs in despair to Lheureux, then Léon, who promises to bring money the next day. As the bailiffs sift through her possessions, the thought of Charles's forgiveness drives her away from her home. Neighbours watch her appealing in vain to Binet. Before the last two dreadful resorts of Guillaumin and Rodolphe, Emma goes to Mme Rolet's house.

> 'Mère Rolet,' she cried as she arrived at the nurse's house, 'I can't breathe, unlace me!'
> She fell on the bed, sobbing. Mère Rolet covered her with a petti-coat and stood near her. Then, seeing she said nothing, the woman went off, sat down at her wheel and started spinning flax.
> 'Oh stop!' she murmured, thinking the noise was that of Binet's lathe.
> 'What's the matter with her?' the nurse wondered, 'Why has she come here?'
> She had come running, driven by a sort of panic horror that chased her from her house. (p. 313)

Emma stares vaguely at the walls and ceiling of the hovel. A 'long spider' crawls above her head down a crack in the beam. All around her, people, animals and objects are spinning. No longer the masculine aimlessness, the pointless copying, of Binet's lathe but the weaving-unweaving (lacing-unlacing) of women's work. As Lowe and Tanner point out, the wetnurse and the spider point the way to the final reification of Berthe's job after both her parents' and her grandmother's death: sent to an impoverished aunt, she ends up working in a cotton spinning factory.[26] As for Emma, at the moment of despair, turning to the corrupted site of a feminine world, she finds only a production-reproduction in which she has no part.

Both lovers, after the nurse, refuse her money and love. The only nourishment left, she guzzles poison. At her deathbed (of which the author and every available character make a hearty meal), she takes her leave of Berthe. The child, dazzled by the candle-light, thinks it is New Year's morning and looks around for her presents:

> 'Where is it, Mama?'
> No one spoke.
> 'I can't find my little slipper!'
> Félicité held her over the bed, but she was still looking towards the mantelpiece.
> 'Has nurse taken it?' she asked.
> And, at this name, which took her back to the memory of her adulteries and misfortunes, Mme Bovary turned away her head as if disgusted by another, stronger poison that was rising up into her mouth. Berthe stayed where she had been put on the bed:

'Oh, what big eyes you have, Mama! you look so pale! why are you sweating? . . .'

Her mother looked at her.

'I'm frightened!' said the child, shrinking back.

Emma took her hand to kiss, but she struggled.

'Enough! Take her away!' cried Charles, who was sobbing in the alcove. (p. 325)

In this last set-piece, Berthe's innocence rests on her mistaking one unique life-event for another, repeated, child-centred and inauthentic one. The details of her error are kindly presented, but when she finds the intended object of her gaze, her Little-Red-Riding-Hood reaction is as much a vomiting of her failed childhood as Emma's rediscovery of her guilt is hers. The mother turns from her child for the last time. Both recognize the false surrogate as somehow the thief of happiness, even though it is, in every sense, rather the fault of masculinity that has brought Emma to her death. Emma's ambitions, her hopeless menfolk, the capitalists that get fat on her stupid despair, these are the places where female institutions have stopped. Convent or brothel, the school that is something of both, these feminized spaces have narrowed down to the girl-child and her false safeties, malnourishing and spidery.

After Emma's death, Berthe is sent to the Homais' house, Emma's father refuses to see her, she comes home and gradually forgets her mother. 'The child's cheerfulness went straight to Bovary's heart' (p. 347). People cease to visit, Charles discovers Emma's infidelities, but adopts her caprices in his own dress and style. As for the little girl, she goes about with shoelaces missing and unpatched blouses, 'but she was so sweet, so gentle, with her little head bent so prettily over her colouring, her good fair hair falling forward over her rosy cheeks, that an infinite delight overtook him, a pleasure mixed with bitterness' (p. 349). His own child's fosterer, he makes and mends her toys. It is Emma's blonde daughter who finds him quietly dead, with a lock of black hair lying in his hands.

Berthe vies with Homais to end the story. As she declines, he prospers, as she is moved around like a pawn, he expands, is centred, becomes a writer, receives the Légion d'honneur. We must not forget that Flaubert accepted the same honour a few years later.

In the last chapter, I proposed the enigma of Anna Karenina's charm. However much she may later degenerate into a distraught and ravaged woman, at the opening of the text she is magical. I want to look at Anna

now as the mother of a daughter, but also more broadly (in this unusually unfocalized text) at the woman–woman relations in which she
takes part.[27]

Anna has a son when we meet her, her daughter is born about halfway
through her story. It is axiomatic that she may not love Ani as she loves
Seriozha. The two children are separated by time, by their different
fathers, their two sides of the blanket, and by sex. How do they mark out
two different sides of their mother?

As I suggested earlier, this text is more difficult to assign among
chapters than my others, and not only because it offers both structures.
Anna is the good mother of the hominocentric text, but also the eponym
of a woman's tale. Vronsky never takes the viewpoint position more than
briefly; it is not his desire that is at issue, even though there is no question that Anna is desire's true object. At the same time, Levin is the hero
of a different story: in love but not in desire, he negotiates with all the
supplicant's comic anxiety the path to true marriage and a reason to
work. The key figure in this confusing pattern is a protagonist of both
structures and the first agent of the desire of Anna – Kitty. Kitty's innocence vouches for the reality of Anna, for it is she who loves her and
is wounded by her before any other person stands to lose. One crucial
clue to the glow of Anna in the opening section of the book is that she
is viewed and loved through the eyes of a young girl.

Altogether, Anna resplendent is a woman's woman. By a subtle thematic reversal, the author opens with her posed in the patrilinear chain
from which she will never emerge, and it is only in the latter stages that
we see her awkwardly, unhappily among women; yet it could equally be
argued that Anna progresses from the fostering mother, daughter, sister
of the opening scene to a point where she has lost all this for a male-
centred and impossible love. The key to Anna's splendour, and to her
temporary similarity to Mrs Ramsay, is that the implicit gaze that desires
her is daughterly. She becomes sexualized, destroyed and an unloving
mother of her children when the implied desiring gaze becomes that of
a son.

Anna Karenina is called by her brother to a home in which 'although
Oblonsky was entirely in the wrong as regards his wife . . . almost everyone in the house, even the nurse, Daria Alexandrovna's best friend, was
on his side' (p. 17). She too is on his side, but it is her sisterly appeal
to Dolly which will solve the crisis. The latter, now and later despite her
frustrations, belongs to her children rather than to her husband, and the
family of which she is the proper head can survive because of this. Her
renunciation of sexual pleasure negates not only adultery but also married

desire: her children (hydra-headed and always plural) are real enough to be irritating bodies but are also the justification of everything else. This is Sonja with dampened anger and the mother Kitty is designed to become. Anna will enter her world and set it osteopathically to rights.

Anna is brought to Vronsky (and us) by his mother who mediates the first meeting. After he has observed her semi-suppressed animation, his mother adds: '"She is very charming, isn't she?"' (p. 76). To Anna herself, she goes on: '"I could travel round the world with you and never be dull. You are one of those sweet women with whom it is nice to be silent as well as to talk."' And as they part – '"Let me have a kiss of your pretty little face. I can speak plainly at my age, so let me confess that I have lost my heart to you"' (p. 77) – Anna kisses the old lady before she shakes hands with the good soldier. The mother's delight opens the way to the son's. This of course offers the opening patrilinear parallel, but it is also a direct encounter. Anna's charm is firstly something for other women.

To be delightful, comradely, helpful to other women keeps Anna seductive but safe; this, not repression, is her form of virtue. She wins Dolly for ever by the directness of her sympathy and a woman-to-woman talk in which Stiva's future is unconditionally negotiated. Kitty arrives a few hours later. Her attachment too is described in terms of sexual love:

> She knew Anna, but only slightly, and came to her sister's in some trepidation as to how this fashionable Petersburg lady whose praise was on everyone's lips would receive her. But she made a favourable impression on Anna – she saw this at once. It was obvious that Anna admired her beauty and youth, and before Kitty knew where she was she felt herself not only under Anna's sway but in love with her, as young girls do fall in love with married women older than themselves. Anna was not like a society lady, nor the mother of an eight-year-old son. Her lithe movements, her freshness, and the persistent animation of her face, which broke out now in her smile, now in her glance, would have made her look more like a girl of twenty, had it not been for the grave and at times mournful expression in her eyes, which struck and drew Kitty to her. Kitty felt that Anna was completely natural and was not trying to conceal anything, but that she had another and higher world of complex interests beyond Kitty's reach. (pp. 85–6)

Kitty's gaze gives Anna her full range of valencies: innocence and experience are visible in equal measure, and the familiar animation holds no promise that it does not already fulfil. But the mutual trust, across an age boundary that conditions the younger woman's mode of desire, allows one danger – that like a mother, Anna's 'world beyond the child's reach' will be sexual.

Kitty's disappointment in Anna (she never forgives her, for the author requires her reliable index always to keep the Anna–Vronsky plot suspended in betrayal) is purely oedipal. It is she who gets Anna to the ball, using a phrase later echoed between Anna and Seriozha, '"you always look nicer than anyone"' (p. 87). Once there, Kitty's gaze mediates everything, beginning with her own narcissism. When she glimpses Anna, the latter's beauty takes shape:

> Kitty had been seeing Anna every day and was in love with her, and always imagined her in lilac. But, seeing her now in black, she felt that she had never before realized all her charm. She saw her now in a new and quite unexpected light and realized that Anna could not have worn lilac, and that her charm lay precisely in the fact that she stood out from whatever she was wearing, that her dress was never conspicuous on her. And the black velvet, with its rich lace, was not at all conspicuous but served only as a frame. It was Anna alone, simple, natural, elegant, and at the same time gay and animated, whom one saw. (p. 93)

Anna is often subsequently viewed within a frame, but here we see her (as we see Mrs Ramsay, inclined also to the colours of mourning when left alone with her thoughts) through a particular mode of desire. Kitty's love has no predation. There is an element of envy potential in the admiration, which can and will become jealousy, but the very visual form of attachment shows how little it is possessive. She would neither capture nor contain Anna: she enjoys her visibility. This whole scene works through a sexuality of vision; Kitty as focalizing position, learning as she looks, makes a dramatic lesson of the optics of innocence. Anna is seen by Kitty becoming the prey of a man's gaze even as she captivates that man away from the lesser spell of Kitty's own loveliness.

The girl's reaction, paralleling Levin's at her refusal, is above all humiliation; this immature, because egocentric and wasteful, feeling is what she grows out of in fitting herself for marriage, exactly as he does. At the same time, her observing eye reads danger in Anna's very charm. From angelic it becomes demonic, a denaturing that predicts (and helps to cause) the fate that love and Anna will undergo. With the adulterous impulse, this view implies, Anna will lose that maternal glow – not just because she must abandon a son but because she removes herself from her innocent place among women. Anna loses Kitty long before she loses Seriozha. When she gives birth to a daughter, it is this relationship that cannot be recaptured. For when she sleeps with Vronsky, Anna enters the diabolized world into which Kitty's jealous gaze first cast her. 'Her sense of shame, rapture and horror at this stepping into a new life' (p. 166) carries all the ambivalence of the author's obsession. This is the mother sexualized: the wearer of the scarlet letter. That sign is visible under the mode of the adulterous daughter, whom we will meet in this and the next text. For Anna Karenina, as for Hester Prynne, self-reproduction is the outward badge of disobedience.

For Anna, the second birth promises an end to suffering: in her imagination, her punishment and resolution will be a childbed death. She has had the same dream as Vronsky of the little peasant (with the resort to the uncanny that many of these authors have in the midst of their fatalistic realisms: blind beggars, ghostly Chinamen, sprites and demon-dreams), and while he shrugs it off with a manly shudder, she reads in it a fatal end.

> 'But don't let us talk of it. Ring the bell; I will order tea. And stay a little, now; it's not long I shall . . .'
> But all at once she stopped. The expression of her face changed in a flash. Horror and agitation suddenly gave way to a look of gentle, grave, blissful attention. He could not comprehend the meaning of the change. She was listening to the stirring of new life within her. (p. 387, ellipses Tolstoy's)

In contrast, the later attention of Kitty to her quickening pregnancy wins Levin's sympathetic engagement: in her voice and eyes he sees the 'gentle gravity . . . found in people continually intent upon one cherished purpose' (p. 388). But hers is the production of a son. Anna's momentary inward turning is destined for no externalization in bliss. Where Kitty's birth (perceptible for us as Levin's learning experience) is a hard struggle to make a new man, Anna's, unwritten, is a labouring for death.

Karenin arrives back from Moscow, summoned by her telegram: '"I am dying. I beg, I implore you to come. I shall die easier with your forgiveness"' (p. 435). He arrives to find her 'safely delivered' (p. 436) and feels a pang of disappointment. But the safety is the child's; Anna is very ill. Vronsky weeps, she raves:

> 'Because Alexei – I am speaking of Alexei Alexandrovich (how strange and terrible that they should both be Alexei, is it not?) –

137

Alexei would never refuse me. I should forget, he would forgive . . .
But why doesn't he come? He is good, he doesn't know himself
how good he is. Oh God, what anguish! Give me some water,
quick, quick! Oh, that would be bad for her, for my little girl! Very
well, then, give her to nurse. Yes, I agree, it's better in fact. He'll
be coming: it will hurt him to see her. Give her to nurse.'

'Anna Arkadyevna, he has come. Here he is!' said the midwife,
trying to attract her attention to Karenin.

'Oh, what nonsense!' Anna went on, not seeing her husband.
'No, give her to me; give her my little girl! He has not come yet.
You say he won't forgive me, because you do not know him. No
one knows him. I'm the only one, and even for me it has become
hard. One must know his eyes . . . Seriozha's are just the same –
that's why I can't bear to see them. Has Seriozha had his dinner?
I know they will all forget. He would not forget. Seriozha must be
moved into the corner room, and Mariette told to sleep with him.'
(p. 437, ellipses Tolstoy's)

This speech is all about alternatives, an economics of scarcity: Karenin
or Anna, mother or nurse, one child or the other, one pair of eyes or
another, one Alexei or another. Anna can attend to the newborn or to
her husband, but not both, for one means life and the other death, and
death is a food she must take in the form of forgiveness. So, as she consumes the indigestible milk of Karenin's goodness, she becomes unable
to nourish her baby.

Anna eats morphia, embraces her two incompatible menfolk at once,
and through her hours of agony and recovery, equalizes and inverts
them: 'they had suddenly exchanged roles. Vronsky felt Karenin's elevation
and his own abasement, Karenin's integrity and his own untruth' (p. 441).
In this homosocial idyll Anna has no space, still less a meeting-place with
her daughter. If Vronsky attempts to kill himself – borrowing her death
on account or mimicking the duel wound that Karenin refuses him – this
is surely because his is now the foolish role, cuckolded somehow by the
arrangement between Anna and her husband. But, as in all homosocial
triangles, it is the woman who is most surely dispensed with. Nurturance
is displaced. Karenin as saint becomes the good mother Anna cannot be.
He forgives and pities Anna, but

for the new-born baby-girl he felt a quite peculiar sentiment, not
of pity only but of tenderness. At first sheer pity had drawn his
attention to the delicate little creature, who was not his child, and

138

who had been cast on one side during her mother's illness, and would certainly have died if he had not troubled about her; and he did not realize how fond he became of her. Several times a day he would go to the nursery, and remain there for so long that the nurses, who were at first a little intimidated by his presence, grew quite used to him. Sometimes he would sit gazing for half an hour at a stretch at the downy, wrinkled, tomato-coloured little face of the sleeping baby, watching the frowning forehead and the chubby little hands with their curled-up fingers, rubbing the tiny eyes and nose with the backs of its fists. At such moments especially Karenin felt quite calm and at peace with himself, and saw nothing abnormal in his position, nothing that need be changed. (pp. 444–5)

Like Charles Bovary, Karenin discovers the only refuge for the cuckold,[28] paternal love. And his is more exceptional precisely because it is a true fostering: the baby is no part of his genetic family. It is because she has no blood tie to him that he can find respite and refreshment with her from all the others, forgetting the dying Anna and Vronsky, favouring her over his own son and, above all, liberating himself from the snare of convention and concern for the figure he cuts. With her – and, like any newborn, she offers no face of subjectivity, indeed her eyes are closed in all these enounters – he takes time out from his position as 'the husband'. This, rather than his soon-satirized piety, is what lifts Alexei Karenin out of the absurd indignity of cuckoldry, and this concern for the tiny creature at the furthest end of the adulterous chain remains with him, closing the circle in an unexpected, productive way. Ani is Karenin's as she is never shown to be either her own father's or her mother's.

If Seriozha functions as the gauge of Anna's wrongness (or rather, the trauma of her conflict, since her love for him is genuine but forbidden), Ani serves not only as the index of her mother's gradual denaturing but as that of Karenin's rightness. She if anyone takes the 'sick son' position in this text: she twice falls ill – genuinely for Karenin, falsely for Vronsky – and her vulnerability is the test of all the other characters.

For her unkind author, temporarily all on the husband's side, lets her get ill when her mother is still in the sickbed, suffering precisely from the bad milk the wetnurse is giving her. The failure of Anna's maternal doubling is stressed even in the opening sentence: 'at the end of February it happened that Anna's baby daughter, also named Anna, fell ill' (p. 445). Sick herself, the mother has nothing to spare, and the child acts upon a rightful envy in offering to fade away. The name, too, is something that must be divided up between them: contrast the detail given on Emma

Bovary's elaborate searching out of the *mot juste* to give to her new plaything; or is it a sign of the primitive expedient which says we must name the newborn after the recently dead? Where Kitty's conception awaits a death-scene to announce itself in benign reaction, Ani's birth is fraught with death, as if the space between one Anna and another should at all costs be closed. Coexistence is impossible – but there will be no such spiritual love-test as is offered to the tempted Mmes Arnoux and de Rênal. Thus the sickness of a daughter seems to require not so much the re-entry of the mother into patriarchal chains as her expulsion into a space where self–other doubling is disallowed.

Socially an object for mockery, sexually and morally unattractive in his magnanimity (Emma after all also preferred suicide to her husband's forgiveness), Karenin is on the edge of our refusal and can appear likeable briefly and only in the hands of the smallest of the book's family of characters. Anna and her husband agree nervously about her not seeing Vronsky, but over Ani they reach crisis:

> 'Oh, I have just sent for the doctor,' said Karenin.
>
> 'I am quite well – what do I want the doctor for?'
>
> 'No, it's the baby. She keeps on crying, and they say the nurse hasn't enough milk.'
>
> 'Why didn't you let me nurse her, when I begged to? Anyway' (Karenin knew what she meant by that 'anyway') 'she's a baby and they will be the death of her.' She rang the bell and asked for the baby to be brought to her. 'I begged to nurse her, I wasn't allowed to, and now I'm blamed for it.'
>
> 'I am not blaming you . . .'
>
> 'Oh yes, you are! Oh God, why didn't I die?' And she broke into sobs. 'Forgive me, I am upset, I am not fair,' she said, controlling herself. 'But leave me . . .'
>
> 'No, things can't continue like this,' Karenin said to himself decidedly as he left his wife's room. (p. 450, ellipses Tolstoy's)

At this point he decides she may see her lover again 'provided the children were not disgraced, that he was not deprived of them' (p. 451). This plural is instructive. Nowhere else but in the mind of the cuckold will those two children form a family together.

If Anna begged to be allowed to feed her baby, it is Tolstoy who has refused her. *La mère jouissante*, she can enjoy neither the legitimate child nor the other, too available as the fruits of illegitimacy. When she leaves the family home she does not depart childless. But, again by the agency of the author's censoring fatality, she refuses divorce, forbidding herself the fulfilment of a fantasy ('is it really possible that we could be like husband and wife, alone together, with our own family?': p. 460) and later increasingly using this refusal against Vronsky. That idyll is negated in the name of Seriozha, carrier of the paternal right: what is in dispute is the *nom du père* and that can never belong to a daughter.

After the painful visit to Seriozha, Anna returns to the hotel and to Ani. The 'chubby, well-nourished little baby' (p. 567) crows and waves her arms around.

> Anna . . . took her in her arms, danced her up and down on her knee, and kissed the fresh little cheek and bare elbows; but the sight of the child made it plainer than ever that the feeling she had for her could not even be called love in comparison with what she felt for Seriozha. Everything about the baby was sweet, but for some reason she did not grip the heart. On her first-born, although he was the child of a man she did not love, had been concentrated all the love that had never found satisfaction. The little girl had been born in the most painful circumstances and had not had a hundredth part of the care and thought bestowed on the first child. Besides, in the little girl everything was still in the future, while Seriozha was now almost a personality, and a beloved one, already struggling with thoughts and feelings of his own; he understood her, he loved her, he judged her, she thought, recalling his words and his eyes. And she was for ever separated from him, not physically only but spiritually, and there was no help for it. (p. 567)

All these reasons are good ones, though again they rely on the economics of scarcity that offers Seriozha the love that is not going elsewhere, while implicitly Vronsky uses up all that could have been Ani's. Similarly, the boy is lost, the girl too available. But it is the last reason that grips and disturbs: the son's hold is something to do with his separateness. Able to understand, he does not understand but judge. This is Anna's fantasy. Understanding, everywhere in this text, is a function between women. But the wish for understanding, this belongs to the sphere of heterosexual relations. Anna is entrapped in her patrilinearity, condemned to look for love (and here her author is crucial) where there must instead be judgement.

Tolstoy, we recall, differs from Flaubert by the broad generosity of his vision. The materiality of his fictional world has a glow of affection, in contrast to the ironic glint of Yonville. But on Anna Karenina he settles the gradual refusal of that generosity. For her initial splendour she pays the price of wanting only what is impossible and falling away from the things that are physically near. In particular, she is condemned to respect what she cannot be, and to look for her reflection in a son.

Critics have argued that Tolstoy is 'in love' with Anna, and I have suggested that the desire by which we perceive her visualized at the beginning is indeed that of the author – but the author as a daughter. As son, he can fantasize only the fraught fairytale of a Levin attaching himself to a Kitty, or the passion of a Vronsky whose background condemns him to make the mother a whore. Judith Armstrong puts it well when she describes Anna as 'both the subject and object of her creator's sexuality',[29] but she forgets how Anna acquires this ambiguity: through the non-predatory desire of a daughterly gaze. As soon as plotting begins, this immanence disappears; rivalry, the marriage story, jealousy among women and then among men, these fix Anna in her patrilinear function and in her fate. What she loses when she loses Kitty is the possibility of a female mutuality without sacrifice of her maternal uniqueness. By the larger jealousy of her author, who like Flaubert cannot bear very much real Tiresian identification, she is not permitted to regain this in the person of her daughter.

Kitty, meanwhile, has entered a totally sororial state. Henceforth, skipping from crisis to reconciliation with her oafishly sensitive husband, she lives for sisterhood and the promise of motherhood. Dolly is hers as we know her also to be Anna's; she is the first without conflict and the second heroically – loving Kitty with maternal affection, sharing with her the saving of her six children from scarlet fever, while for Anna she has a sisterly concern made up of respect as well as gratitude. The latter attachment, conditioned not by shared blood but precisely by Anna's crossing over blood-ties to a more than in-law sympathy, is more fostering, more tested, more Ruth-like in its strength. But as the Levin narrative takes a rising path, and as Kitty settles into her rightful queenship, her territory too becomes the centre from which Dolly will divagate into transgressive thoughts on visiting Anna.

She goes for the best of reasons: '"I am sorry for her, and I know her. She is a fine woman"' (p. 601). Before she leaves she has made up tenderly with her daughter after a childish misdemeanour. On the way to the Vronsky estate she thinks about her 'lot of unfortunate, badly brought-up, penniless children' (p. 638) and daydreams of such romantic happiness as Anna is now enjoying. The two women greet each other with delight and again we see Anna through the eyes of non-predatory admiration:

Dolly was dazzled by the elegant *char-à-banc* – she had seen nothing like it before – by the fine horses and the elegant, brilliant people about her. But what struck her most of all was the change that had taken place in her beloved Anna. Any other woman who was less observant, who had not known Anna before, or who had not thought the thoughts Dolly had been thinking on the road, would not have noticed anything special in Anna. But now Dolly was struck by that fleeting beauty which comes to women when they are in love, and which she saw now on Anna's face. Everything about her: the pronounced dimples in her cheeks and chin, the curve of her lips, the smile that seemed to hover about her face, the light in her eyes, the grace and swiftness of her movements, her ringing voice, even the manner in which she replied, half-crossly, half-fondly, to Veslovsky when he asked permission to ride her cob, so as to teach it to lead from the right leg when starting to gallop – it was all peculiarly fascinating, and it seemed as if she herself were deliciously aware of it. (pp. 642–3)

This is true generosity, as was Kitty's gaze in the opening phase of the book. Dolly does not envy but enjoy because her love for Anna is unconditional – but the gaze is turned negative by something like the author's revenge. In her discontent with her own marriage, Dolly enables us to see the excessive awkwardness of Kitty's home, from which Veslovsky has been ejected because that couple cannot tolerate a degree of worldly levity. But bit by bit her delight in Anna is tainted by a sense of the brittleness of this household in which children provide no workaday centre and adults pass their time in play.

They visit the nursery, whose luxury impresses Dolly 'painfully' (p. 649). Ani is looked after by a collection of women who are absent or neglectful, heterogeneous in nationality, 'smart' and 'wanton' at the same time. Dolly expresses surprise at the contrast between her attitudes to her two children:

'It is often a grief to me that I'm so useless here,' said Anna, lifting her skirt to avoid the playthings lying in the doorway, as they left the nursery. 'It was not like that with my first.'

'I should have expected it to be the other way round,' said Dolly timidly.

'Oh no! By the way, I have seen Seriozha, did you know?' said Anna, screwing up her eyes as though peering at something far away.

143

Thus Dolly sets herself on the side which Anna can no longer reach, that of an economics of plenty and the love of a daughter. We are not told why Dolly is surprised, but it is clear that she has not thought of the stark patrilinear division between desire and maternity which Anna has now chosen. The latter underlines it when they speak of the future.

Vronsky has asked Dolly to intercede to persuade Anna to press for a divorce, for the sake of their future children. What is at stake is the *nom du père*. Not only this daughter but potential sons 'would not be heir to my name or my property . . . They would be Karenins. Think of the bitterness and horror of such a position!' (p. 658). In this insistence, he mistakes both Anna and her husband: the latter in the end a truer father to Ani than he, the former determined to pre-empt the dilemma. Both refuse to allow illegitimacy any real parenthood.

Anna tells Dolly she will have no more children. In an elliptical parenthesis, she enlightens the other woman about contraception – 'precisely what [Dolly] had been dreaming of on the way to Anna's that morning, but now that she learned it was a possibility she was horrified' (p. 668).

> '. . . Do not forget, I have a choice of two alternatives: either to be with child, that is, an invalid, or to be the friend and companion of my husband – practically my husband,' said Anna in a tone intentionally superficial and frivolous.
>
> 'You may be right,' said Dolly, hearing the very arguments she had used to herself and not finding them so convincing as before.
>
> 'For you, for other people,' said Anna, as though divining her thoughts, 'there may be reason to hesitate; but for me . . . Remember, I am not his wife: he loves me so long as he loves me. And how am I to keep his love? Like this?'
>
> She curved her white arms in front of her stomach. (p. 669)

The circularity of this argument – he is and is not her husband, she refuses to seek divorce despite the latter problem – proves its main aim: to separate, in Anna Karenina's adulterous partnership, sexuality from motherhood. Into this scheme, Seriozha fits with perfect logic, but the daughter is a piece of excess, produced but not received, irrelevant both to desire and the death that results from cramped maternity.

Among Anna's new (and for her author, substitute) activities are two that are of particular interest. She writes a children's book, just as Tolstoy did at this period, and she takes a fostering interest in a young English girl. The lovers will later quarrel about this child, Vronsky accusing Anna of favouring her absurdly over her own child. This is no chance. Like

Ruth, the daughter-substitute is foreign and culturally isolated. Anna can adopt her as she once adopted Dolly and Kitty. Interestingly too, she has her name. It has rarely been observed, but around Anna Karenina is a small circle of women marked by their shared name. Her maid is Annushka – '"I grew up with Anna Arkadyevna; my lady's dearer to me than all the world"' (p. 648) – the person from her Petersburg world who accompanies her on the first, crucial visit to Moscow, who is beside her on the train journey back, and whose 'kindly grey little eyes' gaze sympathetically moments before her death. The daughter Ani ('Annie' in some translations) is named after her mother; and her foreshortened version is expanded again in the name of the fostered Hannah, 'a pretty, red-haired child' (p. 729) whose wardship is something that, along with Anna's interest in women's education, her menfolk refuse to take seriously:

> 'Well, did she pass her examination?' asked Oblonsky.
> 'Yes, and very well, too. She's a very clever child, and has a sweet disposition.'
> 'You'll end up by being fonder of her than of your own daughter.'
> 'How like a man! In love there's no such thing as more or less. I love my daughter with one love, and this girl with another.'
> 'I was just telling Anna Arkadyevna,' said Vorkuyev, 'that if she were to devote to promoting the education of Russian children a hundredth part of the energy she bestows on this English girl she would be doing a great and useful work.'
> 'Yes but say what you will, I can't do it . . . Energy is based on love. And love does not come at will: there's no forcing it. But I took to this girl, though I don't myself know why.' (p. 731)

This attachment in Anna is similar to Karenin's for Ani. Neither can, once the primary legal ties of parenthood are strained and severed, be simple parents. Of Vronsky's feeling towards his daughter – though he hurries home when summoned by Anna on the excuse of Ani's illness, which he believes false – we see nothing except a thwarted wish for the hereditary tie. Where the Levins end up under the benediction of an iconic parenthood which must make up (the text frankly argues) for the conflicts and divisions of marriage, Karenin and Anna, that odd couple, are vouchsafed – the one without issue, the other half-absurdly – the privileged relation of the fosterer.

This is a womanly relation. Anna is full of it at the opening of the text: she exudes it so far that the first three creatures to fall in love with her are women whom she has welcomed in like Naomi. This perhaps is the

145

true femininity of the figure whom Vronsky, in his grief, recollects as 'mysterious, exquisite, loving, seeking and bestowing happiness' (p. 815). By the end, she has none of it left. The closing scene from which she is ejected is the cosy partnership of Dolly and Kitty around the figure of the nursing son. For all Kitty's impulse of reconciliation – 'Kitty was torn between her hostility to this bad woman and a desire to make allowances for her; but the moment she saw Anna's dear, lovely face all her hostility vanished' (p. 792) – Anna derives no comfort from the moment. Once the least judgemental of her women proves her dispensable, she is ready to die. Her thoughts immediately before death are full of woman-to-woman ill-will: '"We all hate each other – I Kitty and she me"' (pp. 793–4). Thoughts of her girlhood attend her fall.

When the railway companions Koznyshev and Countess Vronsky ('half-relatives' both) talk through the events since Anna's death in the penultimate scene of the book, we learn that Karenin '"took the little girl. Alexei was ready to agree to anything at first. But now he is dreadfully distressed at having given up his own daughter to another man. He can't go back on his word, though"' (p. 812). Anna's two menfolk unite, then, only in their good breeding, agreements among gentlemen being as arbitrarily binding as later in Fontane: the men's world, in this at least, has mended the unseemly breach. For Vronsky, the 'bitterness and horror' of his child as a Karenin has become real. But we observe the rightness of this ending. The father has no time for anything but mourning and suicide. The cuckold will, as fosterer, bring together what Anna's body could not: the unity of two moments of different love in the blood-siblinghood of two bereaved children. He then becomes what Anna as adulteress has been forbidden to be: a good mother.

The Scarlet Letter, surely one of the most unpleasant books ever written, offers the most extensively and intensively presented mother–child relationship of my seven novels. Hester Prynne's daughter Pearl is not only the result of adultery, she is its sole and sufficient evidence. If the scarlet A which the Puritan fathers force Hester to wear on the breast of her costume is matched by the little girl she clothes in elaborate fabrics, the relation is also more fundamentally reversed: the A has followed the child.

Everything in this painful text is interpretable – so much so that, while critics congratulate the author on his use of indeterminacy and 'multiple readings',[30] the excessive legibility of everything could better be described as sending everyone stupid. No writing is further from the restfulness of realism, where relations are presumed natural. Here meaning is so searingly omnipresent that a compensatory blindness seems to set in. If the towns-people fail to see from the first second that Dimmesdale is the child's father, it must be because not-seeing is what they, and he, are all about. Pearl's quest for a father, the ending of which kills him and makes her 'human',[31] traces the moral direction of this story from vulgar visibility to poignant invisibility. What Freud calls the 'advance in intellectuality', the superiority of inference to sense-evidence in raising paternity over maternity, centres this myth. Mother is visible, displayed and lesser, so that her punishment, fastened only to the garment, serves to strengthen her; father is secret and his torment saps and refines him until he comes out in the open, blossoming and withering in an instant. The profound weakness of the paternal relation is marked by the regular health which enters the elf-child when it is known. The mother–daughter pair exudes a breath of uncanny upon which everyone may feed except them.

Reading this novel after *Anna Karenina* feels like suffocation; but, as Carol Bensick points out, *The Scarlet Letter* is less morally pessimistic, perhaps because it is so saturated in the language of sin that nothing en-ables the reader to enter into it. It is true that the machinery of punish-ment whose effects we spend two hundred pages following is ineffective because 'it leaves the basic emotional issues untouched.'[32] The book has nothing to say about either love or desire. It is entirely about the genea-logical relationship, and men's and women's place in it.

We cannot imagine how Pearl (elf-child and witch-baby indeed) could ever have been conceived. If Hester and Dimmesdale have bodies, they are Kafkaian ones, skins to be written on, not matter to be moved by nerves and hormones. At the centre is the marginalized couple Hester and her daughter, united by the scarlet letter which declares their femin-inity against the seething black ground of their Puritan world. Around them group the father and husband, another more bitterly wedded couple, and then the generations of male judges among whom are two ancestors of the author and a certain Surveyor Pue among whose ghostly remains the preface's author-editor claims to have found the faded scarlet letter.

Patrilinear reproduction is all. Hester is the chance intervention in the encounter between Pue and 'Hawthorne', as she is between Chillingworth and Dimmesdale or the author and his best-meaning readers. In this text, most strikingly, women readers, teased with some proto-feminist pearls, are deeply unintended; the quarrel over whether it is Hester's book or Dimmesdale's began with Henry James and has struggled on against the odds ever since. We are not allowed to reckon punishment publicly borne against the anguish of guilt suffered within. The personal history

147

Hawthorne does not tell is instructive here: on the maternal side, an ancestor arraigned in 1680 with double incest escaped into the forest while his two sisters, one single, one married, paid a massive £5 fine (rather than be whipped and imprisoned) and sat on repentance stools throughout the service at the Salem meeting-house with the word INCEST written on their caps.[33]

Authorship is both public and private. The preface traces out the ambiguity that this text exists to split down gender lines. Let us go back to Freud. Paternity is the superior knowledge because it is more risky, unprovable, cannot be seen. Maternity is of course *semper certa*. But the young man, the penis, the hero, is the thing on display, Freud's earlier theory being entirely based on the little boy's reasoning that a visible genital is the one everyone wants. This reversal is not simply the routine attribution of the plus sign to whatever is male, it is also the difference between a young man's and an old man's eyesight. We know that the woman on display is another phallus, we can see the two sisters sitting under their caps as adequate fetishes for their brother's virility. But by bearing Pearl, in both senses, and holding her up as the marker of her womanhood, Hester becomes something out of the control of the visible-invisible that would make her phallic. Her doubling is genealogical, if only for an interim. Her adultery *is* her motherhood. Pearl is simultaneously the decorative art that sits upon surfaces and the hidden bleeding it fails to gloss. We all know about bleeding; only heroes put it on display.

The narrative opens at the outside of a prison, standing with the citizens of Boston gathered to see the adulteress emerge marked into their disciplinary space. Into this over-lit open, Hester walks unled, carrying her baby who blinks with the unfamiliarity of the prison-born.

> When the young woman – the mother of this child – stood fully revealed before the crowd, it seemed to be her first impulse to clasp the infant closely to her bosom; not so much by an impulse of motherly affection, as that she might thereby conceal a certain token, which was wrought or fastened into her dress. In a moment, however, wisely judging that one token of her shame would but poorly serve to hide another, she took the baby on her arm, and, with a burning blush, and yet a haughty smile, and a glance that would not be abashed, looked around at her townspeople and neighbours. On the breast of her gown, in fine red cloth, surrounded with an elaborate embroidery and fantastic flourishes of gold thread, appeared the letter A. It was so artistically done, and

with so much fertility and gorgeous luxuriance of fancy, that it had all the effect of a last and fitting decoration to the apparel which she wore; and which was of a splendour in accordance with the taste of the age, but greatly beyond what was allowed by the sumptuary regulations of the colony. (pp. 52–3)

Hester is in excess of the regulations of the colony by her presence in its gaze. Marked and positioned by her punishment, she is above all a visible surface whose inside (her womb and its production, her thoughts and desires, her 'soul') is turned outward to be seen and appraised by the community. In her scarlet all women stand exposed and their cruelty covers them, and all men get to see the wound they covet and abhor. Policing Hester, they arrange their virtue around a precise centre. To measure her excess is not difficult: it has the dimensions of the child she holds. As the child has come forth from internal darkness, the female sin has issued with it.

If we eventually learn more about Hester Prynne's prehistory than that of our other mother of an illegitimate daughter, Anna Karenina – for example hearing explicitly the way in which she came to marry an unlovable husband – we never know anything about the passion that her society criminalizes. She is criminal, with the negative and positive connotations of this appellation, from the moment she appears; where she comes from is a prison door. What is clear is that her criminality is embodied in her baby, who makes the private public exactly like a verbal slip. The word 'adultery' famously appears nowhere in the test; the letter instead, in its compulsive interpretability, incarnates the word in the body of a child. Of course the child is female: the act that makes her is a woman's act; she is the evidence of the scarlet inside the clothed undressable body. But in the course of her function in the story she centres, the little girl will push repeatedly against her role as adequate clone, insisting on her paternal provenance and the effective reality of male desire. Like her mother, she cannot win because a particular kind of blindness is against her. The evidence (the letter) is right there on the town's mantelpiece, but it cannot be read.

Hester is large and tall, 'with a figure of perfect elegance' (p. 53), dark-haired, strong-browed, black-eyed. Her deportment is dignified and ladylike: 'her beauty shone out, and made a halo of the misfortune and ignominy in which she was enveloped.' At the same time, her wild, elaborate costume, which she has made herself, expresses her defiant mood, and at its centre stands the letter, 'so fantastically embroidered and illuminated upon her bosom' (pp. 53–4). All this wildness will in the following years be transferred to her daughter, whose position in front of the fabric is repressed in this image. The figuration as 'lady' and the halo, however, belong to the iconic couple of the Madonna and Child.

> Had there been a Papist among the crowd of Puritans, he might have seen in this beautiful woman, so picturesque in her attire and mien, and with the infant at her bosom, an object to remind him of the image of Divine Maternity, which so many illustrious painters have vied with one another to represent; something which should remind him, indeed, but only by contrast, of that sacred image of sinless motherhood, whose infant was to redeem the world. Here, there was the taint of deepest sin in the most sacred quality of human life, working such effect, that the world was only the darker for this woman's beauty, and the more lost for the infant she had borne. (p. 56)

We have not yet been told the sex of Hester's baby but we could have no doubt of it now. This figuration is an anti-icon because the traditional paintings to which the narrator refers – the old ways, England and Catholicism carrying connotations throughout the text of centuries-sanctioned superstition – are, despite appearance, triangular structures. Making the mother–son couple holy is the implied third element, divine paternity, which frames and separates the woman and infant, so that she, familiarly, is also this baby's child, and both are subordinate to a gaze at once background and formal. Mother and son are set always in a larger, patrilinear chain only waiting to become oedipal. The couple of the scarlet letter is doomed because it has no link upwards. Hester's baby must be a girl because the couple is scandalously complete; and just as in nature the exact reproductive pair, issued by cloning, can only be female, so the generic sinfulness of this woman must carry itself forth into a child that is exclusively hers. The shock of the text is that this punitive idyll is not possible. The Puritan audience will try to hold the mother–daughter pair outside genealogy in a marginal place, but there it will survive to threaten because two is both less and more than three. Admission of paternity, even of desire, is the secret this book holds forth and publishes.

The adulteress's genealogy stops here. She has no more history: 'the scaffold of the pillory was a point of view that revealed to Hester Prynne the entire track along which she had been treading, since her happy infancy' (p. 58). With a shock (she clutches her child painfully) she recognizes her long-lost husband in the crowd. At the same time, the Reverend Mr Dimmesdale is called upon to demand that Hester name her lover. Brilliant, eloquent, 'with a white, lofty, and impending brow, large brown, melancholy eyes, and a mouth which, unless when he forcibly compressed it, was apt to be tremulous' (p. 66), he has 'an apprehensive, a startled, a half-frightened look' which shuns company and keeps him 'simple and childlike', letting him, when he comes forth, offer 'a freshness, and fragrance, and dewy purity of thought, which, as many people said, affected them like the speech of an angel'. The Christ-child indeed, big-eyed, fragrant and unsafe as a well-powdered newborn and unpossessed by original sin. Already he is so far the obverse of adultery's daughter that we know he must be her missing link. He speaks of course with forked tongue. If it will make her feel better, he says, Hester must name the name; if she thinks of protecting her lover, she must know that her silence can only '"tempt him – yea, compel him, as it were – to add hypocrisy to sin"' (p. 67). Her advantage, the '"open ignominy"' that expiates, would be denied to her accomplice '"who, perchance, hath not the courage to grasp it for himself"'. And so it is. Hester by definition cannot do right; she refuses to tell. Her infant double tries to speak for her: 'it directed its hitherto vacant gaze towards Mr. Dimmesdale, and held up its little arms, with a half pleased, half plaintive murmur.' But the populace is illiterate, and Hester opts '"to endure his agony, as well as mine!"' (p. 68).

> 'She will not speak!' murmured Mr. Dimmesdale, who, leaning over the balcony, with his hand upon his heart, had awaited the result of his appeal. He now drew back, with a long respiration. 'Wondrous strength and generosity of a woman's heart! She will not speak!'

From now on Dimmesdale casts Hester into an isolation from which he will redeem her only to castigate her for abandoning him. His hypocrisy, hammered and racked by Chillingworth's psychoanalytic arts, will always be as forgivable as Hester's generosity is dangerous. By a laboured but insistent logic, the degree of suffering of each parent is consistently measured by its kind; and feminine, visible pain, deemed to give strength, is always a good, whereas the inward, secretive pain assigned to the man is what it is. Hester's punishment is the equal of her power: exposure exposed, it decorates her; her only secret will be a blackness of thought guaranteed to unwoman her as her pain does its good (for she must not prosper); but Dimmesdale's falsity hides something that is truth, and all

151

the scalpels with which he is penetrated only recharge our sympathy. The pillory that opens the story is a brothel-window for her, the one that closes it will be a crucifix for him. This is the real difference in which she is caught.

Hester returns to the prison cell; both she and the baby are ill; the jailer suspects she will commit either infanticide or suicide. When the doctor is called to administer calm, he is of course her disguised husband. Their discussion is not only cruel: Chillingworth, as he chooses to call himself, freely admits his own fault in marrying her when she was too inexperienced to recognize what was not love. A manner of reconciliation comes out of this mutual admission. But when Hester refuses to tell him too the name of her lover, he vows to penetrate the secret:

> 'Believe me, Hester, there are few things, – whether in the outward world or, to a certain depth, in the invisible sphere of thought, – few things hidden from the man, who devotes himself earnestly and unreservedly to the solution of a mystery. Thou mayest cover up thy secret from the prying multitude. Thou mayest conceal it, too, from the ministers and magistrates, even as thou didst this day, when they sought to wrench the name out of thy heart, and give thee a partner on thy pedestal. But, as for me, I come to the in-quest with other senses than they possess. I shall seek this man, as I have sought truth in books; as I have sought gold in alchemy. There is a sympathy that will make me conscious of him. I shall see him tremble. I shall feel myself shudder, suddenly and unawares. Sooner or later, he must needs be mine.' (p. 75)

Halfway through this speech, the object of uncovering and penetration changes from the woman to the other man. Henceforth the homosocial bond is established: Chillingworth's object is his wife's lover, whoever he may be, and specifically the tremulous mouth of the man characterized by public eloquence and private continence. Under this continence is the swirling of desires as excessive as if they still poured, although – critics surmise a single miraculously reproductive act on the forest floor – the directedness of Dimmesdale's heterosexuality is always unimaginable. The orgasm, it seems, could only be the husband's: one trembles, the other shudders.

The three protagonists are all artists: Hester's art is decoration, the minister's all in his voice, Chillingworth's (the epithet 'leech' carrying its double meaning safe inside the author's crashing quaintness) a blend of all the sciences old and new, the art of the scalpel. If the first covers surfaces – what else can she do? – the second is the son's art, the question of issue that must come from inside, and the third is the paternal art of penetration. The real couple must be that of phallus and mouth. The womb is only apparently an inner space: its vulgarity, its certainty, makes it outward just as it thrusts the female shape out of kilter and, in an ideology of the hymen, necessarily out of true. Hester alone has knowledge, but hers is never the knowledge of the container, she cannot have secrets – both because only the blindness of men explains their unreadability (she intends two names who are already locked on each other's lips) and also because she cannot tell what she knows. The silence that is her choice becomes their unity, and inside this unity there is no space for her, so little is she even briefly a patrilinear mother.

So when Chillingworth binds her to silence – ' "Thou and thine, Hester Prynne, belong to me . . . betray me not!" ' (p. 76) – he only apparently releases her from the infamy of adultery. Why, if no one will know her husband is still alive, could she not become a respectable, even a marriageable, widow? Stupid question: ' "I leave thee alone . . . with thy infant, and the scarlet letter!" ' (pp. 76–7). That is her place, and with her lover is his.

When she leaves the prison, Hester does not leave the colony but settles in an isolated cottage which immediately becomes tainted with 'a mystic shadow of suspicion' (p. 81). An exceptional seamstress, she lives by her needle, and the most virtuous townspeople (patriarchs, babies, all but the brides) go about in her artefacts. She herself wears nothing but plain grey; her letter and her child grow more ornate as her own body sinks into obscurity. However, even though she spends much time sewing simple things for the poor, art brings pleasure and pleasure guilt, and this too is 'a rich, voluptuous, Oriental characteristic' (p. 83), excessive to her due.[34]

She is everywhere spoken, always subject to/of 'the ever-active sentence of the Puritan tribunal' (p. 85). In church she is 'the text of the discourse'; children gang up to jeer behind the back of 'this dreary woman, gliding silently through the town, with never any companion but one only child'. New or familiar people fix their eyes on her chest. 'From first to last, in short, Hester Prynne had always this dreadful agony in feeling a human eye upon the token; the spot never grew callous; it seemed, on the contrary, to grow more sensitive with daily torture' (p. 86). She is, in other words, the unspeaking object of the gaze. The wound is indeed a superficial one, never scarring, always freshly red.

As for her daughter, Hester has named her Pearl – not for any whiteness but because she is

> of great price – purchased with all she had, – her mother's only
> treasure! How strange, indeed! Man had marked this woman's sin
> by a scarlet letter, which had such potent and disastrous efficacy
> that no human sympathy could reach her, save it were sinful like
> herself. God, as a direct consequence of the sin which man thus
> punished, had given her a lovely child, whose place was on that
> same dishonored bosom, to connect her parent for ever with the
> race and descent of mortals, and to be finally a blessed soul in
> heaven! (p. 89)

This is as much as to say that Pearl is and is not Hester's. All she possesses, she is also likely to exceed her at last, redeemed though not redeeming, and failing to share the mother's eternity of retribution. Hester is made to suspect Pearl of every profanity she locates in herself. Pearl is dressed in the gorgeous scarlet Hester denies her own body; she is also rich in imagination: 'imbued with a spell of infinite variety; in this one child there were many children' (p. 90).

It is Pearl's role, obviously, to play the outward form of Hester's repressed passions. Much critical ink has been spilt over how far the portrait is realistic – the very uncanniness of her wild ways suggests an oldish father's shocked recognition of his first child's independent being – but it is clear that she stands midway between semi-fixed symbol and obtrusive female.[35] The character is the outgrowth both of a buried desire and of the punishment of transgression. Hester's attempts to control her show the mother's struggle between social submission and the minimal freedom she has to act upon the world. Mixed into the moral choreography we get a sympathetic portrait of the burdens of single parenthood. Hester tries discipline and kindness by turns; Pearl acts by caprice and often casts her a 'peculiar look . . . so intelligent, yet inexplicable, so perverse, sometimes so malicious' (p. 92) that, with the impoverished vocabulary of her position, the exhausted mother attributes it to devilishness, spritehood, the uncanny. Pearl's laughter, violence, or the occasional 'rage of grief [when she would] sob out her love for her mother' (p. 93), none of these are consistent enough to evoke the latter's confidence. Like a Proustian lover, she is only secure when the child is asleep.

Pearl is as isolated as her mother, her sole and perpetual companion but also her champion. Knightless, Hester lets her shout back at abusive children. She tortures her mother too with a compulsive interest in the scarlet letter, her own effigy and 'the very first thing which she had noticed, in her life' (p. 96). But not everything is a matter of surfaces: sometimes, Hester looks – more calmly than the hero of the *récit* – into 'the unsearchable abyss of her black eye' (p. 97):

> Once, this freakish, elfish cast came into the child's eyes, while Hester was looking at her own image in them, as mothers are fond of doing; and, suddenly, – for women in solitude, and with troubled hearts, are pestered with unaccountable delusions, – she fancied that she beheld, not her own miniature portrait, but another face in the small black mirror of Pearl's eye. It was a face, fiend-like, full of smiling malice, yet bearing the semblance of features that she had known full well, though seldom with a smile, and never with malice, in them. It was as if an evil spirit possessed the child, and had just then peeped forth in mockery. Many a time afterwards had Hester been tortured, though less vividly, by the same illusion.

She is after all the child of two parents, the absent one reliably contained within, but transfigured through the bitterness the mother will not admit. If Pearl can only become human by finding her father – and her quest for origins begins as soon as she can speak, with her refusal to accept '"thy Heavenly Father sent thee"' (p. 98) as adequate answer to Hester's own question '"art thou my child, in very truth?"' – she can also only present him to her mother's similar quest as the traitor he is. To one critic's argument that Pearl enables the text's salvation by bringing Dimmesdale out of hypocrisy to his moment of suicidal truth,[36] I would suggest that she rather exposes what it is her role to hide, so that in revealing paternity as betrayal, her function ends. The bond between mother and daughter is always fraught by the child's difference; labelled as they together are in their extremity, their refusal to be entirely readable, invested in the child's desperate freedom, is as doomed as the unity that can only be sin.

Two or three years pass. The town patriarchs threaten to take Pearl away from Hester, an unfit mother by definition. Hester defends herself angrily:

> 'God gave me the child!' cried she. 'He gave her, in requital of all things else, which ye have taken from me. She is my happiness! – she is my torture, none the less! Pearl keeps me here in life! See ye not, she is the scarlet letter, only capable of being loved, and so endowed with a million-fold the power of retribution for my sin? Ye shall not take her! I will die first!' (p. 113)

But the silent woman, bold for once, is inaudible until she turns to her lover and charges him to speak for her, since he knows better than anyone 'what is in my heart, and what are a mother's rights, and how much stronger they are, when that mother has but her child and the scarlet letter!'

'Careworn and emaciated', his hand over his heart as usual, Dimmesdale repeats her arguments in his 'sweet, tremulous, but powerful' (p. 114) voice, and with a 'strange earnestness' that impresses Chillingworth. Only then is the reasoning heard. Pearl takes his hand and caresses it with her cheek; shocked by her tenderness, he puts the same hand on her head and kisses her brow. She bursts out laughing again and runs off. As they leave, Hester cites her child (and by inference, Dimmesdale, who has twice given her to her) as the sole reason she does not go into the forest with the local witches, led by Mistress Hibbins, the governor's sister. This, the only female community available to her, is the lost (but mortal) alternative to ostracism. We know of no higher motive in Dimmesdale than to mask Hester's appeal, with its scarcely guarded threat of revelation. But his help not only wins the gratitude of author, readers and the helpless heroine: it also makes Pearl begin to move across from the nightmare space of her mother towards her father's side.

He needs her. Closeted with Chillingworth, he has become an involuntary analysand. The doctor recognizes in him a permeable space, worn hollow by a mystery illness, trapped in an intellect crippled by unoriginality – 'in no state of society would he have been what is called a man of liberal views' (p. 123) – and wasting away in his musty interior. He starts to dig,

> probing every thing with a cautious touch, like a treasure-seeker in a dark cavern. Few secrets can escape an investigator, who has opportunity and license to undertake such a quest, and skill to follow it up. A man burdened with a secret should especially avoid the intimacy of his physician . . . at some inevitable moment, will the soul of the sufferer be dissolved, and flow forth in a dark, but transparent stream, bringing all its mysteries into the daylight. (p. 124)

The same sexual imagery reappears. Dimmesdale refuses to talk, but his body speaks for him. His psychoanalyst turns into the demon he carries in his conscience. Moving into the same house, he cohabits with him in a symbiosis more tense and perfect than that of mother and daughter. In this homosocial partnership we find, disguised as the war of two equal intellects, a remarkable battle of stupidities, each failing to reach what the

156

other cries out silently in every exchange. What is this encounter but a question of *le nom du père*? Neither will admit where the women stand inside their intimacy, for neither has, in the end, a stake in anything but this: that they agree on the silence of each other's paternity, the fault of one and the omission of the other. Instead, the oedipal struggle is engaged without its pretext, the very crisis refusing what brings it into being.

Between them and in their intercourse, passing occasionally under the embattled window, two incarnations of female knowledge intervene, Hester with Pearl, canny and uncanny; what the two women say, and how they say it together, is inaudible against the thunder of their theory and the '"disease [which] is what I seem to know, yet know it not"' (p. 135). To know and not know, to speak incessantly and say nothing, these acts take over centre-stage from the women's marginalized negativity. When the minister sleeps, the doctor uncovers his chest and all the text reveals is that what he reads on the other's flesh makes him caper like a fiend. Yet even here ignorance is the essence: 'what distinguished the physician's ecstasy from Satan's was the trait of wonder in it!' (p. 138).

Every event in this narrative is emblematic. Seeking a sham exposure as relief, the minister slips out one night to stand on the scaffold; here, gradually, the other three protagonists gather too, the two women joining him with Chillingworth as audience. The child stands between her mother and father, the latter taking her free hand.

> The moment that he did so, there came what seemed a tumultuous rush of new life, other life than his own, pouring like a torrent into his heart, and hurrying through all his veins, as if the mother and the child were communicating their vital warmth to his half-torpid system. The three formed an electric chain.
>
> 'Minister!' whispered little Pearl.
>
> 'What wouldst thou say, child?' asked Mr. Dimmesdale.
>
> 'Wilt thou stand here with mother and me, to-morrow noontide?' inquired Pearl.
>
> 'Nay; not so, my little Pearl!' answered the minister. (p. 153)

Only for a moment, then, the three stand together as a family. Pearl's presence unites but also divides, because her insight ranges the dichotomous principles – the known and unknown parent, the body and the soul – that split the text. She judges Dimmesdale's refusal with fair severity: '"Thou wast not bold! – thou wast not true!" [said] the child. "Thou wouldst not promise to take my hand, and mother's hand, to-morrow noontide!"' (p. 157).

And Chillingworth leads him away. The father's helplessness, consigned forever to a sonhood which is self-destructive, is hereafter the central issue of the narrative. Hester will fall (again) for it, and no strength she can derive from the exercise of her independent brain will compensate. As the following chapter – painfully adopted by feminism to prove the author's half-digested sympathies – demonstrates, she alone has had the opportunity of intellectual development throughout these years. Hawthorne glimpses what must happen to the ostracized mind trapped in the exposed, recessive body. 'Little accustomed, in her long seclusion from society, to measure her ideas of right and wrong by any standard external to herself' (p. 159), Hester dreams a dream of feminist revolution which she has no place to realize. We puzzle at the libertarianism of the submissive figure; have her downcast eyes had anywhere to gaze? They are, the narrator admits, fixed upon the child: witch or revolutionary, Hester might only have been either if she were not a mother. Her feminist speculations must unwoman her.

> A woman never overcomes these problems by any exercise of thought. They are not to be solved, or only in one way. If her heart chance to come uppermost, they vanish. Thus, Hester Prynne, whose heart had lost its regular and healthy throb, wandered without a clew in the dark labyrinth of mind; now turned aside by an insurmountable precipice; now starting back from a deep chasm. There was wild and ghastly scenery all around her, and a home and comfort nowhere. At times, a fearful doubt strove to possess her soul, whether it were not better to send Pearl at once to heaven, and go herself to such futurity as Eternal Justice should provide.
>
> The scarlet letter had not done its office. (p. 166)

On the contrary, of course, it has done it very well. She sees so clearly the doom into which it has cast her – perceiving after all a great deal more than the implied author – that a total suicide of both her and her double would make simple sense (it is perhaps their only way of finding a home together), if it were not that another Big Daddy waited in the only place they could go to. Pearl is responsible, it seems, for both her staying and her going, both the wandering and the submission of her thoughts. What concerns Pearl concerns all women.

Twice in the following chapters, we see the plural Pearl doubled by a Narcissus image, finding her reflection in rock-pool and brook. Both times, Hester has sent her off to play while she talks to the fathers. As the woman accepts responsibility for the degeneration each man has wrought in the other, her bond to her child is not just diffused and en-dangered. The child retreats into a more simply maternal Nature. Against this, fully social relations are those of the woman with the men: either version consumes and wastes her power. Morally, Hester can only opt from a justified hatred of Chillingworth to a sympathy for Dimmesdale, and ultimately Pearl must follow her there.

Only once do the mother and daughter briefly accede to a kind of companionship. Pearl takes the initiative:

> She took her mother's hand in both her own, and gazed into her eyes with an earnestness that was seldom seen in her wild and capricious character. The thought occurred to Hester, that the child might really be seeking to approach her with childlike confidence, and doing what she could, and as intelligently as she knew how, to establish a meeting-point of sympathy. It showed Pearl in an un-wonted aspect. Heretofore the mother, while loving her child with the intensity of a sole affection, had schooled herself to hope for little other return than the waywardness of an April breeze . . . But now the idea came strongly into Hester's mind, that Pearl, with her remarkable precocity and acuteness, might already have approached the age when she could be made a friend, and intrusted with as much of her mother's sorrows as could be imparted, without ir-reverence either to the parent or the child. (pp. 179–80)

Hester gazes again into the abyss and sees in her daughter 'the stedfast principles of an unflinching courage, – an uncontrollable will, – a sturdy pride . . . and a bitter scorn of many things, which, when examined, might be found to have the taint of falsehood in them' (p. 180); these things, along with early affections which in time will ripen into rich fruit, are surely a simple list of Hester's own best qualities. The mirror has shown her neither the father's fiend-like features nor the circular narcissism of the natural metaphor; instead the minimal social structure, difference be-tween intimates, has suddenly appeared possible. But into this the familiar vocabulary of the symbolic quickly re-enters. 'With all these sterling attributes,' Hester is made to think, 'the evil which she inherited from her mother must be great indeed, if a noble woman do not grow out of this elfish child.'

Their discussion focuses once more on the scarlet letter; but if now Hester can imagine the child's role as its effigy in a positive not just punit-ive light, she still cannot take the step to break its spell. At the third time of asking, she betrays the symbol by more precisely betraying the child:

159

'What does the letter mean, mother? – and why dost thou wear it?
– and why does the minister keep his hand over his heart?'

'What shall I say?' thought Hester to herself. – 'No! If this be
the price of the child's sympathy, I cannot pay it!'

Then she spoke aloud.

'Silly Pearl,' said she, 'what questions are these? There are many
things in this world that a child must not ask about. What know
I of the minister's heart? And as for the scarlet letter, I wear it for
the sake of its gold thread!'

In all the seven years, Hester Prynne had never before been false
to the symbol on her bosom. (pp. 180–1)

Pearl might at this juncture have been able to 'become human', as she
only does in the moment of her father's discovery and death. That this
opportunity is lost because the other is necessary shows how far (but also
how near) the text must hold the possibility of a mother–daughter
society. If friendship is almost possible, the scarlet letter might be spoken
aloud and thus lose its efficacy; but if the scarlet letter were disempowered
there would be nothing to hold Hester where she is, the patriarchy
would have no control at all of what is bred from women. The uncanny
of mothers and daughters must remain intact if fatherhood is to be both
essential and secret.

Hester does wear the letter for the sake of its gold thread. What she
has made it holds it in place as it does her. The girl too is made both
by the negative social definition and her mother's aesthetic choices. But
the letter is gold only after it is red. Pearl's growing-up – '"will not [my
scarlet letter] come of its own accord, when I am a woman grown?"'
(p. 183) – is a menarche that will make her dangerous, for to be a
woman is to be never covered enough.[37] Gold thread, like the sunshine
that covers the child but never the woman, only adds to the visibility of
what is natural and therefore abominable.

From the total exposure to Pearl, Hester turns to Dimmesdale. They
meet in the forest and she confesses the identity of Chillingworth. However
vaguely foreknown, this revelation gains its real meaning for the lover in
the confrontation with her.

'Woman, woman, thou art accountable for this! I cannot forgive
thee!'

'Thou shalt forgive me!' cried Hester, flinging herself on the
fallen leaves beside him. 'Let God punish! Thou shalt forgive!'

With sudden and desperate tenderness, she threw her arms around him, and pressed his head against her bosom; little caring though his cheek rested on the scarlet letter. He would have released himself, but strove in vain to do so. Hester would not set him free, lest he should look her sternly in the face. All the world frowned on her, – for seven long years it had frowned upon this lonely woman, – and still she bore it all, nor ever once turned away her firm, sad eyes. Heaven, likewise, had frowned upon her, and she had not died. But the frown of this pale, sinful, and sorrow-stricken man was what Hester could not bear, and live! (pp. 194–5)

To understand the full import of this distasteful scene we must recognize Hester's gesture for what it is. Forcing the patriarchal gaze away from her, she impales the man in the position originally assigned him, and the only one his religion will allow her: Christ-child redeemer, he must take his place on her bosom. Can his pallor ever efface the letter? it seems unlikely, but the only way open to her unfortunate heterosexuality is to try to restitute the positive icon from which Pearl outlawed her. Dimmesdale's frown, followed by his forgiveness, wipe out the mother–daughter bond.[38]

Only here, and under each other's gaze, can 'the scarlet letter . . . not burn into the bosom of the fallen woman [and can] Arthur Dimmesdale, false to God and man, . . . be, for one moment, true!' (pp. 195–6). His name, her mark, her outside, his inside. The man's truth is his subcutaneous weakness: that is safe in Hester's keeping. Her truth is that it is not simply her body which he needs: '"Think for me, Hester! Thou art strong. Resolve for me! . . . Advise me what to do"' (p. 196).

Arthur listens like a novice to Hester's free speech. His position as patriarchal head, hers as object of scorn, bring them together to the point where at last his voice falls silent. But what he hears can only be sacrilege. Like Des Grieux in the seminary parlour, he vows his spiritual loyalty henceforth to the witch-woman as his '"better angel"' (p. 201). They agree to leave the colony together. Inspired by hope at last, Hester undoes the scarlet letter, casts it on the water and takes off her cap, letting down her hair in an emblematic disrobing:

Down it fell upon her shoulders, dark and rich, with at once a shadow and a light in its abundance, and imparting the charm of softness to her features. There played around her mouth, and beamed out of her eyes, a radiant and tender smile, that seemed gushing from the very heart of womanhood. A crimson flush was glowing on her cheek, that had so long been pale. Her sex, her youth, and the whole richness of her beauty, came back from what men call the irrevocable past, and clustered themselves, with her maiden hope, and a happiness before unknown, within the magic circle of this hour. (p. 202)

This delightful sight is simply that: here is Hester visible at last to the eyes of desire, less those of her lover (we have still seen nothing of sexuality in him) than of the implied author and reader, whose objectification is momentarily released from the vocabulary of condemnation. The sun bursts out, at last consenting to shine on her – surely a warning sign. If narcissism is implicit here as well, it is, we must not forget, in the form of display not reception: Hester does not share the pleasure of her appearance for she has no reflection of her own. The release of her sexuality, even as a promise, is not for her, and we know this most surely because it is not for the only figure of her narcissism thus far, her daughter.

Pearl must be absent from this least chaste scene of the book (in which, however, only a hat is removed and only words discharged) not simply because of *bienséance* but because her absence makes it possible. The lovers are looking backwards to their only moment of unity, before her conception – that is, before disgrace and betrayal as Hester's worst birth-pangs. Dimmesdale, we know, cannot be Pearl's father but only her rival; and in the scene that follows, what is most pitiable is Hester's everyday optimism in the face of the two who dispute over her maternity. Like a good soap opera, the narrative uses prattle to demonstrate the impossibility of domestic peace, the differences between men's and women's hopes:

> 'Dost thou not think her beautiful? . . . She is a splendid child! But I know whose brow she has!'
>
> 'Dost thou know, Hester,' said Arthur Dimmesdale, with an unquiet smile, 'that this dear child, tripping about always at thy side, hath caused me many an alarm? Methought – O Hester, what a thought is that, and how terrible to dread it! – that my own features were partly repeated in her face, and so strikingly that the world might see them! But she is mostly thine!'
>
> 'No, no! Not mostly!' answered the mother with a tender smile. 'A little longer, and thou needest not to be afraid to trace whose child she is.' (p. 206)

Dimmesdale's unwillingness is irreparable and Pearl is no fool. On the other side of the brook, dressed up as a dryad and reflected in a sudden pool, she is doubled into real-life child and a 'shadowy and intangible' (p. 208) other. Precisely where the two parents want her to sink herself in them – 'Pearl was the oneness of their being . . . the material union, and the spiritual idea, in whom they met' (p. 207) – she manifests herself as the plurality that exceeds them. Neither her feelings nor her identity can be subordinated to the triangular structure in which she, as synthesis, would be an end of others' stories.

The double child refuses to come across to them. Hester feels an estrangement 'as if the child . . . had strayed out of the sphere in which she and her mother dwelt together, and was now vainly seeking to return to it' (p. 208). But as the narrator notes, it is the mother who has caused the rift by admitting 'another inmate' to her space. Dimmesdale nags her to get the child over for the sake of his nerves, Pearl gesticulates, Hester cajoles. Only when the woman has put back her scarlet letter will the child return to her – not simply because she is shocked by the unfamiliar and can only find her own mother with the latter's '"shame upon her, – now that she is sad"' but because the only relation between the two women is one which excludes the child-man. The offer of a family, she knows, can only be fulfilled by the three of them together assuming their outsiderhood under the eyes of the town. When this happens, and Pearl's uncanniness is finally abandoned, all the relations will fall away, leaving the group of three equally estranged, all human, the man outside as ever and the women forever apart.

The final climactic scene, in the village centre in front of the pillory, has Hester reclad in her red and grey, Pearl adorned for the last meaningful time, the world staring anew at the shameful breast and, all the while, the minister pouring his oratory into the air. The social difference between the two lovers is at its most marked: yet his place 'on the very proudest eminence of superiority' (p. 249) is hidden from view, hers in the furthest obscurity always trapped in sight. Pearl wants to run to him, see if he will kiss her again, but '"kisses are not to be given in the market-place"' (p. 240). Only Mistress Hibbins knows that the minister's mark is ready to be revealed.

At last Dimmesdale processes, tottering, through the crowd, calls the two of them with 'a ghastly look' (p. 252), and the people

> beheld the minister, leaning on Hester's shoulder and supported by her arm around him, approach the scaffold, and ascend its steps; while still the little hand of the sin-born child was clasped in his. Old Roger Chillingworth followed, as one intimately connected with the drama of guilt and sorrow in which they had all been

actors, and well entitled, therefore, to be present at its closing scene.

'Hadst thou sought the whole earth over,' said he, looking darkly at the clergyman, 'there was no one place so secret, – no high place nor lowly place, where thou couldst have escaped me, – save on this very scaffold!'

'Thanks be to Him who hath led me hither!' answered the minister.

Yet he trembled, and turned to Hester with an expression of doubt and anxiety in his eyes, not the less evidently betrayed, that there was a feeble smile upon his lips.

'Is not this better,' murmured he, 'than what we dreamed of in the forest?'

'I know not! I know not!' she hurriedly replied. 'Better? Yea; so we may both die, and little Pearl die with us!'

'For thee and Pearl, let it be as God shall order,' said the minister; 'and God is merciful! Let me now do the will which he hath made plain before my sight. For, Hester, I am a dying man. So let me make my haste to take my shame upon me.' (pp. 253–4)

The forest dream is dead and, with the death of the man, so is not only the impossible idyll of family but finally the unity of mother and daughter. Dimmesdale steps a pace in front of the other two, tears open his clothing and reveals a scarlet letter engraved on his heart. His last demand is to Pearl.

> Pearl kissed his lips. A spell was broken. The great scene of grief, in which the wild infant bore a part, had developed all her sympathies; and as her tears fell upon her father's cheek, they were the pledge that she would grow up amid human joy and sorrow, nor for ever do battle with the world, but be a woman in it. Towards her mother, too, Pearl's errand as a messenger of anguish was all fulfilled. (p. 256)

The child is at last a redeemer, she blesses where no one else can, and at that moment she leaves aside her role. To be human and a woman, she must both find and lose a father, and in doing so she is cleansed at last of the bloody birthright which made her a mother's child. Dynasty is made possible: Pearl will marry under normal auspices. What is lost here is her unforgiving knowledge, which alone bound her in the female couple; if the letter leaps from her mother-made adornment to his failing flesh, it leaves only Hester marked out. Motherhood, at the end, is loneliness.

The closing pages gather up remaining fates. Dimmesdale is buried, loyal parishioners still failing to believe what they heard or saw; Chilling-worth shrivels away in fury, his occupation gone; but before he dies he makes the least expected gesture, leaving 'a considerable amount of prop-erty, both here and in England, to little Pearl, the daughter of Hester Prynne' (p. 261). For all Pearl's paternity, betrayal and fostering, must be both posthumous and dynastic. No Karenin, Chillingworth-Prynne has nothing to love, if not the rival he devoted himself to (with whom, the narrator quirkily surmises, he may still be united in heaven) and for whose sake he gives the child a line. Hester and Pearl vanish one day, and only the former returns, ending her days in good works and reassuming the scarlet letter, choosing 'to [take] up her long-forsaken shame' (p. 262). This, it seems, is her place. Her child lives on far away, marrying, as her heiress status permits, someone with a European heraldry, 'happy, and mindful of her mother' who at last gets to embroider a lavish golden baby-garment for an unseen and unsexed grandchild. The letter becomes a badge of worth rather than stigma, but over Hester's grave (separated by a pace from her lover's) stands another heraldic emblem, '"ON A FIELD, SABLE, THE LETTER A, GULES"' (p. 264).

This text is, of all, the most intensely matrilinear. In its mother–daughter couple, marked solely by their emblem of sin, all the complexity of an outlawed intimacy is developed. They love, know and struggle. But between them irrupts always the question of paternity that nothing can entirely clothe. What the redness declares, the blood shed in defloration, birth, menarche, menstruation, the involuntary counters of women's time, is that visibility of the woman's body that men cannot repeat. Dimmesdale must scarify his heart in order to create a wound where female blood marks life. But he alone (and his system and his paternal rival) reclaim the child and the continuation of a line. Hester is too blatant, too evid-ent a sign of her sex, either to redeem or to lose her place in the living chain. The anti-icon must collapse.

There are many scarlet As: the narrator's faded rag, the letter on Hester's dress, Pearl dressed up as emblem, the sign in the sky, the mark on Dimmesdale's chest and the heraldic headstone. Pearl herself imitates her mother's gilding art with her green one: flowers, burrs, eel-grass form further As.[39] Neither black nor green can quite cancel out the [read] red. However loaded this text is with its semiotic burden, however dragged under by its absurd locutions, that very embarrassment depends on the simple colour of blood. With all the effort of the implied author to

165

diffuse and control meanings upon the body of women, the scarlet speaks against even the internalized symbolic, leading finally to the question of where the issue began. Menstrual blood is magic because it has potential charge of life within before it emerges, odorized, uncontrolled and signalling death. The unfertilized egg comes out, still hormonally female, of the mother who is not a mother. Upon this evacuated mark masculinity must put its appropriating prohibitions. But the once-spoken taboo lets in a woman's place, however brief, a menstrual hut of a place supposed to hide but inevitably enclosing, a place that starts to suggest synchrony, unity and a matriliny both outside and central. We shall return to these questions in the next chapter. What all the mother–daughter stories point to is the occulting of a kind of inside-body where even castration is absent – pre-oedipal, anti-oedipal but not necessarily crazy.

Effi Briest (1895) is the last-published of my main texts, written by a man in his middle seventies. Many critics note that its delicate geniality has something grandfatherly in it; above all, more than any of the other texts, it seems to lack even an inverted interest in desire. Effi's notion of happiness is familiarly Romantic, paradisiacal and retrospective: there is a garden in which we first meet her, to which she returns after her misfortunes and where she lies buried in the closing conversation between her parents; but what she wants, let alone what her body might desire, is so understated and underknown that she seems almost there only to mark a missed opportunity for other people's sympathetic good sense. As adulterous, no woman's body was ever less motivated. Only the reader best-bred in bowdlerism will be able to figure out where transgressive sexuality might begin; it ends with little effort; versions of nice-minded or embarrassed liking serve in the place where most novels want to put love. And lack of love is nothing even so positive as undesire. The most famous conversation scene has two *Junker* functionaries debating painfully on how many years can elapse after an infidelity before a duel is less stylish than absurd: as one of the sharpest articles comments, the novel is above all the study of 'an uncertainty about the status of "tact", about its human possibilities in late-nineteenth-century Prussia'.[40]

Where is the woman in all this? She provides the disarmingly small-proportioned scope of a social analysis which is never quite bitter or angry, only just about as uncomfortable as an imaginative person at a boring dinner party. Effi is young enough to be a Romantic heroine but has little more yearning than Catherine Morland: no moors or Earnshaws in sight, and her moustachio'd lover is less than the subtraction of

Rodolphe Boulanger from Rhett Butler. Yet somewhere in this text there is an idyll sweet enough to lose, and the fact that the thirty-year-old daughter who dies content in her parents' garden is able to forgive even their convention-bound inadequacies for the sake of her own gives us a text which psychoanalysis has a strangely hard task to read.

As a latecomer, the book offers a number of useful parallels and differences from our other feminocentric texts. Most often compared to *Madame Bovary* – in the teeth of a virtual certainty that Fontane had no interest of any kind in Flaubert – but usually for incongruously unexamined likenesses of content (two villages, two pharmacists), it has also been set against *Anna Karenina* on occasion, and even the maternal attitudes have been compared by one author.[41] I want to begin by raising a number of points of similarity which put Effi in her undoubted context as matrilinear woman, and in certain ways the most extreme of all. With Emma Bovary she shares the legitimacy of her motherhood, a daughter born not out of but alongside the question of adultery. Like Emma she also never functions as a mother in any phantasmatic sense: that both take the child as an occasional plaything testifies not so much to their immaturity as to their fixity in an author's phantasy of irredeemable daughterhood. Each protagonist founders on not being able to contain anyone's store of *le désir de la mère*, neither subject nor object. Both young women want something exotic, though they want it differently; both (though Effi scarcely consciously) perceive that sexuality is the nearest available way of achieving that exotic against the tedious contingencies of provincial life, both go horse-riding as a preamble to the 'real thing'. Neither loves. Finally, they share a set of initials, though Emma's eponymous status depends on her author's unkind use of a surname no less hers than any other, while Effi's is her choice and stands on her grave, her 'maiden name' attesting to a certain untouchedness as well as shame, and even the *particule* dropped as if to make the merest of negative judgements on a rule-bound society she almost learned to despise.[42]

Effi resembles Anna Karenina in very little other than an arranged marriage and a husband more uncongenial than unpleasant: Innstetten hasn't any physical tics but he has sententiousness right down to the bone, the masculine version of her girlish taste for conventional *idées reçues*; he shows an occasional sensitivity but only as far as a few ghosts and an anti-semite's appetite for Wagner. Like Karenin, he is not nasty, but imagination visits him too rarely for him to be able to think much about the human beings around him. Like him also, his real centre is in a skilless pedagogy of whoever is vulnerable enough to be in his hands – in the end, the child rather than the child-wife. Effi, like Anna, founders on a disappointing scene with her estranged child, but nothing before it has really allowed us to believe that this is based on a deep moral passion of the sort that kills Anna.

Wildly different in tone and in every mode of authorial decorum, *Effi Briest* nevertheless resembles *The Scarlet Letter* by a structure that sets sexuality in a past that is seven years hidden from the problematic present of the text. Something like lovemaking happens out of doors (probably) and outside the words of the writing; seven years later, husband and lover stand in the open and the latter dies. Between these events, the woman belongs more surely to other women than to heterosexuality conceived as either synchrony or diachrony, that is, as the coming together of male and female bodies or as a genealogical line. The mother–daughter relation (and here, a fostering mistress–servant relation that kindly upturns all the failures of other forms of parenting) is central, disrupted, unresolved, and the only source of sense.

The text opens in a sunny family garden; mother and daughter are working together on an altar-cloth embroidered out of patchwork squares; every so often, the girl jumps up and does a few over-energetic gymnastic exercises. At these moments, 'the mama glanced up from her handiwork, but always briefly and furtively because she did not want to show how enchanting she found her own child, though her impulse of motherly pride was fully justified.'[43] Effi is dressed in a boyish sailor-suit outfit of blue and white. 'In everything she did there was an equal share of high spirits and grace; her laughing brown eyes betrayed considerable natural cleverness, a fun-loving spirit and kindness of heart. Everyone called her "the little one", a nickname she had to accept only because her beautiful, slim mother was a good few inches taller than she was.'

Effi is, now and forever, a matrilinear daughter. She works in harmony with her mother, exchanging the latter's company only for that of three girl friends, and her very body is measured by this benign comparison. We gradually see less charm in Frau von Briest than her daughter ever discovers for herself: the older woman turns out more cruelly conventional than this idyll suggests, but the daughter is conventional too and has gladly learned her life-clichés at the mother's knee. Exactly here, sewing and jumping under the maternal gaze, will be Effi's only proper place, and this is the moment that henceforth remains as the locus of safety (inevitably lost because no one can fail to grow up or even, genealogically, to want to). Effi's access to womanhood is in her mother's charge, more precisely a question of deferred maternal desire than we have seen elsewhere. Effi's charm for author, parents, friends and husband will always be that her mother is the woman that she is not, the beautiful rather than energetic one, the one endowed with immobile and adequate grace, who is never out of place and who exactly measures what the right proportions are.

As everywhere in this gentle text, nuances emerge in conversation. Effi leaps into exercise mode and her mother begins:

'Effi, really you should have become a circus rider. Always flying on the trapeze, like a daughter of the air. I almost believe that's what you would lie to be.'

'Perhaps, Mama. But if that's so, whose fault would it be? Who do I get it from? only from you. Or do you think it's from Papa? That would make even you laugh. Anyway, why do you dress me in these things, this boys' smock? Sometimes I think I'm going to go back into short skirts. Once I have *them* on again, I'll start curtsying again like a silly girl and when the Rathenowers come over I'll get bounced up and down on Colonel Goetz's lap hoppity-hop. And why not? He's three-quarters uncle and only one-quarter flirt. It's your fault. Why don't I get grand clothes to wear? Why don't you make me into a lady?'

'Would you like that?'

'No.' And she ran to her Mama, threw her arms round her and kissed her.

'Not so wild, Effi, not so passionate. It worries me when I see you like this.'

This interrupted dualogue sets out the mix of motives that supports the closeness of the two women: too childish at times for each of them, Effi is also the presexual body they both wish to preserve. Who Effi can be hangs, it seems, by her mother's choice; the child not only attributes her differences to a solely maternal heredity but also concedes all imminent changes to decisions she only plays at disputing. Her future is no more than a smile, her past is to be the reproduced, risked evidence of this woman's genes. The next move, which alters her life entirely, is again her mother's, and similarly rests on an ambivalence of protection, identification and exposure.

Effi tells her friends of a family visitor she is about to meet for the second time: '"Mama's old friend"' (p. 173) was once her admirer in what has now become a narrative to be read over by four adolescents. '"A love story ending in renunciation is never bad"', Effi begins. When she names the hero of the narrative, her friends laugh.

169

'Oh Effi, we didn't mean to offend you, or the Baron either. Innstetten, you said? and Geert? Nobody has names like that around here. Of course, aristocratic names are often quite funny.'

'Yes, my dear, they are. That is why they are aristocrats. They can permit themselves such things, and the further back they go, I mean in history, the more they can. But you don't understand anything about it, so don't get cross with me. We'll stay friends just the same. So he is Geert von Innstetten, and a baron. He is exactly the same age as Mama, to the day.'

'And how old is your Mama?'

'Thirty-eight.'

'A nice age.'

'Certainly is, especially is you still look like my Mama. She really is a beautiful woman, don't you think? The way she always knows what to do, she's so sure of herself and always so smart and never improper like Papa. If I were a young lieutenant, I'd fall in love with my Mama.'

'Effi, how can you say such a thing?' said Hulda. 'That's against the fourth commandment.'

'Nonsense. How can it be against the fourth commandment? I'm sure Mama would be very pleased to know I'd said such a thing about her.' (p. 175)

Effi's uncomplicated admiration for her mother not only suggests that her idea of sexuality belongs more to fairytale than desire but also predicts her uncertain place in the system of exchange into which she will be inserted. In her tale of renunciation, she identifies with Innstetten rather than her mother, but accepts the social logic of his rejection and the choice of the twelve-years-older Briest as the right husband for a nineteen-year-old bride, justifying an intergenerational basis for marriage that replaces the gender difference she innocently abjures. The question of her mother's desire (except for her, now, as equivalent of the young admirer, then) is never raised. Whose renunciation does she find appealing in the story whose end result is the simple dialectic of her birth? – '"the rest of the story, well, you know that . . . the rest of the story is me"' (p. 176, ellipses Fontane's). A presumed mutuality is never explored: Effi is utterly without sexual imagination.

The girls play on, wrapping up gooseberry skins in a piece of newspaper and ceremonially dropping them into a pond. Effi recalls hearing in school about women drowned in the same way, '"naturally because of infidelity"' (p. 177). Her taste for the exotic, into which she places all she gradually needs to conceive of sexual experience (the far-northern Kessin, the staid husband fantasized as turbaned potentate, all the paraphernalia of foreignness that she finds in the marital home) and which turns to a haunting uncanny as it moves out of her mental control,[44] here clearly anticipates the place of transgression and punishment in any conception of pleasure. However stowed under the sign of girlish prattle, her ideas of women's place in an other system underwrite her own system of placement.

It is a mystery how this protagonist is kept, in the reader's mind as well as in her mother's, a creature of air rather than matter. Many critics read the Melusine imagery of which Fontane is fond into Effi's trajectory from edenic child to punishable woman. Others observe that she is as embedded as anyone in a structure of snobbery (that is, of noble genealogy, its names, its ghosts, its cross-generational marriages) and that it is her concession to these structures, not any kind of rebellion against them, that makes her vulnerable. Effi is not an outsider except in one thing: that her youth, everywhere insisted upon as an awkward charm but also an oddly irreversible fault, seems to evade responsibility for the system she espouses and which finally victimizes her. She complains only once, then dies. But in what is she innocent, if there is no place for innocence except in a garden already spatially fixed in historical time? Effi's innocence is the missed beat of a noble line. No wonder she has a daughter, leaving even the loss of name to a child that will lose it again in her mother's double absence. Effi's marriage, maternity and death are all accidents in the smooth running of genealogy: she is the substitution for her mother, her daughter, then no one. If, finally, this is not to do with adultery, it is because the system runs on temporal blips like the Briest/Frau-Briest/Innstetten triangle, not the spatial adulterous one that ends in the due dance of a duel; and it is this primary triangle that Effi functions to disrupt, expose and die for.

Soon Effi is called and goes off saying '"Carry on playing; I'll be back in a second!"' (p. 179). To her mother she promises to change outfits at once: '"in five minutes Cinderella will turn into a princess"' (p. 180). But the mother impulsively keeps her in the childish outfit whose waywardness seems suddenly (sacrificially?) apt. Innstetten has asked to marry her:

'My hand in marriage? Seriously?'
'It is not a matter that one would joke about. You saw him the day before yesterday and I think you liked him too. Of couse he is older than you, which is a good thing, all things considered, and

a man of character, well-bred, with a good position, and if you don't say no, which I would scarcely expect of my clever Effi, then at twenty you will have gone as far as other women have at forty. You will overtake your Mama by a long way.'

Both unprepared and worldly-wise in her prescribed reply, the girl will be served up to the erstwhile lover as his late consolation prize. The mother's motive, a deferred identification, is no less self-sacrifice than pimping. She passes her child up, in both senses. The age difference seasons the gesture and makes social logic precisely where the bodies are out of line. The chapter ends with a scene that haunts the text:

> When she caught sight of him, Effi suddenly broke into a nervous tremble; but not for long, for almost in the same moment as Innstetten approached her with a friendly bow, there appeared in the middle one of three wide-open, creeper-framed windows the ginger-haired heads of the twins, and Hertha, the more exuberant of the two, shouted into the room: 'Come on Effi [Effi, komm]!'
> Then she ducked down and both sisters jumped off the back of the seat they had been standing on, down into the garden, and all that could be heard was their soft laughter and giggling. (pp. 180–1)

> [Innstetten] did not believe in portents or anything of the kind, and rejected every sort of superstition; yet he could not quite rid himself of those two words and it seemed to him . . . as if that tiny incident had been something other than mere chance. (p. 183)

With this gesture, and the fleeting understanding of it, Effi is uprooted from the world of girlhood. This is one version of the mistake inherent in Effi's life-change, a Persephone myth in which Pluto plucks his girl from among the other meadow flowers. Another version is the, for us, more telling exchange operated by her mother. The latter herself stifles an impulse of nostalgia, accepting the vicarious solution as 'just as good or perhaps even better' (p. 181). But the vulgar wife of pastor Niemeyer has a sharper eye for a social expedient: '"Ah yes, that's how it is. Of course. If it couldn't be the mother it has to be the daughter. That's well-known. The old families always stick together and to those that have, more shall be given"' (p. 182).

These sentences sentence Effi. Her mother is no Demeter, because something in her own story remained unfinished. In this text, which is more powerfully pro-oedipal than any other – Effi has no other place but in the presexual world of women – there is also the keenest sense of mother–daughter betrayal since *Atala*. Frau von Briest sells Effi into the latter's mistaken fairytale for the sake of her own story: 'the rest' is, indeed, the synthetic only child created out of one's social status and the other's loss. Girls consenting to marry old men make more girls fit only to furnish their mothers' unwritten narrative ending, like Atala or Juliet, sacrificed as something between adulteress and virgin. As Innstetten will recognize and misrecognize (for he is talking about men's matters), it is all a question of time.

Briefly before the wedding, the mother steers Effi away from the innocent exotica of the bedroom (a Japanese screen and a red light) and tries to question her motives. Promised a '"model marriage"' (p. 192), Effi admits she is not at all sure that is what she wants. Equality perhaps, tenderness and love – but if that is impossible, then above all '"being rich and having a grand house, a *really* grand one . . . honour and glory, and then entertainment – yes, entertainment, always something new to do, something to make me laugh or cry. What I can't stand is boredom"' (p. 193). So her mother asks whether she loves Innstetten (whose daily letter she has barely glanced at), and the child answers yes of course, just as she loves her family, her friends, the kindly pastor and

'everyone who likes me and is nice to me and spoils me. Geert will spoil me too. In his own way, of course. He wants to buy me jewellery in Venice. He has no idea that I don't care a bit about jewellery. I'd much rather climb or play on the swing, best of all when I'm scared it will crack or break and I'll fall down. It wouldn't kill me, after all.'

'And do you love Cousin Briest too?'

'Oh yes, very much. He's always so funny.'

'And would you have liked to marry Cousin Briest?'

'Marry him? For goodness' sake, no. He's just a boy. Geert is a man, a handsome man, a man I can go into smart society with, who will be somebody in the world. Whatever are you thinking of, Mama?' (p. 195)

A certain kind of height appeals to Effi. She likes climbing and swinging, and the threat of falling is part of the thrill.[45] But the greater height represented by the distinguished older man also threatens a fall, which is just beginning to haunt her. The Baron is, everyone agrees, '"a man of principles. And I . . . well, I don't have any. See, Mama, that's the thing that worries me and makes me anxious. He is so kind and good to me

173

and so considerate but . . . I'm scared of him"' (ellipses Fontane's). Effi
can get neither equality nor anything like love from her husband. Like
Flaubert over Emma, but with the difference that he will only seem to
have a greater knowledge than she, Innstetten will lean down over his
child-wife. It is a fantasy of authorship, a love story turned ghost story
in which she plays both the dead and the haunted, that Effi falls into; but
she falls willingly because, allowed only temporarily and briefly in the
female world in which she could have been unviolated, a male author is
what she thinks she wants.

After an exhausting honeymoon, Effi arrives in Kessin, where her excitement survives only a short time. There are no women here except hyper-
critical aristocrats who look down their noses at her southern ways, the
maidservant Johanna, more sure of herself and more bound to the master
than Effi can ever be, and the crazy Frau Kruse, the coachman's wife,
who sits all day in an overheated room clutching a black hen. Sleeping
alone below an unused gallery salon, she mistakes the noise of long
curtains swishing in the wind upstairs for the sound of ball-gowns sweeping
the floor and little white slippers dancing. One night when Geert is away
visiting Prince Bismarck, the ghost of a Chinaman seems to brush past
her bed. Her husband gently refuses to come to her aid either by alterations
or by moving house. Her ambition for him is appealed to: what would
the prince think if the governor's wife was too frightened to let him out
at night? The story of the Chinaman only gradually emerges, but it is not
by 'mere chance' that it haunts this house, this woman and this marriage.

The sea-captain who built the house had a Chinese servant and a niece
or granddaughter named Nina. While for Effi and the Christian burghers
of Kessin '"there is always something creepy about a Chinaman"' (p. 205),
the three lived in harmony until Nina's wedding-day, when the girl suddenly disappeared, and the Chinaman died soon afterwards. The exotic
of desire out of the control of class, race and religion, but barely spoken
even in gossip, hovers around the model marriage and its half-innocent
victim.[46]

Outside the walls of her marriage, then, Effi has no one in Kessin
besides the courtly pharmacist Gieshübler, who showers her with the
undemanding and romantic attentions her husband fails to produce.
Through Gieshübler she meets the first woman-friend of her married life,
the singer Marietta Trippelli (née Marie Trippel, a local pastor's daughter),
who offers her a model of such freedom as she will never imagine for
herself. An artist, kept by a Russian prince but also supporting her own
career, Trippelli chooses her name, the hours she keeps, the clothes she
wears '"because the bust and lungs must always be free, and above all

the heart"' (p. 248). The narrator marks her out from the generational women by an introductory portrait – 'la Trippelli, in her early thirties, very masculine and a strikingly droll character' (p. 244) – that sets her mobility of life and manners outside Effi's marital scope. The men enjoy the tame danger of her drollity but Effi confides her fear to the older woman who gives her understanding and some practical advice. Her own insurance against ghosts is a Quaker maid; Effi's will be a Catholic one who will give her the only consistent kindness she will ever enjoy and who, at first glance, for all superficial differences, will remind her of Trippelli.

Meanwhile, Christmas passes and Effi is pregnant. She writes to her mother:

'What I hinted to you recently is now a certainty and Innstetten shows me every day how pleased he is about it. I don't need to tell you how much I'm looking forward to it myself, especially because it will bring some excitement and distraction into my life here or, as Geert puts it, will be "a dear little toy for me". He may be right in using that word, but I wish he wouldn't, as it always gives me a bad feeling and reminds me how young I am, only half out of the nursery myself. I can't get rid of this idea (Geert says it's unhealthy) and it means that something that ought to make me so happy seems to cause me constant embarrassment instead . . . [The baby is due] in early July. Then you must come or, better still, as soon as I am more or less back on my feet, *I* will come, take a break from here and head for Hohen-Cremmen. Oh how I long for it and the air there – here it's almost always sharp, cold weather – and a trip to the Luch every day, all covered in red and yellow, and I can just see how the baby will hold its hands out to the flowers, because it will feel that is its home. But I'm only writing this to *you*. Innstetten must not hear of it.' (p. 252)

Truly matrilinear, Effi offers the baby to her mother in a gift that explicitly excludes the husband who will not let her grow up into maternity; if anyone is to keep her young, let it be the woman who has made choices for her thus far. Effi's guileless search for a female figure of protection proceeds via her girl-child. Not so much Effi as her infant will take them both out of the *unheimlich* back to the place that is home.

The routine of Effi's heterosexual isolation is now established: Innstetten leaves her side every evening to work, returns around nine for tea, asks her to play a little Wagner and then 'at ten o'clock, relaxed at last' (p. 256), indulges 'in a few well-meant but somewhat weary caresses which Effi accepted without much response'. Uncritical affection is available only from the hunchback Gieshübler. Kessin offers little to satisfy her need for diversion except (as she writes a few months later to her mother) the arrival of the new District CO, Major Crampas. After the previous incumbent, whom no one liked, this choice, a brother-officer of Instetten's, sounds so much more interesting that husband and wife '"threw our arms around each other, thinking nothing bad could ever happen in dear old Kessin again"' (p. 257). Nice and sad, the irony is obvious. It is Effi alone who looks to the new arrival as '"a bringer of rescue and consolation"', even though, as she goes on to reveal, the character of his wife looks like preventing this possibility.

It is to the latter she had thought of turning – a woman of forty-five (a year older than her husband) with two young children, potentially a motherly friend. But she is difficult and melancholic, another Frau Kruse, and obsessively jealous over her husband, '"a man of many affairs, a ladies' man"', who has already been through a duel that left his arm shattered. The couple visit the Innstettens, but the wife's bitter surveillance and the embarrassment of both Crampas and Effi make the situation intolerable. Despite all this, when he is on his own he '"can be quite different, relaxed and high-spirited . . . a real gentleman, exceptionally elegant and witty . . . but the wife! Without her of course it's no good, and with her it's impossible"' (p. 258).

The adulteress in Effi is, as we see here in the clearest representation of the lover's awaiting charm, a bored child looking for something closer to maternal protection than sexual excitement. If Frau Crampas offers a double for the uncanny Frau Kruse (and later events will be built by Effi into a telling extension of this parallel), her husband's split from her puts him in the place Effi's own husband has refused to take up, the place of the rescuer from fear and creator of interest. It is at this moment that Effi follows Trippelli both metaphorically and metonymically by choosing, to care for herself and her baby, the dark-eyed, powerful figure of the Catholic Roswitha.

She meets and rescues the latter after her employer's death leaves her suicidal. Between these two women, a mother and the fosterer of her child, a bereaved mother and the child who offers her a kind of granddaughter – the servant is clearly much older than the mistress, but is constantly and safely patronized by her – we see the kindest and most reliable relationship in the whole novel. It is a complex of mutual nurturance in which nothing is intimate enough to require exploitation but in which also each learns by the other's utterly accepted inarticulacies.

Class difference and similarity of fate overturn Effi's daughterhood. Unlike Innstetten or Frau von Briest, Roswitha has no authority. More like the dog Rollo in the true-hearted muteness of her position, she is nevertheless a human model to Effi of what could have been and what continues to be when all other relations founder on the social law. Every genealogical possibility is corrupt; nothing, even motherhood, even the love of finally redeeming parents (the sunny garden, the easy-going father with his safer vulgarities, the mother tender in spite of her harder traits of social rigidity) is able to give the adulteress a companion, except the foster-mother she gets through her child.

With the entry of Roswitha into Effi's household there is a shift in arrangements. Hired to care for the baby, she is moved into the space that Innstetten, Johanna (once) and the baby (potentially) might occupy. Sleeping with her in the alcove, Effi is convinced that there will be nothing more to fear and, sure enough, the ghost noises are inaudible to the Catholic. Roswitha's stories reassure Effi and even entertain Johanna, who has no more sense of rivalry over the mistress's affections than she has with the dog. A week or so later, the baby is born.

The birth is rendered indirectly and is thus painless and centreless. The doctor regrets that the child, born on the anniversary of a battle, could not be a boy. What Effi thinks we do not learn. Instead we glimpse the reaction of Roswitha, whose privilege it is to name the child:

> Roswitha may well have felt the same [as the doctor], but meanwhile she was unrestrainedly overjoyed with the baby just as it was, and without hesitation called the child 'Wee Annie', which the young mother took as a sign. 'It really must have been an inspiration that made Roswitha pick that name.' Even Innstetten could raise no objection to it, so everyone referred to 'Little Annie' long before the christening day. Effi, who was to stay with her parents in Hohen-Cremmen from mid-August, wanted to put the christening off till then. But that was impossible; Innstetten could not take leave. (p. 267)

As in our other matrilinear texts, the naming of the daughter is an issue – no doubt in compensation for the disappointment of a child whose other name will not carry the father's seal. It is left to mothers and 'old wives' to pass their mark to the half-named infant; only in the ceremony, with its speeches in homage to paternal authority, is the naming covered by the reappropriation of a father's place. As the show is stolen from the fruit of her body by the institutions into which children are set, Effi sits on the margins with Crampas and Gieshübler, banters with the one, confides in the other.

In Hohen-Cremmen, Effi enjoys an idyll uninterrupted by any visit from Innstetten, surrounded by her family, Roswitha and the child, her old friends and old activities: 'best of all she would fly through the air on the swing, then stand up and in the sensation "now I'll jump" got that peculiar prickly feeling, a thrill of sweet danger' (p. 269). Where Effi is now jumping, with the habitual lightness of the gentle moves of this text, is into womanhood. However little we see of Annie and however little she impinges on her mother's story at this stage, here bringing Roswitha's voice echoing from the nursery, there the occasion for a stroll outdoors, the baby functions to make Effi something she has not yet been. On her return to Kessin, Innstetten discovers a change:

'You know what, Effi, you seem quite different to me. Before little Annie was born, you were still a child. But now all at once...'
'Well?'
'All at once you are completely changed. But it suits you, I really like you this way, Effi. Do you know what?'
'Well?'
'There's something seductive about you.'
'Oh my one and only Geert, what you've just said is lovely; it gives me a good feeling in my heart... Pour me another half-cup, could you?... Do you know, that's what I've always wanted to be. We have to be seductive, otherwise we are nothing...' (p. 273, ellipses Fontane's)

In this awkward exchange among the coffee-cups, marital love gets its last chance. Good-heartedness without desire blends on both sides with the timid discourse of excitement and the cosiness of the habitual. Changes are never change enough without risk. While this conversation takes place, Effi is on that tamed version of the real seat of pleasure, swinging without danger on a rocking-chair. Crampas comes by, having taken an early cold-water swim, the three chat lightly about death by drowning and the season's entertainment. Then the entrance of Roswitha with Annie disrupts the triangle. 'She took the baby from her arm and lifted it proudly and happily up in the air.' As the child swings high in the arms of the young mother, a female enclave interrupts the men, but precariously, lacking the institutional fixity that gives them their odd unity.

The days lenghten and the two men and Effi begin to go out horse-riding along the beach. They debate whether life is best lived by rules or 'enjoyment [Leichtsinn]' while she looks out for the seal that might be a mermaid. A while later, in a key conversation during a picnic without Innstetten, Crampas tells Effi what he knows of her husband. He has always told ghost stories, perhaps to draw attention to himself for his career's sake (a 'singularity' he has both enjoyed and deplored in his child-wife) but perhaps for less forgivable reasons. It is when Crampas sows the seeds of suspicion that her husband has exploited her fears, not just out of pedagogy for its own sake but as '"a cherub with a sword"' (p. 283) to keep her in check, that Effi begins really to grow up. However suspect the major's own motives, what he has said rhymes with her knowledge of Innstetten: she recognizes the cruel trait of a 'calculated device for creating fear'. Exiled at last from the edenic garden, to whom else might such a woman turn, conventional as she is, but the bringer of rescue, consolation and enjoyment?

After Christmas, all the local society, except for Frau Crampas, gathers at a party in the Uvagla forest followed by a sumptuous dinner; punch, conversation and speeches flow. On the homeward journey, by a series of chances, Effi ends up alone in a closed sleigh with Crampas; her husband's sleigh, which they are following, turns into the woods:

> Effi gave a start. Until then there had been air and light about her, now it was gone and the dark vault of trees was arching above her. She began to tremble, and locked her fingers together as if for something to hold onto. Thoughts and images raced through her mind; one of them was the little old woman in the poem called 'God's Wall', and, like that little old woman, she prayed now that God might build a wall around her. Two or three times the words were on her lips, but she could feel that they were dead sounds. She was afraid but at the same time it was as if she were under a spell from which she did not want to be released.
>
> The one word 'Effi' was whispered softly at her ear, and she could hear the voice trembling. Then he took her hand and undid the fingers she was still holding clasped together, and covered them with ardent kisses. She felt as if she were about to faint.
>
> When she opened her eyes again, they were through the wood, and a little distance off she could hear the other sleighs racing on ahead. (p. 308)

The homeward drive takes them past where the Chinaman lies buried. Effi first looks about her as the sleigh stops outside their house.

Once again, the events of the woman's body are unnarrated. Just as

179

birth is a blurred before/after, so seduction like marriage begins nowhere, opens nothing, barely occurs. The opening eyes in the cleared carriage where Effi reappears alone in the text do no more than reverse the minimal action of a whisper in the ear shutting off her unwhispered prayer and the unclasping of fingers she had knotted together. Where is the body of desire? only in a move from fear to consciousness, a fairytale faint and then the world returning. God's wall can (for she will never become an old woman) never surround her.

Effi begins to find her health necessitating daily walks out by the dunes. What she does out of doors is not told; alone at home, however, there are two places where she mourns for a loss of self – at her bedroom mirror and by the cradle of her child:

> When Innstetten went away . . . she sat by her baby's cradle and her tears fell on the pillow. The whole thing bore in on her again, and she felt like a woman imprisoned for whom there was no way of escape.
>
> She was suffering deeply and longed to free herself. But although she was capable of feeling things strongly, she was not strong by nature; she lacked persistence and all her good impulses passed as quickly as they came. So she went on with it, today because she could not change, tomorrow because she did not want to change. The forbidden, the secret, had her in its power.
>
> Thus it happened that Effi, frank and open by nature, came gradually more and more to play a part. At times it shocked her how easy she found it. In one thing only she remained herself: she knew exactly what she was doing and made no excuses for herself. Once, late in the evening, she stood in front of her bedroom mirror; light and shadows flickered before her and Rollo began to bark outside, and at that moment she seemed to feel someone looking over her shoulder. But she pulled herself together: 'I know what it is; it wasn't *him*' and she pointed towards the haunted room upstairs. 'It was something else . . . my conscience . . . Effi, you are lost.' (pp. 314–15, last two ellipses Fontane's)

Effi divided by dishonesty (Anna Karenina surprised herself too by the ease and artistry of deception but had, after all, more motive for it) reappropriates the haunting of her house, the negativity of her motherhood, the absence of anyone in her bedroom except a reflection of her self. We learn only much later, when the whole thing is so far over as to concern nothing but Innstetten's Prussian conventionality, what there was to know of the lived experience of this relationship. Extracts from three of Crampas's letters to her indicate her attitudes: fear and guilt – '"you mustn't be so afraid of everything. We have *our* rights too"' (p. 371); the desire to escape – '"you say let's go away. That's impossible. I simply couldn't leave my wife in the lurch . . . we must learn to take life easy [Leichtsinn ist das Beste]. Everything is fate"'; and finally relief when the choice of departure is made for her. The course of the affair appears in negative only, implied, retrospective and echoed (as in the servants' parallel of a Molière or a Shakespeare tragedy) in Effi's school-mistressy concern with Roswitha's apparent affair with Kruse.

Roswitha provides her here as everywhere else with the narrative and support she needs; she creates in Effi a woman in charge, more motherly in her admonishments than either her mother is with her or she ever is with her daughter. The nursemaid offers a safer model than any legitimate women may: and her own story, less mysterious but no less extreme, takes over from that of Nina and the Chinaman. Effi chides her for flirting with Kruse, whose uncanny wife offers a handy parallel with Crampas's. In return, Roswitha tells her the tale of how she came to learn the lessons of transgressive sexuality. She says nothing of love:

> Effi was sitting up, with her head leaning on her arm. 'Go on then, tell me. How was it exactly [the first time]? I know what it's like with you people, from our own servants at home, always the same story . . .'
>
> 'Yes, at first it's always the same, and I won't pretend I was anything special, nothing special at all. But when they asked me straight out and I had to say yes, well, it was just terrible. Mother wasn't so bad but Dad, he was the village blacksmith, he went wild when he heard, he came after me with the red-hot iron he'd just pulled out of the fire, he was going to kill me. (pp. 321–2)

Her baby, born in the barn, was taken from her and she was saved by the job of wetnurse to a gentleman's wife. Kissing Effi's hand in gratitude for a second and final rescue, she embarrasses the girl. No less when she offers a simple-hearted parallel – '"the holy Mother of God protect you from sorrow like that, my lady!"' (p. 322) – does Effi bridle: '"Whatever can you mean? I am a married woman."' The parallels give Effi the confidence to assume difference, using Roswitha as her nearest means towards the principles she lacks for herself. Only the foster-mother can offer a mixture of narrative with safety; but that too is no more than an idyll.

Throughout this text – in the protagonist's motives as well as in the society she occupies – women's space is a perfect and fragile expedient. The sunny garden, the nursery in which mothers need never grow up, these replace the embraces of desire as spaces almost outside time. Nothing like ecstasy, but something a little like peace, seems to be available in these feminized moments where narrative counterweighs moral debate and language atones for acts. Why then is Effi directed into adultery at all? Because adultery is the masculine oedipal version of the dangers to the familial. Fontane wants, it seems, both to use it as a device for the outlawing of innocence and also to show how unnecessary it is. Adultery is hardly essential to Effi's failure. Not the spatial misplacement of one man's woman into the embrace of another, but the time-lag that passes a mother's lover down to the daughter as husband and ruins matrilinear unity, this is the central triangle of this text. This is why, however strangely it may read in the realist narrative, Effi must feel nothing impelling her towards Crampas except her own repressed disappointment in women. While Roswitha's tales give shape to her dilemma, her lover's whispers are inaudible.

Innstetten goes to Berlin for a few weeks; when he returns he tells Effi that he has been offered a post there. She sinks to the floor and stammers ' "Thank God!" ' (p. 326). Her two words, his momentary suspicion and a farewell wave from a silent Crampas at the quay when she leaves with Annie and Roswitha are henceforth all that remain of her weeks-long adultery. Effi departs with her womenfolk to join her mother in Berlin and look for a flat. From there she has resolved not to return. A little dissimulation, which grandfatherly Dr Rummschüttel is worldly enough to humour, enables her to call Geert to join her without having to go back to Kessin. After this, almost seven years pass in unclouded married life in the capital.

Now after all, Effi has what she always desired: the social whirl, a smart home, respectability and status and her family not too far away. The child grows, the husband progresses, the wife moves on through her twenties. All that remains is a vague feeling of guilt, not at what she has done but at the lack of real remorse and a sense of the vulgar disappointment of lying so fluently and having had something to lie about. All this fades, though, over six or seven years – years in which (to the puzzlement of readers and characters alike) Effi does not destroy the small number of letters she had received from Crampas. Then one day she goes off to a spa and, shortly before she is due back, Annie falls down on the steps as she is arriving home from school.

Annie's awkward poem of greeting to her mother, the split in her upbringing between the storytelling Roswitha and the snobbish Johanna, is the first sight we get of this child's independent existence. She lives more among these nicely divided servants than with her father and mother, neither of whom seems preoccupied enough with her to bring her into the narrative. But now, as Shieh and Jamison point out, it is Annie who takes the fall in Effi's stead, just as the latter got married in her own mother's.[47] This little girl serves the author as have our others – midway between a Seriozha and an Ani, she enters our interest and leaves it at points that separate her parents – but she also marks a chain in which her final submission to Innstetten's pedagogical authority cuts off something that made Effi live. The latter, adult at last, had begun to fade; it is only, but negatively, through Annie that Effi can recover her loneliness. As the last link in a ruined chain, Annie proves that the man cannot lose: immature for the future Frau von Briest, absurd to his wife, for his daughter at last he can be the pure desexed educator. Annie stands at the end of the matrilinear inheritance, urbanized, neglected and in utter loss of all her mother might have left her. Her fall is as near desire as this child can ever get – unlike Berthe, she does not even need to be pushed – and the blood on her forehead marks nothing more womanly than what will become her lot: paternal justice with the minimum of tenderness.

Annie falls, and as Johanna and Roswitha search in the mistress's sewing table for a bandage, a yellowed bundle of letters drops out. When Innstetten comes home, he reproaches the child (in virtually her grandmother's words) for rushing about: '"You are so wild, Annie, you get that from your Mama. Always like a whirlwind. But never mind, it doesn't do any harm, or anyway nothing worse than this." He pointed to the wound and gave her a kiss' (p. 368). After an awkward dinner *à deux*, he glances at the letters and recognizes the handwriting of Crampas. Moments later, he has called his friend Wüllersdorf. The two men discuss the rights and wrongs of a duel over an adultery so many years old. Innstetten is motivated not by animosity towards either partner but by a sense that, having once chosen to confide his dilemma, he cannot again wipe out the humiliating fact from social consciousness. The '"idol"' (p. 375) of Prussian convention, however unworthy, is not to be gainsaid. What is most striking about this scene is the entire absence of discussion of Effi's place in the arrangement; while Innstetten vows he still loves her and would be inclined to forgive, no question of her motives then or now enters the debate. The rightness of the triangle which overturns adultery by an exclusive encounter between men (and mutually exclusive – one must die) overrides any remaining relation, violent or conciliatory, between the married partners. Effi is disposed of no less

183

surely than Crampas; but it is the lover's dying words and look that will haunt the husband. The total exclusion of Effi seems right to everyone.

When Innstetten returns from killing Crampas, we watch Johanna and Roswitha duelling over who knows more and how Effi is to be judged. Against Roswitha's broad view, Johanna's will prevail: she will remain with the master and help to educate the child. As for Effi, she is at the spa chatting uneasily with the flighty Frau Zwicker when a letter arrives from her mother, which ends thus:

> '. . . And now, as to your future, my dear Effi. You will have to fend for yourself, though as far as material support is concerned, you can rely on us. It would be best for you to live in Berlin (these things are best concealed in a big city) and there you will be one of those who must live without fresh air and sunlight. You will live alone, or if you choose not to do that, you will be forced to live outside your own social sphere. The world you have lived in will be closed to you. And the saddest thing for us and for you (for you just as much, as far as we know you): your old home with us is closed to you too; we can't offer you a quiet place in Hohen-Cremmen, a refuge in our house, for that would mean cutting ourselves off from everyone we know, and really we do not feel inclined to do that. Not because we are so attached to our social life that we could not bear to say farewell to what is called "good society"; no, *not* for that reason, but simply because we have to make our own position clear and must show the whole world – I cannot spare you the plain words – our judgement of your action, the action of our only, and so beloved child . . .'
>
> Effi could read no further; her eyes filled with tears and, after struggling against it vainly, she burst out at last into violent sobs and weeping, which brought her some relief. (p. 391, ellipses Fontane's)

This ultimate abandonment, and the hypocrisy embodied in its justification, brings no reproach at any time from Effi or the narrator. Effi's mother it seems is the prime mover. Her father later, on the instigation of grandfatherly Rummschüttel, is the one to call Effi home in an encircling repetition of the 'Effi komm' of her childhood girl-friends; her mother blames her even in her dying days. Any critique remains implicit. Effi herself, we know, differs in no fundamental way from the world and the parents that bred her. But at this point, with the breaking of the primary mother–daughter bond and the turning out of the beloved child from fresh air into the secluded cell of shame, we see most sharply the betrayal of the matrilinear structure. Effi has no compensating resources in her own motherhood, and this is because, in the end, the idyll of her daughterhood, on which her whole story depends, is revealed as hollow, a matter of surface comfort only. When her father, in the text's closing words, rejects the question of blame with his habitual cosy phrase '"that subject would take us *much* too far afield"' (p. 427), he enunciates the morality of surface that holds back every character in the book from any effective form of love.

Every character, that is, except Roswitha. Childless and parentless, attacked by her father and robbed of her baby, Roswitha alone moves outside the tacit violence of the higher classes to ally herself with the motherless Effi. The latter's excitement when Roswitha reappears reveals what is left in her of the trusting child:

'Roswitha. You. What a joy. What have you brought? It must be something good. Such a dear, good old face can only bring good things. Oh how happy I am, I could kiss you; I never thought I could have such joy again. My dear old friend, how have you been? Do you remember those old days, back there, when we had the Chinese ghost? They were happy times. I thought then that I was unhappy, because I didn't know how hard life could be. Now I know all about that. Oh ghosts aren't the worst thing, by far! Come, my good Roswitha, come, sit down, tell me everything . . . Oh I'm so longing to know. What is Annie up to?' (p. 397, ellipses Fontane's)

Only Roswitha can restore hopes of the maternal relation. In her depleted state, Effi is more than satisfied with her companionship. For Roswitha has the practical and emotional strength to nurture not despite but because of the 'hard times'. '"For Roswitha everything is good enough, if she can share it with mylady, and especially if it is something sad. I am really happy about that. Because, you see, that's what I understand"' (p. 399). What she offers is both unstinting and genuine: the ability to tell stories together, to share the limited resources of women on the social margin – like Hester and Pearl, entombed in an unspoken cell in which words can flow unheard.

And when Annie reappears, glimpsed in the street by her mother and then invited up (through the mediation of the minister's wife and Innstetten's over-civilized ambition), she is brought in and tactfully left by Roswitha to enter her mother's embrace. That this encounter fails is

185

the fault of the same girlish submissiveness that ruined Effi. She too has learned her duty well and alienates her eager mother by an excess of repetition:

> 'And now tell me, Annie – for today we've only just had time to see each other again – will you come and visit me often?'
> 'Yes indeed, if I am allowed.'
> 'We could go for walks in the Prinz Albrecht Gardens.'
> 'Yes indeed, if I am allowed.'
> 'Or we'll go to Schilling's and have ice-cream, pineapple or vanilla – those are the ones I used to like best.'
> 'Yes indeed, if I am allowed.'
> At this third 'if I am allowed' Effi had had enough; she jumped up and threw the child a glance flaming with something like rebellion. (p. 408)

The attempt to reach the child through a re-creation of her own childhood pleasures has failed. She sends her hurriedly away to join Johanna and, in a rare fit of passion, curses all those who have robbed her of her maternal rights and cut off her own girlhood as well as her daughter's:

> 'God in Heaven, forgive what I did; I was a child . . . No, no, I wasn't a child, I was old enough to know what I was doing. I *did* know, I don't want to minimize my guilt, . . . but *this* is too much. This, with the child, this wasn't you punishing me, God, it was *him*, only him! I thought he had a noble heart and I always felt small beside him; but now I know it is he that is small. He's small and he's cruel. *He* taught the child to speak like that, he always was a schoolmaster, Crampas said so, mockingly at the time but he was right. "Yes indeed, if I am allowed." You don't *need* to be allowed, I don't want any of you any more, I hate you, even my own child. Too much is too much. He was ambitious, that's all he was. – Honour, honour, honour . . . and then he went and killed that poor fellow, shot him dead, when I didn't even love him and I had forgotten him because I didn't love him. It was all stupidity, and now it ends in blood and murder. And it's my fault. And now he sends me the child because he can't refuse a minister's wife, and before he sends the child he trains her like a parrot and teaches her to say "if I'm allowed." What I did disgusts me; but what disgusts me still more is your virtue. Get away, both of you. I must go on living, but I suppose it can't go on for ever.'

When Roswitha came back, Effi was lying on the ground, her
face turned away, as if lifeless. (pp. 408–9, ellipses Fontane's)

Effi's deathwish begins here. Roswitha stays with her throughout the rest
of her life, and the old dog Rollo joins them at the end. Rummschüttel
contacts the parents and they invite her home. Reluctantly, they settle
into a calm idyllic period lit up by their daughter's uncritical gratitude.
The kinder, older men offer her sanction and sanctuary, the loving mother
still whispers reproaches. Innstetten lives on alongside the caricatural
Johanna, seriously unhappy but making no move towards his past. After
Effi's death, her mother wonders briefly '"if perhaps it wasn't all our
fault?"' (p. 427); old Rollo shakes his head slowly, and Briest declines to
pursue the thought.

In this last of our matrilinear texts, the light touch betrays a resigned
acceptance of failure. The Demeter-Persephone structure undermined from
within, neglect underlies both the apparently solid base of the loving
partnership of Effi and her mother and that between her and Annie.
There is, in the end, nothing to hold them – not because they are united,
like Anna and Ani or Hester and Pearl, outside the social sanction, but
because they are too firmly rooted in it. Finally, the genetic tie on which
everything here seems to rely is just a series of imitations: if Annie speaks
like a parrot it is not simply because her father has got at her but because
there *are* only unrecognized repetitions, substitutions in which 'wildness'
functions as the flushed face of submission, the wish for air and excitement
is bound within a genealogical structure that overlays this one's mistake
onto that one's fated loss. Desire has no place here. Safety, secrecy and
security are possible only across classes, between the fosterer and her
child; but this is of no consequence because the stories flow on without
real confidence and even their succour is immaterial. Roswitha is absent
from the final scene because she has in the end failed to preserve either
child, or even herself, from the unspeaking danger that surrounds them.

Among the mothers and daughters of male-authored texts, it seems,
the adulterous motive is hereditary. In Chateaubriand's *Atala* (1801), the
eponym's adulterous mother damns her daughter into a suicide of desire
because she herself began a chain of punishable transgression. The virginity she forces on her child is the cruellest heritage, depriving the girl
of life only after it has made her unfit for anything but incestuous
heterosexuality. As a male author bends over his girl (raven-haired from
Normandy or blonde from Louisiana) he turns the horror of maternal

desire into an unfitness to pass on anything good. Almost a century later, the Goncourts' Germinie Lacerteux embodies everything the sensitive aristocracy find most fascinating in working-class vice: her unrelenting suffering, her aphrodisiac ugliness, her inability to resist the horrors of debt and drink; with all these and through her silent martyrdom, she bears a daughter (waiting at table throughout an inaudible labour) whom she loves, sends to a wetnurse and loses in infancy. The reproduction of a female child is an indistinguishable part of both corruption and punishment.

Three twentieth-century texts offer a similar pessimism. *La Porte étroite* gives us a latter-day Atala, condemned to die in a body that cannot create because her mother's sexuality was too wild; her sister fails another way, and the love of the two is disempowered by authorial divide-and-rule. Female virtue, in such a construct, is possible only as a perversion of adultery.

Mauriac's *Thérèse Desqueyroux* (1927) presents a heroine both in revolt and fatally wedded to the small-minded genealogy of her wealthy province; as fascinated by women as Effi, she finds nothing but aggression uniting her to them. Her mother abandoned her in a childbed death, her best friend Anne offers a model of submissive heterosexuality that provokes Thérèse's disappointed cruelty; a transgressive maternal grandmother only whispered of in the family passes down nothing to her but a need for escape. Towards her daughter she shows the same indifference as Emma, pausing occasionally over her cradle but 'detached from her daughter as she was from all the rest'.[48] After attempting to murder her husband she is incarcerated in her own home, and finally cast out into the grim streets of Paris, both times entirely alone. But her author cannot quite leave it at that. In the even more miserable sequel, *La Fin de la nuit* (1935), Thérèse is reunited with her daughter in Paris only to lose her definitively by 'stealing' her quasi-intellectual boyfriend as she once 'stole' Anne's. Women's freedom in Mauriac is above all freedom from God. Thérèse goes further than his other best-known protagonists in evading the conversion that is coming to her: the author, in other words, prides himself in being less coercive than he might. But where she is doomed is by her failure, like Effi, to be able to enjoy the girlhood that should precede desire; this sinner has never really been innocent.

In Breton's *Nadja* (1928) another wild girl haunts the streets of the capital and the narrator's head; but he prides himself more in the fact that *he* haunts her, recurring in her dreams and occultry with unhealthy frequency. We know little of her past: she admires her father but despises and deceives her mother; a seventy-five-year-old man keeps her, putting her to bed every night. Where or how she lives is deliberately left un-known, but we discover she is the mother of a daughter; is it for the sake of the latter that, irritating the narrator's sense of poetry, she works as a prostitute and drug-trafficker? Nadja is eponymous and pseudonymous; the *nom du père* touches her nowhere except in the author's authorship, and there it holds her in absolute thrall. More explicitly than any of our realist heroines, she is the vocable of another's phantasy; both in and out of his text, he polices her excess while deploring her incarceration. Nameless and bodiless finally, she breaks out and is utterly enclosed; and who minds the baby when she is locked up?

189

5

Conclusion

*P*aternally both, 'Flaubert' and 'Tolstoy' lean down over
their heroines. The former enters with distaste, the latter
sighs and lets her have him only when devalued. Both women's bodies
give forth clones they cannot love. Adulterously or non-adulterously,
these girls are copies of a fault. Like Hester and Effi, their mothers name
and misname them: nothing will give the castrated infants the father's
name. For the authors are at pains not to be implicated in the fate of
these lost children: their ending exceeds the text's close only to round
off into further failure; they are unaccepted.

'Hawthorne' and 'Fontane' know that the girl-child belongs to the
outside of her mother's body. She marks her. She can only be scarlet.
Daring safely, as they surmise, to offer up to the reader's vision the
couple formed by mother–daughter passion, they keep it in its place,
within the walls of a cell, a garden, but always exposed, always declaring
its scandal freely to public notice. Seven magic years pass to delay desire,
unfitting it for a consummation only to be remembered. During these
seven years, the children grow as their mothers' heterosexuality grows
distant. At the end, exhaustion puts a halt to danger: the men regroup
and one dies; the mark of the mother is wiped from the daughter, so that
she may re-enter the genealogical chain from which adultery satanically
removed her.

Men's part in reproduction begins with alienation and ends in appropriation. Patriarchy's narrative begins at the end of this process, and at
the beginning must recognize, if it dares, something deadly to it. Patriarchy's prehistory (pre-narrative) is assigned at the moment of loss. The
seed given in what must often be a private moment of ecstasy goes on
to start something in a dangerous place: if the phallus returns safe but
no longer phallic, the product reproduces beyond his jurisdiction (beyond hers too, but this is not his danger). She has, it seems, in becoming
the site rather than the object of his alienation, taken more from him

than anyone since the moment of birth. He thought he had her threat under control: he had returned safely enough times. Now she exceeds him, even without knowledge of the event she enables. (What is authorship beside this?) She fills with blood. Without harm or castration, she is the container of blood, unspilt because nurturing. Just in time he escaped engulfment, and if that is because he has caused it, he cannot help suspecting it might have drowned him.

If what emerges is a male child, he is somewhat rewarded. He appropriates the son, takes and marks him with something better than birthblood, the blood of a wound made at the giving of the paternal name.[1] The mother, in Leviticus 12:1–5, rests for forty days in a state of defilement. If she has a daughter she is occulted for eighty days: this child can less in any case be redeemed from the parturitional flow. The daughter can neither be wounded nor named. Nothing done to her can stick. She is, on the contrary, already so far of her mother's blood that, even if she is named Pearl, she will be coloured dark red. Her emergence signals that which cannot be appropriated. Born in a prison, she blinks when she first sees sunlight. There is no point cutting her, they say, because she is already wounded, castrated.

Actually, if she were, there would be none of the danger that requires her to be incarcerated. Quite the contrary, she is not castrated. As Hawthorne vividly conveys, she is rather castration itself. The girl-child bears witness to what the boy-child risked: she is a thing utterly removed from the man's body.

Thus Hawthorne desperately and Fontane delicately set their girls to redeem their mother's excessive femininity by seeking the daughter–father relation where it seems most unpromising and where finally, in however murderous a way, it reappears to collect them. Hester and Effi exceed their womanly bounds in and by means of the mother–daughter relation, but it stops with them: only fatherhood can come next and stay last – as it does also in the final fostering of Bovary and Karenin. Paternity as authorship steps in to save the phantasy from what would be the real risk of castration. The sick son is a moderate expedient, it plays with danger; the living daughter might take away all hope of return.

The daughter is the place where the man stops. He can write a mother's agony at the seeming death of her boy, not the father's crisis (except in negative) at the birth of his girl into a world in which she does not prove him. She carries no sign of him; if she is his sign, he may no longer be a man. We thus find in our seven novels of adultery two stages in the phantasy of the man's alienation (the hero's singleness, and narrative plot) and reappropriation (punishment of the woman, and authorship).

The first is that of mothers and sons, in which the author-narrator-protagonist remains inside a protective patrilinear structure; the second is that of mothers and daughters, in which patriarchy cracks open and is restored only by a panicked expediency. In both versions, of course, the woman suffers and dies; but the risk rehearsed in the first goes out beyond the death principle in the second to become a portrait in negative of the potential dispensability of male authorship.

In the remaining pages, I want to conclude this book's analysis by tracing through a number of broadly connected ideas that arise from it and from the problems of parenthood, masculinity, femininity, authorship and desire. In seven nineteenth-century male-authored novels we have seen the motif of adulterous desire founder on the real other of the beloved's child: the phantasy-act of authorship as oedipal expediency both creates and solves – evades, co-opts or almost murders – that other who focuses the impossibility of having and wanting. As in my Introduction, it is inevitably the question of difference that underlies all these issues. In the always internourishing worlds of action and phantasy, how do we perceive what is other without suspicion or terror? How do we know? How do we desire?

The two terms I used above to speak of men's reproductive role come from Mary O'Brien's admirable book *The Politics of Reproduction*. In the second chapter she sets out 'the moments of reproductive process':[2]

The moment of menstruation
The moment of ovulation
The moment of copulation
The moment of alienation
The moment of conception
The moment of gestation
The moment of labour
The moment of birth
The moment of appropriation
The moment of nurture

Of these, only 'alienation and appropriation are male moments ... copulation and nurture are generically shared moments; all of the others are women's moments' (pp. 47–8). She continues:

Ovulation and conception are not tangible moments; they are not only involuntary, but are not immediately apprehended by consciousness. We therefore have quite a complex process, in terms of several factors quite out of the realm of simple biology. When we speak of voluntary and involuntary moments, we have entered the realm of the human will. When we speak of copulation and nurture, we speak of social relations. When we speak of appropriation, we speak of a relationship of dominance and control. Clearly, there is much more to reproduction than meets a narrow physiological eye. (p. 48)

I shall speak more later of menstruation and how it too is demonstrably made the basis of a social relation of dominance and control, one directly linked to the scarlet letters of patriarchal culture. The important point here is that the two 'male moments', occurring towards either end of the system, are the only ones not centred upon the woman's bodily experience. They differ significantly. The first occurs inside the woman; the second in the public place in which men reign and relate to one another. Alienation (or separation, the masculine obsession) is not unconnected to the key trope of our linguistic world, castration. It is the unmanning – so he must feel – of the phallus; as it occurs, the phallus loses its consistency and the man his power: she takes them over. Only by the reappropriation that occurs beyond her skin, after the child's emergence and by a system that differentiates gender at the instant of naming, does the man (does masculinity as a system) recover from the trauma of alienation.

I began my Introduction with the question of why we have such trouble conceiving the mother as a knowing or desiring subject. As desirer, she must have preceded us, and preceded also the man's 'possession' of her in engendering us. Fathering, by definition, happens in an instant; mothering is for ever after. If we are fathered by the father's desire, the mother's desire is the mystery, the extra, to that logic. We shall see soon what problems sociobiology has with the awkward fact of an experience, the orgasm of human females, and an organ, the 'supernumerary' clitoris, which exists against the hard truth of Darwinian genetics with the sole purpose of providing that orgasm. Of course there is more to the mother's desire than this haunting prehistory: mothers can desire after and extra to the reproductive process, as poor Pierre Roland spends his crisis discovering. The patrilinear novel of adultery especially is dedicated to accepting and then policing that difficult truth. Here is another version:

In the old times the moon lived on earth as a young man of very tiny size and he was covered on his whole body with light colored hair. It was his habit to follow the women and girls to the garden.

For a long time none of them paid any attention to him, until one day he began to scream, whereupon a married woman lifted him up and set him in her woven basket that hung on a limb. (According to another version, he himself climbed into a basket and from here he started to cry.) Then the woman told him to be quiet, she would fetch food for him and cook it.

While she was digging out a yam root for this purpose, the little one slipped out of the basket and broke off a piece of sugar cane and ate it. Thereupon he cohabited with the woman, with the result that she became pregnant.

Her husband accused her of adultery with the boy. Although she denied it, he was nevertheless suspicious and lay in wait for her. In a short time the pair came together, whereupon the youth climbed back into his basket which now hung in the garden-house, and here he again started to cry.

The woman said he should be quiet, she would give him to eat and then go back to the village. Her husband, however, lit a fire in front of the house and behind it so the boy was unable to escape and was killed.

His blood squirted up to heaven and here turned into the moon. The moon announced that in retribution all girls and young women shall bleed when he appears, but old women and pregnant ones are excepted, the latter since he was responsible for their condition.[3]

This sick son is a lunatic; like Freud's Oedipus he is preferred to the woman's husband and may make love with her, cry and feed by turns – that is, as long as he is the pre-oedipal penis/child she always desired. What does Freud's woman want? to be the double object of a son who never grows up. This is of course the son speaking. The woman in this story is nurturing before she is sexual; her married status is more or less incidental, except as the occasion of the lover's martyrdom. Husbands may be literal-minded and good at plotting; like Laius, they attempt murder against the son; but he survives in the women's monthly cycle, controlling it from on high. Thus O'Brien's reproductive process is, if you like, inverted: and the fact that the story ends with the woman's regulated bleeding suggests again a myth of origins that precedes the whole patriarchal argument.

And the mother's knowledge? What actually occurs in the body of a pregnant woman and how does she know it? How is she, even before birth, other to her internal double? Her knowledge comes on the one hand from bodily sensations interpreted as best they may be and on the other from the 'advice' provided by booklets, ultrasound screens or other women – all sources of difference and uncertainty as much as of knowledge. The only certainties are the temporal anticipation of a new relation and the spatial given of containment. What is it to contain a presence which can neither know nor be known by us?

I want to trace some of the modalities of knowledge in pregnancy through their paradoxes and into the final politics of their conclusion, the baby's moment, when knowledge enters a new brain by a terrible route. Two people occupy the same body; one dreams, paddles and sucks its thumb; the other one dreams of it while carrying on her everyday life. Who are they and how are they bound to one another?

Conception is the term used not for the entry and acceptance of seed into ovum but for the moment of implantation into the uterine wall, some days later. So the possibly ecstatic orgasm or the momentary cold flush the next morning are events without significance in the reproductive process. Equally peculiarly, the forty weeks (or 'ten common law months',[4] as Shuttle and Redgrove quaintly put it) are measured not from any time when the small life can be said to have begun but from the more convenient dating of the last remembered period. Thus for the first two or three weeks of pregnancy she is not pregnant at all – a fact that comically splits knowledge from reason.

As for the unknown or half-known pregnancy: miscarriages tend to occur at the four-, eight- and twelve-week points of suppressed menstruation. Is there ever a month after the rite of menarche when women do not watch their unpredictable regularities with either fear or hope? At those anchoring times, we wish into being that creature we know only by our discomforts: whether the pregnancy is wanted or undesired, the creature has to exist in order to stay or go, its contrary being the scarlet letter that tells us if it will stay or go.

It may, indeed, have gone before the evidence of its absence is available to anyone. In a blighted pregnancy, the joke is on the confiding mother, who contains all the extra equipment of placenta, foetal sac, etc., but no child, the fertilized ovum having failed to implant. What is her knowledge in such a case? When she miscarries, she realizes that she has been talking to herself, addressing an other who, like God, has not needed to exist in order to be believed in. Like God again, that non-existent but well-loved child was in theory ungendered.[5] In fact, all foetuses, whichever their genetic coding, are physiologically female until about the sixth week, when the reception of androgens will make the XY child into a boy. But there is no doubt that – with not wholly convincing exceptions – we all tend to anticipate a child of one sex or the other, according as

195

we are patrilinear or matrilinear mothers, how much we want the penis, or how many male or female children we already have.

In a supplement to the literary focus of this book, I interviewed a number of pregnant women to examine how they gendered the unborn child at the twentieth week. One said: 'it doesn't bother me one way or another . . . but I *know* it's a boy.' Strictly speaking, she did 'know', since the child turned out to be male. Asked at the time how she knew, she gave several reasons – 'well, everything about it has been so much trouble, it's bound to be a man . . . I've got this feeling, it's restless, determined, forthright . . . a cunning little thing' – and gazed across affectionately at her husband whom she said she wanted the child to resemble and who she felt was more decisive and determined than her. Mild-mannered, he did not comment. After the birth and although the child was somewhat delicate, this mother insisted that indeed he had the qualities of aggression and forthrightness that she lacked, as well as being so beautiful that people stopped to lean over his pram. She herself had, exactly as Freud argues it, acquired something of the masculine qualities she wanted, from the husband via the son: she was more assertive in shops, more prepared to argue and take decisions, in a word more grown-up.

Now we all recognize a certain achievement of 'womanhood' when, with our birth-story and sleepless nights under our belt, we join the ranks of mothers. It is a delusion of course – childlessness is no doubt an equally testing way to maturity – and as much a myth as the transferential separation of motherhood and desire. This woman was more exactly celebrating the accession to a sort of adulthood that gave her something of phallic normality, as measured on the Bem scale.[6] An important component of the sense of achievement comes from the sense of an ordeal of passage, vividly feared beforehand, undergone and survived; the only real adulthood derived from being a mother is the day-by-day accumulation of sense and expediency in dealing with a tirelessly demanding other. But that is for later.

Another interviewee, whose first name resembled that of a boy, glowered somewhat when her husband went out jogging, said she resented the way people at work pick at your stomach and tell you what to eat, and revealed that she was not entirely gratified at finally having conceived after four years of trying – it was too much what everybody wanted of her, she felt 'invaded'. Concerned not so much with 'how it will be but with how I will be . . . sometimes I think my life will be over', she had started out 'absolutely convinced I was going to have a boy', now was less sure. I asked whether she came from a family of girls, and she told me she did, but then remembered there was a youngest brother, the least sporty one in the family. Her parents had 'desperately wanted a boy', so that her mother was repeatedly pregnant until they got one; her father, the only child of a widow, had longed for 'someone to project all those things onto', and had got her, the sporty eldest daughter, next two more girls, and then the quiet artistic brother. 'I am definitely doing it for my parents,' she concluded, having already told me that her mother had only done it for her husband; 'I know I'm doing it and there's nothing I can do about it.' Her sense of doing what other people wanted was both the expression of and an interference with desire; whatever sex child she had, she could feel resentful that her body had been, for a time at least, other people's rather than her own. In fact she had a girl. To see where that child's invasion by others' expectations might take her, we would have to wait a generation.

The genderedness of pregnancy must affect the life of the child from the moment of birth. In Ann Oakley's *From Here to Maternity*, one of the mothers when told she has a boy reacts with a disappointment very like Emma Bovary's. The doctor asks what it is, she replies: '"a substitute girl"'.[7] Weeks later she still feels her '"feelings about his personality aren't right"', finding a disturbing dissonance between what she feels and what she knows: '"I just feel that he's a wilful minded little fucker. He wants his food. But I know that's ridiculous. I know that he's just a little animal that needs feeding"' (p. 158).

When we collect the chickens and eggs to try and trace how our children turn into 'real little boys and girls', measuring out our own influence against the large- and small-scale practices of the child's social world, we cannot ignore that the 'knowledge' that predates birth has a part to play in our own reception of the person we have contained. The child we bear is after all never the child we expected to bear, down to hair colour, size or frailty, but, in many cases, in its sex also. Many mothers wisely do not admit their wishes, either to others or to themselves; but it must be rare not to have them. For God and the foetus are never neutral but perceived through our prescribed or devious imaginations, themselves as unable as language to go without a sexed grammar. How we use that grammar to order our world into subjects and objects, we shall see.

After the interviewing I circulated a total of seventy friends and acquaintances, all mothers, with a questionnaire asking about the sex, anticipated sex and desired sex of their children, as well as the resulting relations – whether they perceived them to be gender-dependent or not – with the children they had. This has no pretensions to being a scientific or socially representative survey: almost all the women are middle class, in their thirties or forties, most professional, many academic, many Jewish and a fair number consciously feminist. I was looking, obviously, not to develop statistics or theories, but to see what kinds of response I got to very openly phrased questions. Of those who described themselves as wanting one sex of child or the other, a number wanted boys because they expected them to be challenging and 'exciting'. The middle one of five daughters, whose first child was male, 'couldn't believe I'd be lucky enough to have a boy'; another wanted a son for the 'unknown' experience; a third specified that being one of three sisters had made her want a boy. A considerable number wanted to reproduce their husband or father; two, married to men who already had daughters by previous wives, wanted to offer them something new; though some who themselves preferred boys noted that their husbands would have liked a girl. Two women who never lived with the fathers of their children consciously took those men into account in their own prenatal desires: the one wanted to reproduce the man in any case, the other hoped he might be more interested if the child were male. Another woman, very strongly motivated to have children but whose lover had abandoned her, chose to have an abortion rather than risk having a child who would resemble him; a fourth, wanting a child by a lover after her marriage had ended, found herself for the first time thinking it might be nice to have a son. A number of the respondents admitted to wishing for a boy first for conventional reasons; some wanted or at least tolerated their family's wish for a celebratory circumcision (though this put others off); many wanted two children of different sexes,[8] only one claiming that this was for the feminist motive of seeing how well she could raise them undifferentiatedly. Only one respondent actively wanted a girl because she had had no sisters; more commonly, people who were unfamiliar with boys hoped for daughters because they desired the easier task of coping with someone similar to themselves. One mother of daughters took a special pleasure when those daughters turned out different from herself; most, however, enjoyed a sense of close companionship and shared, particularly verbal, experience. Rather more wished to follow their mothers than differ from them, though the latter group expatiated further on painful past histories. Only two positively said they wished for a child who would differ from themselves in every way – both, of course, preferring to have boys. The longest list are those who wished for girls – though my group is of course somewhat self-selecting, and culturally highly specific – and of these many cited feminist motives, or a strong relationship to their mother; one frankly said she 'regarded little boys with alarm and distaste', another that 'the more I see of little boys, the more pleased I have been that she was a girl!' Very few admitted to a negative reaction at the birth; those were all women who had had boys when they wanted girls. Among the more general observations of their own parenting, about an equal number considered sons to be closer, more 'cuddly' and dependent than daughters, and daughters to be closer, easier to bond with, than sons. Some worried more about their daughters, especially as they grew up, many specifying that they had higher expectations about what a daughter should achieve; one, who strongly wanted girls, felt only pity at their births because she herself had suffered painful Caesarians. Two were relieved to have a son followed by a daughter because they believed an older sister would be 'bossy' or make him a 'sissy'. Virtually all agreed that 'most mothers' treat children differentially, though a few considered that children (or their children, at any rate) sex-stereotyped themselves.

What this material, however diffuse, suggests is that there are patrilinear and matrilinear mothers, influenced respectively by a sense of genealogical link to men and to women, although a woman may feel this impulse only lightly and may well change around from one to the other during her reproductive lifespan. If I hold to these terms despite some reservations it is because I think the two modes do argue for two distinct positions taken. The clearest instance of patrilinear motives was in the mothers who insisted, like my first interviewee, that they wanted a child who would not resemble themselves; this child is, by our crude habits of thinking differentiation, inevitably gendered male. He functions, like Emma's Georges or Freud's Oedipus, to make the mother no-thing with respect to a very specific other; like the phallus-double for the thinking man, she finds in this son an excess to her possibilities but also (as far as it goes – not far, for he must fly) an extension to her possibilities. In monogamy, patrilinear women may find a sort of peace or a comfortably sexual place in their own singularity or isolation; single patrilinear mothers may enjoy playing football or learning the vocabulary of boys' prescribed interests, because they never did these things when they were young. Matrilinear mothers, on the other hand, are more of a piece with themselves. They need not be feminists but, in a sense, they also must be and must have been before the word was even available. They take from their mother's strength and contentment in herself a similar narcissistic strength and they hand this on to their child. As parents they must learn difference slowly and with some strain. Single matrilinear mothers – and are there inevitably more of these than the other kind? – produce extremely powerful daughters, wild and brilliant like Pearl, girls about whom we might worry (or not worry) how well they will in future life succeed in living with men. Such women, empowered by a voluntary or involuntary separation from their children's fathers, centre their children on themselves. How do their sons fare, looking up to 'bossy' mothers or sisters, learning competence unattached to the figuration of masculinity? Feminists hope, of course, their sons will learn maturity with the grace of a man for whom gender identity is not tied by anxiety to domination, and perhaps even discover another kind of Oedipus complex without the deadly politics of gender contempt. If they do, it will be because their parent has learnt (at her mother's knee) how to love sameness and difference first of all in herself, then in her child-other.

The link between prenatal anticipation and how we go on to live with our children is, then, as various as its motives. It is there long before we, in any sense, 'know' our child as a body separate from our own or a mind to confront ours. It affects all we do during the months of living plurally, both ignoring and dwelling on the creature dwelling in us.

Two other key moments structure the experience of pregnancy. The first is the moment of 'quickening', when the foetus is perceived by the mother to kick inside her. The truth that perception depends on knowledge rather than pure sensation is proved by the fact that quickening seems to come earlier in a second pregnancy – this time round, it is easier to recognize. What makes this a striking moment is the sense that this is the first signal from a living child. Of course the foetus does not really 'quicken' then: but the entitlement of life, the living proof, is dated from the moment it becomes a possible object of perception. That internal perception never seems quite sufficient – apparently gastric sensations have, after all, never before come from someone else. She tends to place a hand on her belly (her own hand or another person's) or wait to see the movement actually expressed on her flesh – so much does the visible evidence seem necessary to prove what comes from the interior where the creature actually lives. The two-tier experience, apprehended inside and 'verified' outside, is the crucial beginning of the child's perceived personhood. Not uncommonly, people gender the foetus male at that point: 'he's going to be a centre forward', they remark. Quickening is, deludedly, the first occasion of what feels like communication. To know that it is not signalling takes quite an effort of the imagination – the effort to understand that our child does not know us in an utterly distinct way from the way we do not know it. It does not realize we are there, because *there* is all we are.

Possibly the most important but also the most difficult aspect of the knowledge of pregnancy is to understand that we are not so much the director as the theatre of the production with which we are so concerned. To be the site rather than the agent of an event gives us a sense of both secrecy and freedom, always active on two fronts at least, as women like to be. It also dislocates the body from the mind – as illness does similarly but negatively. That very dislocation, however, is the key object of knowledge – to be the knowing theatre of an event to which one concedes is to be remarkably alive. The point is that this is not an unconscious knowledge or an unconscious relation. It is experienced, thought about, in daily living, it is already – though necessarily blurredly because the boundaries are precisely blurred – the confrontation with and reception of an other. This other is abstract; by such expedients as gendering it (in conviction or wish) we attempt to structure it as a concrete being as vaguely bodied as the implied author – but the bodiedness of this being is our own, we have incarnated it. As we bear this abstract but indubitably (only) physical other, we are always thinking, working strenuously and constantly to understand the separability/individuation of ourselves.

Before every first-time mother, finally, lies an effort of anticipation which challenges all her knowledge. To get off the roller-coaster is to expect pain; it is rarely possible, in a first pregnancy, to think much beyond that. It is not simply fear, but a more existential concern: how will she behave in the labour ward, will she cease to be herself, will the pain be beyond her mental control? No reassurances can be adequate. The male equivalent, they say, is the first battle, the first parachute leap. Women are accustomed to every physical rite of passage being announced in terms of pleasure mixed with pain; but the moment of parting from and receiving as another the double-within is a moment no amount of anticipation can control. Giving birth, many women experience incomparable agony; others comparative ease, delight at being so cared for and so clever; some something close to orgasm.[9] It is our big moment. But what about the child?

In a discussion of accounts of perithanatic or near-death experiences, Carl Sagan suggests that what the people are describing is a dim memory of the moment of birth.[10] Passing out of a state of stillness into a period of darkness or pain, the near-dead finally seem to emerge into heavenly light and are, they say, greeted by a godlike figure, sensed as male, who is waiting to receive them. Sagan lists, in parallel, four stages in the birth process: the first stage is the 'blissful complacency' of life in the womb (p. 305); the second, labour contractions experienced as 'a cosmic torture chamber'; in the third the child might begin to perceive 'a tunnel illuminated at one end and . . . the brilliant radiance of the extrauterine world' (pp. 305–6); in the fourth stage, the child is received, wrapped up, cuddled and fed. This is all extremely convincing. What I remain curious about is the gender of the figure who greets, wraps and receives the child: why is he male? Perhaps because we have always learned about a masculine God; but not, I think, only because of that. In so far as literal memory is concerned, most babies are surely received and wrapped by women, and have been since human birth began. Rather, I think, by a negative reasoning: what the receiving person is not is the mother. It cannot be the mother, it must be her inverse (just as, later, we learn to expect fathers and other male figures to 'take us out into the world') because the mother is that other thing, the world recently left. If it is true, as every empirical evidence tells us, that neonates and infants have a very dim sense of separateness from the mother, sensing their body as vaguely, not always successfully coterminous with hers, this is nevertheless a kind of intellectual perception: the mother is what is not there to be known. When she takes the baby to her, gazes at its opening eyes and calls its name, this is not anyone the child can possibly know. Precisely where the mother (deludedly of course) seeks and almost inevitably finds a sense of recognition, the child encounters a stranger than whom, in a way, everyone is less strange. She smells and feels familiar, perhaps – she is once again, though in such a different way, there – but she is not to be known.

Hence the ending of *Le Rouge et le noir*, where there must, as well as Julien's re-entry into death as an intrauterine state, be a child suspended before birth; a painful conflict of wants shapes the doubleness of this ending. Mme de Rênal cannot at one and the same time be the mother and be loved; she cannot both be the womb and share it; she must be replicated by the now grotesque Mathilde, a bad womb still unseparated and holding aloft Julien's severed head. One effigy is inside her (denatured already by all the talk of fostering, Julien's talk of course, not her own), the other is the piece of him that he has now surpassed. The good mother, by contrast, is tragic: to be good, she cannot be loved, for to be the mother, she cannot be there. The perfect mother is unknown; she is simply the universe. How can she be loved? She cannot; the mother is always imperfect.

In the perceived similarity of subjecthood for mothers and daughters, which I discussed in the Introduction, a continuum is intuited which is not exactly to do with 'effortless communication', parallel body images or social arrangements (though it produces these) but to do with a kind of 'thereness'. The daughter is just as other, when she is born and ever after, as the son; but the son's knowledge of the impossibility of true sitedness with the mother immediately after birth will become irrevocable as the daughter's will not. The daughter will potentially confront as internal event but also as epistemological test the nine-month experience of containing the other/not-other; the boy will not. Being and having of the maternal body are the different modes of filial knowledge, the female one an anticipated ontology, the male one a phantasized possession. It is difficult indeed to know how the mother's differentiating practices are directed towards sons and daughters: difference is, as I shall suggest later, infinitely too complex probably to be analysed by the gross tools of a myth-making psychoanalysis. What I should argue instead is that the female child will have access to a bodily knowledge of the other as internal, which she recognizes as maternal knowledge, while the male child has to devise other modes, and other attitudes, to regain access to the mother's space, modes which tend to the desperate, predatory, invasive or domineering (tragic) expedients of conventional masculine sexuality.

My long discussion has led to this point: of course mothers *know*, they even know their children, though the child they know is never quite the one they have. But for a child to know is never to know the mother. For 'know' read also 'love'. Mothers normally love their children, though never quite the child they have. Children love their mothers in a state of unknowing shaped by the trauma of birth and impossibly retroactive to it.

The rest of the story is too long to tell here. Many excellent studies examine, from a more or less enlightened point of view, how children are reared well- or ill-meaningly as boys and girls.[11] Every actor in the drama both chooses and does not choose the gender stereotypes made insistently available by our culture. It is observable that – now, in the West at any rate – boys have a harder time if they resist expected norms than girls. (For girls, after all, as Freud knew, normality is a neurosis, there is thus less to lose.) The best discussion of the whole sorry process, from a psychoanalytical-feminist standpoint, is Jessica Benjamin's *The Bonds of Love*,[12] in which she argues with patient cogency for a more rational understanding of mothers' and fathers' part in each child's socialization; for the complex and rich reciprocity of pre-oedipal dynamics between infant and adult (especially with the rational, reasoning mother); and for a dissolution of the gender split in our transferential thinking – between 'the holding mother and the exciting father' (p. 131), 'a mother of attachment and a father of separation' (p. 136), 'paternal rescue and maternal danger' (p. 148), or, worst of all, 'regressive maternal warmth and the icy paternal outside' (p. 177). Universally blaming the 'archaic mother' for everything both tempting and terrorizing, we assign reason and adventure to the male principle, and both sexes suffer. She directs us to observe that mother–child relations are a site of negotiation, learning and spacing, holding and adventuring and above all *mutual* mirroring in the process of quasi-linguistic exchange – what Winnicott calls the environment of play. This simple discovery, well known to the empiricists, is most often ignored by the psychoanalysts and, it seems, by grown-up sons and daughters who prefer to resent or forget. Like Sara Ruddick before her,[13] Benjamin speaks for the restitution of reason. In the site of pre-oedipal play, she comments usefully, 'begins the sense of authorship' (p. 42). Here indeed it should begin – but perhaps it usually begins elsewhere.

Mothers' freedom to choose arises in another theory, but with oddly narrow consequences. I turn now to the area of sociobiology, into which I shall tread only a little way and with rightful trepidation. I used to think, like everybody else, that the mother had no choice in the sex of her child. Natural historians disagree: the sex ratio of an animal population or even the sex of the next offspring she wishes to bear can apparently be influenced by a mother's preference. Reading these books, it seems that nature even more than Freud criticism provides a target impossible to miss. In the multiform ways of male and female animals, in the domestic arrangements of birds or primates, every possibility is possible, it appears. The female seahorse, for example, penetrates the male; he carries the young and gives birth to them; then he nurtures them. Why then, you say, is he male? Because the female is the one who contains the egg, an egg being a gamete (sex-carrying cell) which includes its own food supply. In birds, it is the male that is XX and the female XY. Among bees and the like, sisters are more closely related genetically than parent and child; hence their industrious social system. Non-sexually reproducing species, like greenfly, consist understandably of mothers and daughters, though turkeys made to clone in laboratory conditions produced only males. The maze is as brilliant as it is complex.[14]

Most natural historians show some contempt for the all-female cloning species: these are 'lower down' the evolutionary scale, and should not be able to survive. However, one group called the bdelloid rotifer has survived up to now and has never contained a single male.[15] The idea of the expendability of sexual reproduction, in other words of males, is understandably somewhat unpalatable to some people. As a glance at the rise of the reproductive technologies will show us, male scientists holding up triumphant test-tubes like new-age Frankensteins or legislators busy redefining the rights of paternity could be demonstrating the proprietorial anxiety of a threatened species.[16] This fear of expendability and the authoritarian response to it is not new or especially 'modern', however: we shall see another version later in the primitive expedient of blood rituals.

In a similar intellectual cloud to that from which anthropology is just emerging,[17] natural history always takes the male as the norm of any species group; and only one text I know of contains sentences such as 'Green turtles swim 2250 km from Brazilian coastal waters to Ascension Island, [where they] lay and cover their eggs.'[18] Despite Elaine Morgan's remarkable and somewhat influential *The Descent of Woman*,[19] the female norm is an idea still to be accepted. However, the idea of maternal choice in the sex ratio of offspring, as in her mate, is well accepted. Tim Clutton-Brock is a zoologist who works among the red deer of the Scottish island of Rhum. His team has tagged every one of the population and discovered how the sex ratio is adaptively determined. Now sociobiology, like all evolutionary theory, works according to an economics of scarcity: adaptation is the least wastage for the best use of resources and the optimal chance to pass on one's selfish genes. Male deer are polygamous: one or two dominate the others, so that these, the biggest and strongest, will impregnate most of the does and the rest of the stags may pass on no genes at all. What choice is therefore in the mother's best interests? Her breeding success depends less on body size than on her wise use of the resources of her home range and her own body. 'Several lines of evidence indicate,' Clutton-Brock writes, 'that mothers invest more heavily in their sons than their daughters and that the costs of rearing male calves are greater than those of rearing females.'[20] Males gestate longer, suckle more and are heavier at birth. 'Hinds that rear a male are more likely to be barren the following year than those that rear a female.' In addition, the chances of the hind's male offspring being among the few who would pass on her genes are not good. (Other influences, such as lifetime sharing and inheritance of home ranges among females weigh the argument somewhat the other way.) That would indicate, one might think, that having a daughter was a better bet. But in discussions with friends in the field, I found a gambling streak perpetually entering into the argument. After a reasoned exposition of the complex factors at work, the mythology of depletion and sacrifice is exchanged for one of prowess and strength when it comes to estimating the more desirable choice. Gamblers do not like safe bets; sociobiologists assume females are the same. The hind will, in their eyes, more profitably risk all – her genes and her body strength, including her next opportunity to breed – on the chance of a 'big, strong male' than on a smaller and therefore less depleting and reliably breeding daughter. Among humans too, in whom males are more frequent and markedly weaker at birth, mothers tend to feed sons longer and more assiduously. This may be due to the pressure from all those who say 'he'll need plenty of milk' variously because the boy baby is unusually big or unusually small. There is some sense of a phantasmatically 'strong' boy in the minds of everyone, it seems: we all know that the smaller a male child is the more eagerly (anxiously) he talks about bigness and strength, we all read fairytales and fiction full of Romantic bastards making good and finding princesses.

The term 'sex ratio' itself is often used in a biased way to indicate the number of males in the group: thus it goes up or down according to the preferential proportion of males.[21] Of course bias is never absent from human thought; but a belief in the self-evident good-heartedness of scientific reason remains strong, particularly in questions of sex/gender. Another theorist in this area, Robert Trivers, opens an article disarmingly: 'no attempt is made [here] to review the large, scattered literature relevant to sexual selection. Instead, arguments are presented on how one might *expect* natural selection to act on the sexes, and some data are presented to support these arguments.'[22] Is it ever otherwise? As Rosalind Coward observed some years ago: 'it is rare for these [natural history] programmes to comment on female groups as anything other than "harems". Who is to say that these are not primarily female groups which have marginalized males, except for one good-looker tolerated for his reproductive function?'[23] This might sound funny, but it isn't. When I pressed a scientist friend to answer the challenge, she agreed that 'harem' was indeed an anthropomorphically biased term with political implications we should not ignore. Evolutionary theory is an elegant structure accounting for a multiplicity of evidence with a minimum of rules – but that precisely is its problem. What falls outside the structure is difficult to justify. What is the theory to do, for example, with the 'unnecessary' female orgasm in humans (and probably some primates) or with the clitoris, which exists solely to provide that orgasm? Some people argue that it motivates monogamy; the reverse is more likely to be the case, as the rite of clitoridectomy surely suggests. The clitoris is, if you like, a purely aesthetic object: it provides women with an organ of purposeless purposiveness with no use value at all. In the economics of utility, it exceeds. Mary Jane Sherfey has argued that the 'excess' of female pleasure explains the punitive and incarcerative structures of patriarchal (that is, human) society.[24] What is most obvious here is the parlousness of the economic model – however nuanced. It has no place for things that flow both ways, refuse to take risks, or fail to prize the maximum gain at the least possible cost. I shall return to this critique of the economics of scarcity at the end of my argument.

I have spent many pages on the mother and the extent and limits of her choices. I want now to return to the problem of masculinity and to the main matter of this book, which is textuality and its expedients. In Chapter 2, I called the *récit* the son's story and the realist novel the father's. In this section, I shall trace a further link between them in a common image of French Romanticism, one where we find the move from alienation/separation (Romantic bastardy, adventure) to appropriation (authorship, paternity). That is the image of the bird.

Flight is an obsessive theme in Romantic poetry. Baudelaire, the first modern and last Romantic, bases his whole aesthetics of pleasure on a dialectic of incarceration (spleen, boredom, the enclosure of rooms, heads, cities) and free flight, which departs from the fog of material things but relies on that very physical starting-point (despised love, buzzing cityscape, oppressed imagination) to set off the soaring of fantasy and the flow of words. Here is the third poem of *Les Fleurs du mal*:[25]

Elévation

Au-dessus des étangs, au-dessus des vallées,
Des montagnes, des bois, des nuages, des mers,
Par delà le soleil, par delà les éthers,
Par delà les confins des sphères étoilées,

Mon esprit, tu te meus avec agilité,
Et, comme un bon nageur qui se pâme dans l'onde,
Tu sillonnes gaiement l'immensité profonde
Avec une indicible et mâle volupté.

Envole-toi bien loin des miasmes morbides;
Va te purifier dans l'air supérieur
Et bois, comme une pure et divine liqueur,
Le feu clair qui remplit les espaces limpides.

Derrière les ennuis et les vastes chagrins
Qui chargent de leur poids l'existence brumeuse,
Heureux celui qui peut d'une aile vigoureuse
S'élancer vers les champs lumineux et sereins;

Celui dont les pensers, comme des alouettes,
Vers les cieux le matin prennent un libre essor,
– Qui plane sur la vie et comprend sans effort
Le langage des fleurs et des choses muettes!

Elevation

Up above the ponds, up above the valleys
The mountains, the woods, the clouds and the seas

Up beyond the sun, up beyond the ether,
And beyond the confines of the starry spheres,

My spirit, you move with agility
And, like a good swimmer swooning in the wave,
You joyfully forge through the immense depth
With an ineffable and masculine delight.

Take off, fly far from the morbid miasma,
Go to be purified in the higher air
And drink, like a pure divine liquor,
The clear fire that fills the limpid realms of space.

Behind the cares and the endless griefs
That load down with weights this foggy existence,
Happy is he that with a vigorous wing
Can leap and fly towards the bright serene fields.

He whose thoughts are like the morning larks
That take off soaring freely to the skies,
– Who hovers over life and can read without strain
The language of flowers and of silent things!

'Elévation' is a special and especially erotic case of Baudelaire's aesthetics, for it encapsulates (right at the start of the text) the central paradox of this pleasure. In every other line – 'Au-dessus . . . par delà . . . tu sillonnes . . . envole-toi . . . va . . . et bois . . . derrière . . . s'élancer . . . prennent un libre essor' – movement is marked, with a powerful onomatopoeic rhythm (readers brought up in British schools will start humming 'Faster than fairies, faster than witches . . .') and repetitious vocabulary of 'take-off'. But where does he go? Nowhere it seems, having (like the poor old codger of pornographic fantasy) to keep on starting and precipitating himself again; the idyll is one of sheer zooming, movement not just *from* but *off*, yet never movement to.[26] At the other end of the book, the poet avows that 'les vrais voyageurs sont ceux-là seuls qui partent / Pour partir [the only real travellers are those who leave / For leaving's sake]',[27] showing again that pleasure is never in arrival. The text ends in the uncoiled spring of a suicide just about to be imagined – for 'to die', as Barrie reminds us, 'will be an awfully big adventure'.[28] 'Charles Baudelaire' and Peter Pan can, of course, never grow up into real men or people, essentially because the fantasies of zooming must be immaterial to give such excitement. And hence their suicidal pretence.

But 'Elévation' does not entirely end in this frantic idyll: at the close it offers what is surely a clear politics of the necessary other. The poet has got nowhere also because, like the albatross, his final wish is not to go away but to hover over. Hovering over that humanity defined as miasmic because irredeemably material, he can of course read – flowers (of evil?) and things that never answer back.

Baudelaire's flying and hovering implicitly carry an idea of swooping, an erotic and predatory closure that is never enacted. In order to come down on deck, the albatross has to be captured; then his weakness (read 'genius') is the object of cruel mockery. Thus the Romantic poet carries his predatoriness up on high where he can look down, but never swoops – and never really zooms.

Baudelaire is not alone. Hugo's *Les Contemplations* (1856) is a veritable aviary of beating wings – swans, doves and butterflies in sweeter moments, eagles and whole flights 'd'oiseaux blancs dans l'aurore et d'oiseaux noirs dans l'ombre [of white birds at dawn and black ones in the dark]' as the tone rises.[29] In him too, flight, rebellion and knowledge are tied together: the aim of the 'songeur ailé [winged thinker]' is to 'voler Dieu [rob God]' (pp. 338–9) – but does he? Never; rather, he does a great deal of hovering, leaning down, contemplating and reading the book of nature. The oedipal-promethean gesture is overt in its sufficiency; but the leaning remains a solution it is essential not to admit. For this leaning is a form of erotic interruption. Below the poet must be a maternal/material object (flowers, mountains, 'the world': in a word, the mother's body) upon whom his excitement forbears to act.

Most sexy of all is another bird, Leconte de Lisle's doughty predator in 'Le Sommeil du condor'.[30] The poem begins, exactly like Baudelaire's, with a repetition of 'Par delà' and presents a map-like panorama of great complex shapes and features, above which this 'vaste Oiseau, tout plein d'une morne indolence [vast Bird, filled with a gloomy indolence]' floats in the air 'comme un spectre, seul [like a spectre, alone]', gazing at America fron where night slowly unfurls, putting everything to sleep. When the darkness arrives:

> *Il râle son plaisir, il agite sa plume,*
> *Il érige son cou musculeux et pelé,*
> *Il s'enlève en fouettant l'âpre neige des Andes,*
> *Dans un cri rauque il monte où n'atteint pas le vent,*
> *Et, loin du globe noir, loin de l'astre vivant,*
> *Il dort dans l'air glacé, les ailes toutes grandes.*

He groans out his pleasure, shakes his plumage,
Erects his muscular, hairless neck,
He rises up, whipping the acrid snow of the Andes,
With a harsh cry soars to where the wind cannot reach,
And, far from the black globe, far from the living star,
Sleeps in the icy air, his great wings outstretched.

Again, the extreme erotic effect of this poem comes from the idyll of tension unappeased: this bird can sleep on the wing, so utterly does 'he' combine erectile power with pure serenity. Nothing so small as an outlet is envisaged; instead, the world has diminished to a round dark thing, still material and living but no longer consumable prey: he is above.

The promethean gesture, the excitement of take-off, leads to this: a paternal-dispassionate position of knowledge, hovering on high. This is as clear and dazzling a portrait of the phallus as Flaubert's idealized 'book about nothing . . . with no external attachment, which would stand up by the internal force of its style'. It is, as Flaubert's own case so precisely shows, a portrait of the author as phallus, the paternal phallus of course, whose less stable filial copy struggles and disports himself in the text. My point is that the two fantasies, zooming and hovering, are of one movement, and that each is the failure of the other. Each refuses precisely the consummation it sketches: the first does not fuck, the other does not know, because neither will admit the possibility of an autonomous, reciprocal object. At the end of this chapter we shall see a version of phallic masculinity which at last is heterosexual, in the person of Oshima's Kichi. This masculinity is, by contrast, cowardly and self-important. We find it again in Camus's image of *l'homme absurde*,[31] the man who is always on the mental *qui vive*, always erect, as it were, ready for a struggle with no opponent. They look pugnacious, they look authoritative – but only because there is no one else there.

Hence Flaubert's discomfort with his Emma, hence his inevitable aesthetic of belittling, ringing the doorbell and running away. The modernist version, found in such diverse sources as Marinetti and Saint-Exupéry, is the cloacal phantasy of the bomber-pilot who wreaks pits of destruction without even dirtying his hands; and both writers come round full circle to the imagery of the Bible, with the machines as a flock controlled by a stern, watchful shepherd.[32]

Men can, of course, be pastoral. Though Bernanos's curé can only envy the fostering of working-class women, Karenin achieves a tender masculine version of it. We really should not forget that nowadays Anna's murderous conflict is more likely to be a man's dilemma: today it is not adulterous mothers but rather adulterous fathers who have to make the impossible choice between love and children. I shall return to this point later. The insistent theme of male fostering in the matrilinear texts is surely a signal of that future reversal in an age of somewhat improved maternal rights. But it also has a warning ring: Karenin and Chillingworth rescue the wee girls in order to put them back in their place in the chain, to control and pre-empt a naming that otherwise might have been a matronymic.

Mothers' knowledge and authors' knowledge: two modes without real object. I have suggested, though, that presence/acceptance is the mother's usual mode and absence/refusal the author's. Such nuances in the relation of self to other, whether gendered different or not, act in any moment of knowledge or desire. What, now, do we mean by gender difference? In order to begin answering that we need to look where gender difference seems least, by turning to that good younger brother of feminism, gay studies. He is a very old young brother, because some of his most radical exponents are the classicists. David Halperin and John Winkler have both recently turned our attention back to the Greek literature of pederasty, 'the sexual pursuit of adolescent males by adult males'.[33] We need surely not to forget that such father/son sexualities are always dangerous, but we need also to understand that the 'homo-' of homosexuality is simply the dulling term for inevitably other differences. Between the subject and the object in these relations (the textual relation never varies from a subject/object structure of penetration) was an implicitly negotiated bargain in which desire was exchanged for knowledge, political maturity for political apprenticeship, established for potential citizenship – power, in a word, for pleasure. Power among men may have operated as a genuine exchange (economically phrased as it, familiarly, was). As Foucault's and Winkler's use of Artemidorus illustrates, sexuality in the Greek texts is perceived exclusively as a relation of penetrator to penetrated: the subject–object difference is perfectly poised, and something we would nowadays call exploitation is a very real element in the positioning of higher- and lower-status beings via their bodies. Difference, then, with or without predation, always persists in same–same relations. What, then, is sameness? Many theorists, most recently the ever-eloquent Sedgwick, have reminded us with Foucault that homosexuality, until a hundred years ago, designated not a thing one was but a thing one (anyone) might do.[34] The relentlessly taxonomic scientism of the late nineteenth century ranged it among the fine-split hairs of the perversions but, as Sedgwick puts it, 'why the category of "the masturbator", to choose only one example, should by now have entirely lost its diacritical potential for specifying a particular kind of person, an identity' (p. 9), is a parallel and equally mystifying question. Difference needs to be acknowledged precisely where the categories of existentialism make us feel most safe. Feminism in the last decade has included the recognition of internal differences (and the hierarchies that uncomfortably go with them) among its most urgent means to maturity. Judith Butler has lately challenged feminist and gender studies by insisting that, prior to the resolution of the incest taboo by the breakdown of the Oedipus complex, a preceding homosexual attachment to the same-sex parent has been repressed and remains everywhere buried by the effigies of gender. I am not sure. Benjamin argues I think more convincingly for the readmission of differences, positive and usable ones, in the relations of parents and children (same-sex and other-sex) before and outside the oedipal drama, and these are differences of a subtlety to make 'sexual' an over-blurring term.[35] Similarly, in the richest adult sexual relationships, it is not the exact fit of man and woman that excites but the way that male/female and female/male find a vocabulary of multiple exchange among two bodies.

Of course we have only patriarchy to read ourselves by. In that great culture, we have – along with the exceptions, because of course it is an all-too-elastic safety net – four masculine phantasies at work: the father/daughter plot (regulation of exchange), the father/son plot (the homosocial treaty), the son/father plot (what Bloom calls 'strong' poetry) and the son/mother plot (the *récit*, the novel of adultery and all their adjuncts). Women-authored culture still has not much room of its own and, if it is neither written in men's discourse nor mumbled/scrambled in the body-language of the semiotic or *écriture féminine*, it is generally an oral one. Old wives' tales are communication by chat and allusion, lore rather than science but nevertheless just as securely based in knowledge. As students of social psychology have noted, cultural identities that are prevented from developing internally coherent groupings will tend to go underground into a communicative system based seemingly on inexplicable recognitions, but more accurately on a subtle form of allusiveness.[36] Thus women communicate with each other in supermarket queues, clinics and seminars. Jean Baker Miller has shown that this, in any institutionally subordinated group, will be supplemented by the ability to listen to and speak with the powerful via 'intuition', hint-taking and rhythm.[37] Subordinate groups are for good reasons bi- or multi-lingual. This skill with language is, as Sedgwick shows, inverted by the hegemonic group into an epistemological disadvantage:

Knowledge, after all, is not itself power, although it is the magnetic field of power. Ignorance and opacity collude or compete with knowledge in mobilizing the flows of energy, desire, goods, meanings, persons. If M. Mitterrand knows English but Mr. Reagan lacks – as he did lack – French, it is the urbane M. Mitterrand who must negotiate in an acquired tongue, the ignorant Mr. Reagan who may dilate in his native one.[38]

Reagan may therefore run rings around Mitterrand, or at least, he is almost certain to think he has. Ignorance, we could for simplicity's sake argue, is that which thinks itself to be knowledge. (Of course I cannot stand unarraigned by that discovery.) To step out of danger, then, I want to go back to the language of allusion and lore, the old wives' tales that women speak when they foster each other.

Effi and Roswitha, Naomi and Ruth, Hester and Pearl even, foster one another precisely by the recognition that crosses the differences. Like my questionnaire respondent who felt relieved and excited when her daughters behaved in ways unlike her, these women use the space between the apparently same as their area of reciprocation. Identifiable differences like gender, colour, class do not exclude this kind of relation – but it happens more allusively across the conscious bridge of 'the same'. All mutualities (like metaphors) are a balance of contrast and likeness – but where we begin, where we go, is essential. Women exchanging narrative knowledge focus often on their acquired experience of the body or of children, or familiarly of men as 'big babies' (this is the equivalent to having rhythm, the strategies of subtler control that keep strengths secret) – one explanation perhaps of the attraction for women of psychoanalysis, which is after all, with its gestures of overbearingness, all about big babies. But these areas, children, the body, 'how to manage men', are precisely the ones where the tales really are knowledge. Such knowledge raises people. It holds and separates them. It may lie to them, mislead them, gender them, but it is the space in which they get grown up. What men remember as the archaic or primitive mother is a repression of those areas of experience which had to do with her acquired knowledge. Of course daughters separate less from this area. That is why, in adult crises, men tend to remain in the unhealthy state of unspent lore, unspent talk, and women tend to share their suffering – from mutual moaning to the shared laugh – in curative evenings of commiseration.

If the talk is said to belong to old wives, to *babushkas* or *nonne*, that indicates its basis in age, experience, and the accumulation of maternal knowledge in the fostering state. As modern urban society separates white middle-class daughters from mothers, making us (like Effi) dependent on non-related women to care for our children and talk to us, other societies continue to rely on kin-bonds to supply women with each other across endogamic differences.[39] Age, class and race truly do divide, but female knowledge continues to cement.

I must return to men. I want to come, via a few remarks about the gender difference in the phantasy of doubling, back to the question of castration and culture. A few paragraphs ago, I set in unexplained parallel two groups: mothers and authors. We know it is a rotten lie that we make babies and they make books; we know we can do both if the arrangements are available, even though Mrs Gaskell was the only one of the canonical English women writers to have combined the two knacks in one lifetime. That is no longer a problem; we are after all bilingual. (Or we exploit our fosterers – yes, that too, we are not innocent.) And men are, of course, often authors and fathers too, even Flaubert taking over the upbringing of his dead sister's daughter. But I suggest for the sake of the impossibility of symmetry that there may be two modes, men's and women's, of phantasizing the double, in which the man's is authorial, the woman's maternal. The relationship of self to double is a metonymic one: it turns on two conceptions of *bearing* and, based on them, on two versions of separation. The masculine metonym, as I observed in Chapter 3, is that of self to phallus. Their books depend on doubling in a number of ways, crucially by the fantasy of the doubled implied author and intended reader, both male, one in charge of the other; and we have seen endlessly how the protagonist is double to the author. Separability is essential here, as it is to all control. One of Freud's most startling, grotesque and telling phrases, used in passing of course, describes the young boy as 'the small bearer of the penis [der kleine Penisträger]'.[40] We glimpse an impossible weight, a sort of Obélix lugging around a terrible responsibility; no wonder he is haunted by castration. He bears, and cannot bear; he is always too small. The male body, it seems, is always at risk by its own transcendence: it or he must zoom, take off or be taken off. What remains behind would be a sort of woman's body then; or rather it would be the body in itself, familiarly assigned in our culture to female immanence or work, the dirty province of domesticated women, nurses to his shame.

The woman has a different kind of doubling. We too bear: we carry babies and from them too we must separate. But this 'must' is different: we really must and we really do separate from them; for love or knowledge to exist in action, separation turns into the only possibility of recognition, beyond the body. To 'bear' a child is simultaneously to have it inside and to give it forth; the term shifts as the action does, from keeping to parting – and thus to another kind of keeping. It is not castration. It goes via fear, but again, a material fear of the threshold of pain to be borne between bearing and bearing. That fear is an event, not an *hantise*.

Men's *hantise* has created culture. We must not underrate the magical creativity that has come out of patriarchy's psychic life: sublimation is a justly beautiful word for it. But if the results are lovely, complex, intellectually enriching, the basis is rotten. All those texts and images are scarlet letters. They rely for their motive, like the institutions housing them, on the repressed envy of women's maternity, the fear of biological expendability and, focusing both of these, the terror of women's power-ful blood. As long ago as 1955, Bruno Bettelheim wrote about the symbolic rite of adolescent circumcision and its extreme refinement in penile sub-incision. More than twenty years later menstruation as experi-ence and magic got its first book-length treatment in Britain by Shuttle and Redgrove; their ethereal harmony is supplemented by Paula Weideger's wonderfully sane *Female Cycles*, and most recently by the contributions of Chris Knight and others to the anthropological collection *Blood Magic*.[41] The literature continues to grow. (Sanitary 'protection' is even advertised on TV now – though you have to be very grown-up to understand what is being sold.) What all these writers agree is that the perceived power of menstrual blood is at the base of the complex cultural practices in rituals that create, on the surface of men's bodies, a regular and shared bleeding which they make in envy.

Knight, after Bettelheim, concentrates on the terrifying (to us) rite of sub-incision, practised by the aborigines of West Arnhem Land.[42] These men gather in groups to cut open their penises in a line underneath from scrotum to tip, then they hold them opened up against their bodies to imitate the vagina. From these wounds they bleed, smear the blood on each other and celebrate together. The same tribes isolate women who are bleeding by reason of menstruation or birth. Grouping and the pre-vention of grouping is crucial. It has long been known that women who live together will, in a matter of months, begin to menstruate synchron-ically. (It is also known that light really does affect the timing and form of menstrual flow, as the moon-boy myth suggests.) All the laws of menstrual taboo – perhaps, rather than the incest ban, the deepest structure of patriarchal societies – exist to mark off women whose power is felt to be inordinate at these times. This power may, paradoxically, be increased in practical ways by the separation rules: the menstrual hut may be a place of talking, cooking, shared eating for women under the ban, just as it is the walled garden, the prison cell, the closed bedroom in which our matrilinear women, mothers and daughters, lovers, friends, stayed together. There are just too many women to keep each alone on her pedestal or in her hut for long. Men's envy and men's greed make harems where unknown kinds of desire and unity must exist.

Their fear is that, in us, bleeding is not from a wound. They must cut, we bleed whole and healthy. They make wars, we give birth. We are not castrated – nor, indeed, are they: shall we tell them so? No one is castrated, and both the sexes are needed to make children.

Let us come out of the blood magic of culture into daytime reason. I want to take one everyday example to suggest that, beneath the buried terrors of the female body as maternal, magic and enviable, something else is buried deeper. Suppose a man loves a woman passionately and tenderly (I shall expand on this in a moment) and then leaves her. Earlier I observed that Anna Karenina's painful dilemma is now more likely to be that of the adulterous father. Men's responsibility and love for their children, men's dilemma, leads most commonly not to suicide, Anna's solution, but to departure. Indeed, in this conflict, he must leave someone. Why does he choose to leave passionate love?

In a moment I shall take on the familiar answer that they cannot bear the strain of this passionate state, too much concentrated on the body and the experience of ecstasy because the body is the domain of the archaic mother whose embrace is deadly to autonomy. For now, I want to suggest another, still less admissible motive. There *is* a fear of engulfment but there is also, more exactly, a fear of the same/different equipoise that comes from the relationship of knowledge. It is the adult-to-adult (father to mother – how irresistible the politics here!) encounter that they cannot face. We saw, in the twin fantasy of zooming and hovering, a masculine thematics of desire without reciprocation. We have observed the politics of authorship exercised on the petty character. The thing men most fear about their own desire is the confrontation with the woman's daylight reality. Maternal knowledge is, I repeat, sure to be mistaken some of the time – but no more than other kinds of knowledge. Like other epistemologies, it is a mode of domination or narcissism, but good relationships are a reciprocation of dominances, narcissisms and many other things. Maternal knowledge is a scandal so deep as to require repression because it is actually authority, not unreason. Just as a woman's bleeding is not primeval, not mysterious, but a physiological logic as simple as her orgasm (not excessive, in other words, just excessive to science, another fallible knowledge), just as her body is complete, not lacking or entrapping, so her reason is as whole, as energetic, fallible and keen, as a man's. She can, in other words, think without the phallus. If it is an organ of logic, so is the brain. The missing piece, which is *not* missing, is the humanity, the adulthood of women. We are all children inside, of course – we all search for the impossible, rage and weep – but we are also adults.

And now some more about love. Let us postulate that romantic love is experienced similarly by the two sexes. A man and a woman alike may feel the same passionate concentration on a single other who, for whatever arbitrary reasons and despite the imperfections we all wish ignored by a loving gaze, exactly meets the deepest need we know. Both sexes, in the fully reciprocated state, find the precision of desire matched to desire in a sexual encounter as graceful as dance but with no need of choreography. Orgasm to orgasm or hand to hand, bodies represent whatever else we have made our lives to be. Sexual love, like the parental sort, is based on the expectation of attention – but unlike the parent's, it is startlingly voluntary. After the *post partum* honeymoon we rarely have the complete safety in our child's presence that we have in the embrace of a lover. A number of elements enter into this grace, and if I offer a partial version, the reasons are obvious. First, pleasure is play: purposeless purposiveness, it has the aesthetic exactitude of a rhyme carelessly found. Connectedly, it is also innocence: something of childhood recovered in a momentary escape from taboos, the delights of 'dirt' rediscovered. Then nurturance: in love we are protected and nourished – fostered if you like – by the lover of either sex; without this there would not be the safety to experience bliss. Fourthly, narcissism: as in the maternal gaze, we become visible through the pleasures given and received without being counted out. If these are all too idyllic, let me add a measure of the politics of love – for a woman, the brief or sustained effect of having power over the powerful male. In the successful union, however, this is another kind of play. He gives, she takes (but without predation) the phallus which really is the phallus, donated without danger but in an excitement that creates an element of competition, two temporary equalities imitating the process from struggle to truce. To live such love beyond the erotic moment means a level of attention often too intense to be borne for long – hence the grim logic that leads the narrative, inevitably it may seem, from love to death.

Romantic love is rarely practical; it feeds on loss. Perhaps this is due to the real constraints of the claims of mutual spontaneity: to force ourselves to be loving is something we might offer anybody but a lover. It is not chance that, while our body is clearest in satisfaction, our heads are most focused by refusal. It is then that we prowl round the places the beloved might be, hunting in his absence the effigy of a moment or exploring in all other faces their absurd failure to be his. If Serpuhovskoy argued that women are 'more materialistic . . . more *terre-à-terre*' than men, he must, as I suggested earlier, have meant something to do with the anchoring effect of maternity. This may but need not be literal parenthood; it is often enough to have a house, or even just a half-sussed life, for the man to depart in horror. Availability keeps us on the earth, while masculine phantasies, as we have seen, are all of flight. The very intoxicating mutuality that they savour exactly as we do tastes of entrapment; as we have seen, this is tied up with the identification of the woman with the mother's body perceived, despite all the actual pre-oedipal negotiations that every child grows up by, as regressive and hazardous to autonomy. Attention seems to remain, objectless now, in our hands. Availability is our trap, for the refusal of availability is the last (perhaps only) card they can play. As for their children, they control their potential – human males, unlike animals, have arranged things so that they do the choosing – to deny us the child we want or to leave us with the ones they have settled on us. I began with Mary O'Brien's male dialectic, across the whole span of the reproductive process, of separation to appropriation. Once the child is born, they reverse this process: appropriation comes first (sometimes called passion, sometimes maintenance), then comes separation.

A few weeks ago I saw a film released from censorship after almost a decade: Nagisa Oshima's *Ai No Corrida* (*In the Realm of the Senses*) (1976).[43] The intense and exclusive sexual passion of Kichi and Sada, which takes them indoors into an ever narrower private/artificial space heavily scented with their shared pleasure, ends in his slow strangulation by her followed by a careful castration that had the audience hiding its eyes. What was most seductive, and most unusual in a film portraying desire and violence in a heterosexual context, was the extent to which the man and his pleasure were the willing instrument of the woman's pleasure. Kichi was never predatory – on the contrary, he was, increasingly as their mutual absorption developed, always lovingly available to her. In a striking and exact way, the man fulfilled the phantasy of the hoverer: he was always ready, always phallic, reliably available to the woman's desiring presence; not absent, neither aggressive nor removed, never 'above', he seemed to present simultaneously for himself and the other the ideal of phallic stillness. His serenity was represented by a smile, often a giggle, which oddly perhaps took nothing from his masculinity. From this remarkably benign base, pleasure grew from her pleasure. Although the geishas who were the frequent audience of their lovemaking accused her of perversion because she was apparently always sucking him off, we rarely saw that portrayed – except on the only occasion that his orgasm was represented, not as a *jouissance* of his body but as the liquid that slowly emerged from her mouth as she gazed up in a rare moment of quasi-humiliation, quasi-pornography.

Kichi, for instance, offered Sada an escape from Sade in one scene where, returning from an expedient episode of prostitution with an aged college director, she recounted how she stimulated the man (or herself? it is not clear) to the loveless act. Whether for his or her sake, she played out a typical male–female encounter based on violence, asking the old man to slap her, pinch her, pull her hair, until they were both ready for sex. Kichi asks whether she wants to do the same now. She agrees; we expect a precise repetition. Instead, he asks her (he is lying on his back, as usual) to slap him, and we see how, by a reversal that mirrors, he can enable her to rise out of the object-politics of heterosexuality.

In Kichi, or in the lover of my earlier definition, availability is gendered masculine. Of the pregnant woman or the matrilinear daughter whose motherhood will be self-reproduction, I have used such terms as 'there-ness', 'sitedness'. If Kichi signifies availability by his Rilkean smile, if he becomes by it more rather than less human, the woman's availability is too often co-opted as immanence, failure to rise, incarceration in a body which men find fearful. But we have seen that when in phantasy men lose their immanence, they rise into a kind of flight without meaning, zooming or hovering, never reaching, and that this male transcendence irresistibly becomes castration. I want to suggest that the two versions of immanence I have described need not be gendered divisively or negatively. They both have to do with a body in and out of control (desire), and a mind that assents to it (knowledge). If they are grounded, they are not still. They are always bodies in relation.

The narrative of *Ai No Corrida* founders, as narrative must, on the move from spatial exactitude to temporal change. At the end, death and blood are the inevitable conclusion of the anti-social act of love, it seems. When I spoke above of 'desire and violence in a heterosexual context' I was knowingly incorporating into the story the bloody ending which caused all but one of my women friends to refuse to go to it with me – despite the fact that *The Silence of the Lambs*, notorious for its normal exploitation of women's terrorization as the medium of suspense, was showing the same week and they were prepared to go to that. There are some shocking scenes in *Ai No Corrida*: I am thinking not so much of the moment when he puts an egg inside her and she squats to eject it, which drew gasps from some, but rather the cruel *Liebestod* of an old geisha and, especially, the scene where Sada suddenly grabs the penis of a cheerfully playing little boy, in what is perhaps her only real moment of perversion. However these, in my reading, are part of the thematics of violence which Oshima cannot, after all, eschew, and which moves through the narrative as the preordained story of the woman's necessary madness.

Sada's madness is her professed obsession with the phallus. It is also presented in her resentment of other women's envy and mockery, pushing her back to a shameful past, her jealousy of the rights of the wife, which glance through occasionally in the flash of a knife and the glimpse of fantasized blood. There are, I have suggested, two modes through which phallic presence is evoked in the film. The first is the crucial identification of Kichi's kind availability, his adult masculinity, as wholly phallic for their mutual sakes. At the same time, we are textually directed to believe Sada interested, increasingly as her world narrows, in his penis for its own sake, and obsessed with it as detachable from the man, as if its magic did not rather reside in him. In the closing section, Sada accepts Kichi's suggestion that the greatest buzz imaginable is in coming while being strangled; but what more precisely happens is that, with the culmination of the theme of the translation of his *jouissance* into hers, she is co-opting his orgasm as her own. She is the sole enjoyer; he after all dies as it happens. At the instant of his death, his phallus, which hitherto she has borrowed in mutuality, becomes entirely hers. In the last frames we see the clothed body of Sada curved against the naked body of Kichi, he smiling peacefully, gashed red in the place where a woman is said to have 'no sex', and carrying on his chest the avowal of their love that she has written with his blood, while the director's voice-over announces the historical facts: the original Sada wandered through Tokyo for four days with the severed genitals in her hands, 'radiantly happy', and her case inspired a strange sympathy. Why is this woman happy with her lover's castrated remains? why do the public and private systems of censure forgive her both her passion and her gesture? What masculine phantasy is it that we see in this fiction, so willing to represent the whole phallic man via his gentle availability to the desire of play and pleasure in a woman, and yet which then makes her cut him into pieces, preferring the part to the whole?

I recently spoke to a man who, after fifteen years of loving a woman at a distance, agreed enthusiastically to have a child with her, saying he understood that, if he were to die, she wanted to have something (someone) that would keep their love incarnate. After changing his mind, he was appalled by her grief at the loss of that potential child, almost as if the broken promise was proved a mistake by the woman's transfer of bereavement from him to a child. Similarly, the logic of *Ai No Corrida* suggests that the woman cannot for long have both Kichi and his phallus; male-made and male-conceived, the film of course forms her wish out of his ambivalent wish, representing in his cheerful willingness a man's desire to be separated whole from part and in her violence his equal wish to remain undivided. If a man is (in his own phantasm, perhaps in ours) as self to double the metonym of a metonym, is castration not the logical desire and fear that motivates his relation to us?

I suggested a moment ago the two distinct modes of the phantasy of doubling, one focused on the phallus and one focused on the child. Both are anchored on the twin moves of introjection and projection, and lead to something like an obsession with separation – in other, more homely terms, attachment and loss. Psychoanalytic theory of our day has returned to this dialectic of attachment and loss, concentrating, against Freud, no longer on the essentially masculine idea of castration (masculine but assigned to women too of course, in the skewed logic of the first stage) but now on the child's phantasized loss of the primal mother and accession to autonomy as an adult individual. Men's inability to stay with us (either in physical removal or in the petty resentments of domesticity) is understood, rightly I guess, as their fixed belief that their autonomy has to be as near as possible to the bleak ideal of emotional independence, the residue of practical needs being fed by a wife who pretends to be (and usually financially is) more dependent than they. The argument that adults never quite let go of the archaic mother, always perceived as regressive, natural, ideal and therefore terrorizing, and contrast with her a father who belongs in the outside world and alone can lead there, remains persuasive; it can certainly still haunt us all, men and women, feminists and unregenerates alike. It routinely murders the heroines of the novel of adultery and leaves us all with unbalanced domestic arrangements. In the optimism of Chodorow, Keller, Gilligan, Benjamin et al. that changing social structures will change these phantasies, I long to concur.[44] I am still not sure, however, equally persuaded by my more Lacanian friends that no direct route of influence can be found between social and psychic reality. We cannot forget that the unconscious remains a bourn from which no traveller returns, and which is evident only via the interpretative arts of the modern-day shaman. But if this is so, if the act of interpretation is all we have to know our deepest motives by, then it is perhaps not impossible that we could change our metalanguage and thereby change our souls.

Conclusion

The French feminist theorists shock everyone by offering other bits of the body, the female body this time, to think with. Empirical feminism meanwhile doggedly describes, identifies and tries to inculcate practical measures for demanding equal choice. Men are, however tentatively and however much with one eye on the ejector seat, learning parenthood as a daily operation, sometimes idyllic and phantasmatic, often bitty, irritating or amusing, just as women have learned it one by one. It comes to all of us to realize that parents and children, like the body and its really inseparable organs, are day-by-day arrangements. This is daylight knowledge: can it enter our dreams?

Well, perhaps it can, since we dream and desire after all with the material vocabulary our waking life gives us. The symbolic order is only the sum of images we have, like Emma Bovary, stupidly consumed. None of us is born outside the great patriarchal building, bricked and decorated by fathers and mothers, in power and out of it. But the stucco may be a *trompe-l'œil*. Feminism says it is. Knowledge of its dips and curves, knowledge of our own, is always the possibility of change.

If today, to return to poor Sada (or is it poor Kichi?), the lover is still metonym to his metonym, servant to the phallus that may serve the woman better than himself, remaining finally in her body or in her hands, are all men still similarly dependent on, afraid of and *necessarily* separable from their children? Then, when they leave us, must they experience the shock of endorsing, in dismay or gratitude, the proof of their voluntary redundancy now that they have left us with child? We have seen how nearly expendable the male is in sexual reproduction, how entirely redundant in the species that reproduce asexually – how, to rephrase Samuel Butler, a man may simply be a woman's way of making another woman.[45] At this moment, the matrilinear mother stands in that position, a little further on than the patrilinear mother who, in our society, looks less but is rather more enchained. But humans are not natural.

Irigaray and Cixous suggest that there are two economies by which we think, one tendentiously tied to the masculine and one to the feminine.[46] The ever-present risk of feminist euphoria lets Cixous assign *le propre* (ownership, property and propriety) to the man's way of thinking, and *le don* (the gift) to the woman's. We have no way yet of knowing how women might think if released from the position of subordination in which the system still keeps us: euphoria is delightful but it will not really do as a mode of reasoning. In Kichi, we have seen the gift most gracefully assigned to the masculine – no longer paternal, because it acts without power, and finally not stable because the male-female imagination of the fiction cannot preserve it uncut. I want to end by suggesting something we might be able to think by, via the consciousness of gender but pointing beyond it. Only through the feminist exposure of this rich and cruel culture can we know what phantasmatic world we live in. But we might negotiate it differently from before.

Patriarchy is indeed the grand construction of *le propre*, and it is an economical reasoning. It functions by a logic of the economics of scarcity: an either/or, envy, separation, competition and war. It structures capitalism, ruthlessness and jealousy, the homosocial bond which moves through the generations by exchange, suspicion, the harem, and the oedipal contempt for women. In it, adultery is the normal mode of passion, castration its *hantise*, death its consummation. It unites them and divides us. It has written some terrific books, but they are mostly fiction. Balzac and Freud argue similarly by the economics of scarcity, slipping from fluid mechanics by an obvious logic to masculine desire. You have only so much of the vital juice, they say, and you'd better watch how you spend it: virgins are cleverest, says Honoré; civilization creates its best successes out of sublimation, says Sigmund. They are wrong, though. Semen is like breast-milk, both the least bloody, most friendly of substances. If the aborigines of West Arnhem Land choose to call the blood of sub-incision 'milk', that only underscores its motivation in envy. But unlike the sad wetnurses of the last two centuries, we now know that production of breast-milk is increased by demand and that the mother's body can feed three as easily as one (if she has some practical support). We also see Kichi as generous after a morning in bed as he was the night before: his store too increases by being spent. This is the economics of plenty.

Nowadays we have a new fear of body fluids: every mixture is potentially bloody, desire it seems once again leads to a punitive death. Something new called non-penetrative sex is presented, even by blushing leaflets dropped by governments on doormats, suggesting methods of enjoyment without entry. This is not the famous separation of pleasure from reproduction which seventies feminists reclaimed and are now rethinking. It is rather something Sartre (a typically squeamish male) talked of way back in *L'Etre et le néant*,[47] the pleasure of the surface. He favours caress over penetration, but he is thinking of a mode of appropriation or possession a little more refined, more fastidious perhaps, than the other. I speak perhaps as a sixties girl, but I am thinking also of the body's inside where we all wish to be or be known. Sada writes scarlet letters on Kichi after she has taken from him that thing of the surface that she wants for herself. This whole book is about the question of an internal event (love, gestation, the doubly desiring womb, the moment of shared pleasure) turning into an external one (marriage, politics, the visible phallus, the once-born child) – a difference that we must insist is not equivalent to the sad dialectic of separation and appropriation.

Notes

Throughout this book, all translations from French, German and Hebrew, unless otherwise attributed, are my own, and reference is given to the original text. Further references to a cited text will appear after quotations; passages without page reference are from the last-cited page. Unless otherwise stated, all italics are the author's and all ellipses mine.

Notes to Chapter 1

1. Roy Pascal, *The Dual Voice* (Manchester University Press, Manchester, 1977), pp. 45–6. In even so modern and feminist a text as Jessica Benjamin's *The Bonds of Love* (Virago, London, 1990), however, the same scruple shows itself: in a footnote to pp. 13–14, she writes: 'since there is no graceful solution to the problem of what gender pronoun to use for the infant, I shall alternate between masculine and feminine. In those paragraphs where I refer to the mother as "she", I will generally avoid confusion by calling the infant "he". In those paragraphs where I refer to the infant alone and therefore the referent for the pronoun is clear, the infant will generally be "she".' Thus we find isolated girls and interactive boys in her world, which at least has the advantage of originality.
2. Julia Kristeva, *Pouvoirs de l'horreur* (Seuil, Paris, 1980), p. 43.
3. John Forrester, *The Seductions of Psychoanalysis* (CUP, Cambridge, 1990), p. 61. See also the essays in Charles Bernheimer and Claire Kahane, eds, *In Dora's Case* (Virago, London, 1985).
4. I use the masculine pronoun here to stress the politics of the exchange where (on the model of Dora and most other hysterics) what is taking place is a father/daughter countertransference safely legitimated by the abandonment of the seduction theory.
5. J. Laplanche and J.-B. Pontalis, *The Language of Psychoanalysis*, tr. D. Nicholson-Smith (Hogarth, London, 1973), p. 93.
6. Donald Winnicott, 'The theory of the parent–infant relationship', *International Journal of Psycho-analysis*, 41, 1960, pp. 585–95.

7. Donald Winnicott, *Playing and Reality* (Penguin, Harmondsworth, [1971], 1985), pp. 131–2.

8. Judith Arcana, *Our Mothers' Daughters* (The Women's Press, London, [1979], 1984), p. 34.

9. She does, of course, though in far smaller quantity. Such collections as Karen Payne's *Between Ourselves* (Picador, London, 1984) and Tillie Olsen's *Mother to Daughter, Daughter to Mother* (Virago, London, 1985) present writings that go in both directions, and other examples are the article by Sara Maitland in Stephanie Dowrick and Sibyl Grundberg, eds, *Why Children?* (The Women's Press, London, 1980), pp. 78–103, and Marianne Grabrucker, *There's a Good Girl*, tr. Wendy Philipson (The Women's Press, London, 1988). For a full analysis in the context of women-authored fiction, see Marianne Hirsch, *The Mother/Daughter Plot* (Indiana University Press, Bloomington, 1989).

10. Chodorow's recently published collection, *Feminism and Psychoanalytic Theory* (Polity, Cambridge, 1989), despite its inclusive title, adds nothing new to her theory.

11. Dorothy Dinnerstein, *The Rocking of the Cradle and the Ruling of the World* (elsewhere entitled *The Mermaid and the Minotaur*) (The Women's Press, London, [1976], 1987), p. 68; Luise Eichenbaum and Susie Orbach, *Understanding Women* (Penguin, Harmondsworth, 1983), p. 57; Rosalind Coward, *Female Desire* (Paladin, London, 1984), p. 228.

12. Luce Irigaray, *Sexes et parentés* (Minuit, Paris, 1987), p. 15.

13. Verity Bargate, *No Mama No* (Fontana, London, 1979), p. 112. The protagonist embraces her infant son whom she has dressed in girls' clothing and temporarily renamed: 'I picked Rainbow up and held her hard, as Joy had done, to see what she might have felt but she was all softness, nothing male about that sweet pliable body.'

14. The term is from Eve Kosofsky Sedgwick, *Between Men* (Columbia, New York, 1985).

15. Esther Fuchs, 'The literary characterization of mothers and sexual politics in the Hebrew Bible', in Adela Yarbro Collins, ed., *Feminist Perspectives on Biblical Scholarship* (Scholars Press, Chico, 1985), p. 119. I am indebted for help on the Hebrew and midrashic sources to the kind advice of Ruth Kartun-Blum and Nicholas de Lange.

16. The language used in Ruth 4 (see quotation later in this section) does not explicitly say that Naomi becomes the child's wetnurse, though the usual translations into English have the ambiguous 'nurse'. The Hebrew *'omenet* has the main meaning of 'childminder' or 'educator', but can also have the broader and more ambiguous sense of 'foster-mother'. See F. Brown, S. R. Driver and C. A. Briggs, *A Hebrew and English Lexicon of the Old Testament* (Clarendon, Oxford, [1907], 1959), p. 52. See also Phyllis Trible, *God and the Rhetoric of Sexuality* (Fortress, Philadelphia, 1978), p. 69. Despite various disagreements, I have found illuminating the chapters on

Ruth in this book and in Mieke Bal, *Lethal Love* (Indiana University Press, Bloomington, 1987).

17. These lines are from a poem by Hayim Robinson, quoted in W. Gunther Plaut, ed., *The Torah: a Modern Commentary* (Union of American Hebrew Congregations, New York, 1981), p. 154. See also Binyamin Galai's poem, 'Mot Sarah' ('The death of Sarah'), quoted in R. Kartun-Blum, '"Where does this wood in my hand come from?": the binding of Isaac as a test-case in modern Hebrew poetry', *Prooftexts*, 8, 1988, pp. 293–310.

18. The root of the Hebrew verb translated here as 'to get children' is 'to build'; Sarai is thus hoping 'to be built up' by this surrogacy. In modern Hebrew *lehibanot* means 'to take advantage', even more appropriate in the circumstances. Women poets writing in Hebrew have on the whole shunned the figure of Sarah, preferring to identify with the outcast Hagar.

19. Kartun-Blum, '"Where does this wood in my hand come from?"'.

20. L. Rabinowitz, in H. Freedman and M. Simon, eds, *Midrash Rabbah VIII: Ruth, Ecclesiastes* (Soncino, London, [1939], 1961), pp. vii–viii, shows that this midrash concentrates at great length on the figures of Ruth, Boaz and Elimelech – the latter being the oddest, since the Scroll tells us more or less nothing about him. The centrality of Naomi is generally ignored.

21. Curiously, the two pronominal phrases here ('for them' or 'for their sake', and 'on your account') are reversed in gender, the daughters-in-law being addressed in the masculine, the putative sons referred to in the feminine.

22. The Authorized Version tautologously has: 'the man is near of kin unto us, one of our next kinsmen', but the Hebrew *go'el* means 'redeemer', both in the sense of a close relative entitled to 'redeem' the widow by whom his family line must be continued, and also in the general sense of saviour, as it may be used of God. The term reappears in Ruth 4:14, where the baby is both a 'kinsman' (Authorized Version) and – as forefather of David, elided with him – a saviour of the people.

23. The passive formula *yulad le-*, according to Brown, Driver and Briggs, *A Hebrew and English Lexicon*, is used exclusively of the relation of paternity, except in this instance (where I think we can take it as the subtext) and in Isaiah where similarly it is implicit: 'unto us a son is born.'

24. The Scroll ends with a patrilineal genealogy from Phares to David; A. Jones, ed., *The Jerusalem Bible* (Darton, Longman & Todd, London, [1966], 1968), argues in a footnote that since the narrator identifies Obed as legally Naomi's and Elimelech's child, the last four verses must have been added by a different author.

25. H. Freedman and M. Simon, eds, *Midrash Rabbah I: Genesis* (Soncino, London, [1939], 1961), p. 381, quote a rabbinic view that the matriarchs were barren because 'the Holy One, blessed be He, yearns for their prayers and supplications.' But see also Trible, *God*, p. 34, 'in the Hebrew scriptures the wombs of women belong to God'; and pp. 31–71 for a study of images of God as mother.

Notes to Chapter 2

1. Shoshana Felman, *Literature and Psychoanalysis* (Johns Hopkins Press, Baltimore and London, 1977), p. 10.
2. For a more detailed study of these and other *récits*, see my *Narcissus and Echo* (Manchester University Press, Manchester, 1988).
3. Gérard de Nerval, *Œuvres*, ed. H. Lemaître (Garnier, Paris, 1966), p. 624.
4. François-René, vicomte de Chateaubriand, *Atala, René, Les Aventures du dernier Abencérage*, ed. F. Letessier (Garnier, Paris, 1962), p. 185.
5. André Gide, *Romans*, ed. M. Nadeau, Y. Davet and J.-J. Thierry (Gallimard, Paris, 1958), pp. 372 and 375.
6. Antoine-François Prévost-d'Exiles, *Histoire du Chevalier des Grieux et de Manon Lescaut*, ed. F. Deloffre and R. Picard (Garnier, Paris, 1965), p. 15.
7. Prévost, *Manon Lescaut*, p. 134, note 4.
8. Prosper Mérimée, *Romans et nouvelles II*, ed. H. Martineau (Gallimard, Paris, 1951), pp. 627–8.
9. On his way to see Amélie at the convent, René stops to visit his childhood home; the description of his entry through the long avenue and into the nostalgic halls is like a return to the mother's body. He learns that a few days earlier his sister tried to make the same pilgrimage, but fainted away on the threshold.
10. Benjamin Constant, *Adolphe*, ed. J.-H. Bornecque (Garnier, Paris, 1960), p. 59.
11. Alfred de Musset, *La Confession d'un enfant du siècle*, ed. G. Barrier (Gallimard, Paris, 1973), p. 214.
12. Several of the authors of *récits* offer the texts as fictionalized accounts of real love affairs, e.g. Constant, *Adolphe*, pp. i–iii; Eugène Fromentin, *Dominique*, ed. B. Wright (Garnier, Paris, 1966), p. x. It may be no coincidence that the (at least partial) models for Constant's and Musset's texts, Madame de Staël and George Sand, were at the time of writing much more famous and prestigious than their partners: and if the characters seem startlingly exculpated of the 'infidelities' of the originals, this is no simple homage – nothing is so boring as virtue.
13. Georges Bernanos, *Œuvres romanesques*, eds G. Picon, A. Béguin and M. Estève (Gallimard, Paris, 1961), p. 1045.
14. In 1913, Gide chose *Dominique* as one of his favourite novels in French: *Romans*, p. xi. Interestingly, in one he did not choose, Rousseau's *La Nouvelle Héloïse*, another Julie tries to initiate another exchange of the lover with her cousin Claire.
15. If, by coincidence, Gide's cousin really was called Madeleine, he preferred to write of and to her by the less sullied name of Emmanuèle – a name whose connotations suffered an unfortunate reversal for 1970s filmgoers.

16. The number of Juliette's children is ambiguous; according to p. 580 this is her sixth child, according to p. 596 her fifth. It is significant, however, that the eldest and youngest alone are girls, the first known to Alissa, the second reproducing her.

17. Lemaître's edition erroneously has 'que' here; I correct it following Gérald Schaeffer, *Une Double Lecture de Nerval* (La Baconnière, Neuchâtel, 1977), p. 127, note 14.

18. Théophile Gautier, *Mademoiselle de Maupin*, ed. M. Crouzet (Gallimard, Paris, 1973), pp. 74–5.

19. Almost the identical phrase is used in *René*, p. 232, when Amélie has been stripped and shorn in the ceremony of becoming a nun, and in Gide's *L'Immoraliste*, *Romans*, p. 460, when Marceline is nearing her death. In each case, the woman is in a state of physical humiliation identified with saintliness.

20. René Girard, *Mensonge romantique et vérité romanesque* (Livre de poche, Paris, 1961); I quote from the influential American translation, *Deceit, Desire and the Novel*, tr. Y. Freccero (Johns Hopkins Press, Baltimore, 1965), and from Eve Kosofsky Sedgwick, *Between Men* (Columbia, New York, 1985). The latter puts the issue pithily: '"to cuckold" is by definition a sexual act, performed on a man, by another man' (p. 49).

21. That Girard takes it for granted the mediator is male is shown by this disingenuous image: 'the hero's imagination is the mother of the illusion but the child must still have a father: the mediator' (p. 23); tied to this is his nervousness of the female 'parthenogenesis' (p. 17) of Romantic writing and preference for the manly revelation of mediation in the novel. Confusingly, in reference to sexual desire, Girard finds that triangular desire may have no need of a third person (pp. 105 and 159ff); instead the body and self of the beloved are perceived as split and the result is 'coquetry'. This version makes nonsense of the axiom that 'the impulse toward the object is ultimately an impulse toward the mediator' (p. 10).

Notes to Chapter 3

1. Judith Armstrong, *The Novel of Adultery* (Macmillan, London, 1976); Tony Tanner, *Adultery in the Novel* (Johns Hopkins University Press, Baltimore and London, 1979). The former gives a fascinating background in the history of marriage customs in France, England, Russia and America, followed by a survey of a number of texts from the viewpoint of a cheerfully common-sense feminism; the latter is much more theoretically ambitious but is vitiated by a curious concentration on the men in novels, especially fathers, and by a dismal frequency of errors in the French and German.

2. For a full discussion of the motif of doubling, particularly its use in the

récit, see my *The Unintended Reader* (CUP, Cambridge, 1986), pp. 159–93.

3. Robert Scholes and Robert Kellogg, *The Nature of Narrative* (OUP, Oxford, 1966), p. 240.

4. In a less developed form, similar scenes of a son's illness occur in two texts which belong to the category of *récits* rather than realist novels: Sainte-Beuve's *Volupté* (1834) and Balzac's *Le Lys dans la vallée* (1835). Both are first-person narratives in which the young protagonist nurses an unconsummated passion for the mother of a son and a daughter. In *Volupté*, the colourless Mme de Couaën appeals to the protagonist to diagnose her son's hacking cough; he recovers at the time, but dies a while later, leaving both parents equally bereaved. *Le Lys dans la vallée* is unique in all these texts in painting a vividly angry picture of the heroine's husband: syphilitic, petty and self-pitying, he is, as Mme de Mortsauf acknowledges, like a third sickly offspring. It is his life that she and the narrator sit up all night to save, finding a moral consolation in their shared sacrifice, but in her posthumous letter the mother points to her son's illnesses as representing to her a divine threat. (The mother–daughter relationship in *Le Lys* is reminiscent of that in some of the *récits*: passionately attached to her daughter, the mother nevertheless sours the girl's future by planning to marry her to the protagonist; after her death the two young people are irredeemably hostile.) The mother–son scenes have been seen as prototypes for the scene of the croup in *L'Education sentimentale*: by André Vial in 'Flaubert, émule et disciple de Balzac', *Revue d'histoire littéraire de la France*, juillet–septembre 1948, p. 252, and in 'De *Volupté* à *L'Education sentimentale*', ibid., janvier–mars 1957, pp. 53–4; by R. J. Sherrington, *Three Novels by Flaubert* (Clarendon, Oxford, 1970), pp. 293–5 and p. 295, note 2; and by Pierre-Georges Castex, in *Flaubert: L'Education sentimentale* (Société d'edition d'enseignement supérieur, Paris, 1980), pp. 140–3. Extraordinarily, however, no critic seems to have perceived the parallel with *Le Rouge et le noir*, published earlier than any of the others.

5. For a dazzling analysis of *Le Rouge et le noir* from this point of view, see Carol Mossman, *The Narrative Matrix* (French Forum, Lexington, 1984); my own comments will show both parallels and debts to hers.

6. Stendhal, *Le Rouge et le noir*, ed. P. Castex (Garnier, Paris, 1973), p. 427.

7. Ann Jefferson, *Reading Realism in Stendhal* (CUP, Cambridge, 1988), p. 81.

8. Examples of parallels between the two women are given in Roger Pearson, *Stendhal's Violin* (Clarendon, Oxford, 1988), pp. 148–9.

9. See Mossman, *The Narrative Matrix*, pp. 149ff.

10. The term *fils* is used in two other important places: first, to contrast the purity of provincial love with the derivative love of the city, 'in Paris, love is born from novels [fils des romans]' (p. 36); second, in Mathilde's more or less premonitory declaration, 'between Julien and me there is no signed contract, no notary – everything is heroic, everything will be the child of

chance [fils du hasard]' (p. 297). Especially in the latter instance, where a different formulation could have avoided the stress on gender, we can see the specific heroism attached to masculine illegitimacy.

11. See pp. 308, 332, 414 and 484, and pp. 435, 444, 468 and 484.
12. Leo Bersani, *Balzac to Beckett* (OUP, New York, 1970), p. 103.
13. From Stendhal's *Vie de Henry Brulard*, ed. H. Martineau (Garnier, Paris, 1953), pp. 28–9, quoted in the original in Gilbert Chaitin, *The Unhappy Few* (Indiana University Press, Bloomington, 1972), p. 16.
14. Gustave Flaubert, letter to Louise Colet of 9 December 1852, *Correspondance*, vol. II, ed. J. Bruneau (Gallimard, Paris, 1980), p. 204.
15. Gustave Flaubert, *L'Education sentimentale*, ed. P. M. Wetherill (Garnier, Paris, 1984), p. 302. It was with this phrase that Flaubert marked his own edition of the text.
16. These two archetypes, and the mutual relations between them in each of the three major female figures, are well analysed in Lucette Czyba, *Mythes et idéologie de la femme dans les romans de Flaubert* (Presses universitaires de Lyon, Lyon, 1983).
17. Gustave Flaubert, *Mémoires d'un fou*, in *Un Coeur simple, précédé des Memoires d'un fou et de Novembre*, ed. R. Dumesnil (Editions du Rocher, Monaco, 1946), pp. 25–6.
18. Czyba, *Mythes*, p. 242.
19. See Castex, *Flaubert*, pp. 10–27. For complicated reasons of convenience, Elisa Schlesinger's daughter was registered 'of unknown mother', a curiosity she understandably seems to have found hard to forgive.
20. Marie-Jeanne Durry, *Flaubert et ses projets inédits* (Nizet, Paris, 1950), p. 151.
21. Gustave Flaubert, *La Première Education sentimentale*, ed. F.-R. Bastide (Seuil, Paris, 1963), p. 234. See for example discussions of this scene in Jonathan Culler, *Flaubert: the Uses of Uncertainty* (Paul Elek, London, 1974); and Hazel Barnes, *Sartre and Flaubert* (University of Chicago Press, Chicago and London, 1981).
22. Durry, *Flaubert*, p. 137.
23. This point is well made by Czyba, *Mythes*, p. 315.
24. Lionel Trilling, 'Anna Karenina', in *The Opposing Self* (OUP, Oxford, [1955], 1980), pp. 58–66; this quotation, pp. 60–1.
25. Having no Russian, I am obliged to rely on a translation for *Anna Karenina*; all quotations are from that of Rosemary Edmonds (Penguin, Harmondsworth, 1978); this quotation, p. 13. I have however not chosen to follow her usage in changing the name of the book or the protagonist.
26. The phrase is Tolstoy's own; see Elisabeth Stenbock-Fermor, *The Architecture of Anna Karenina* (Peter de Ridder, Lisse, 1975), pp. 75–98.
27. F. D. Reeve, *The Russian Novel* (Frederick Muller, London, 1967), p. 256.
28. Albert Camus, *La Chute* (Gallimard, Paris, 1956), p. 62: 'une manière de s'entendre répondre oui sans avoir posé aucune question claire.'
29. Cf. Stenbock-Fermor, *The Architecture of Anna Karenina*, p. 107.

Notes

30. Cf. J. P. Stern, *Re-interpretations* (Thames & Hudson, London, 1964), pp. 324–5; Percy Lubbock, *The Craft of Fiction* (Jonathan Cape, London, 1921), p. 240.
31. See John Bayley, *Tolstoy and the Novel* (Chatto & Windus, Edinburgh, 1966), pp. 50–1.
32. Guy de Maupassant, *Pierre et Jean*, ed. Pierre Cogny (Garnier, Paris, 1959), p. 97.
33. Cogny, 'Introduction' to *Pierre et Jean*, pp. i–xv.
34. Freud, 'Family romances' (1909), in *The Pelican Freud Library*, vol. 7, tr. J. Strachey, ed. A. Richards (Penguin, Harmondsworth, 1977), pp. 217–25.
35. Less sexual than in earlier drafts, Jean's careful caresses leave Pierre's filial attitude as the most clearly sexual passion in the book, and no evidence but the brief distanced recollection in Mme Roland's voice lets us suppose that masculine desire might be tender rather than violent.
36. Cogny, 'Introduction', p. lxvii.
37. Kate Chopin, *The Awakening* (The Women's Press, London, 1978), pp. 12–13.
38. Evelyn Waugh, *A Handful of Dust* (Penguin, Harmondsworth, 1951), pp. 117–18.
39. David Hare, *Paris by Night* (Faber, London, 1988), p. vii.

Notes to Chapter 4

1. Letter to Louise Colet of 6 April 1853, Gustave Flaubert, *Correspondance*, vol. II, ed. J. Bruneau (Gallimard, Paris, 1980), p. 297.
2. James Joyce, *A Portrait of the Artist as a Young Man* (1916) (Panther, London, 1977), pp. 194–5; though see Michael Black, *The Literature of Fidelity* (Chatto & Windus, London, 1975), p. 69, 'but the nails aren't pared; they are bitten down to the quick in Flaubert's case.'
3. This has been argued by Chodorow et al., and will be discussed in Chapter 5. In a different context, orthodox Jewish men say a daily blessing thanking God 'for not having made me a woman'; this could be understood not merely as a repetition of contempt but more nervously as a compulsion to shore up a difference from the mother (and from the repressed female deity) that is never more than precarious.
4. Terence Cave, 'Introduction' to Flaubert, *Madame Bovary*, tr. G. Hopkins (OUP, Oxford and New York, 1981), p. xviii.
5. Letter to Louise Colet of 16 January 1852, *Correspondance*, vol. II, p. 31.
6. Jean-Paul Sartre, *L'Idiot de la famille*, 3 vols (Gallimard, Paris, 1971–2).
7. Alison Fairlie, *Flaubert: Madame Bovary* (Edward Arnold, London, 1962), p. 20. See also Erich Auerbach, *Mimesis* (1946), tr. W. R. Trask (Princeton University Press, Princeton, 1953), p. 484.

8. The sometimes deplored 'presence of the artist' is always sensed in the perceptibility of 'fine writing'; see M. Lips, *Le Style indirect libre* (Payot, Paris, 1926), p. 192; Roy Pascal, *The Dual Voice* (Manchester University Press, Manchester, 1977), pp. 105–10; Seymour Chatman, *Story and Discourse* (Cornell University Press, Ithaca and London, 1978), pp. 156–7.

9. Chatman, *Story*, p. 153, note 9.

10. See Freud, 'The advance in intellectuality', *Moses and Monotheism*, in *The Pelican Freud Library*, vol. 13, ed. A. Dickson, gen. ed. James Strachey (Penguin, Harmondsworth, 1985), pp. 358–63.

11. Ezra Pound, 'Hugh Selwyn Mauberley', in *Selected Poems* (Faber, London, [1928], 1968), p. 173.

12. Quoted in Victor Brombert, 'Flaubert and the status of the subject', in Naomi Schor and Henry F. Majewski, eds, *Flaubert and Postmodernism* (University of Nebraska Press, Lincoln and London, 1984), p. 107. I have used my own translation.

13. This and the next quotation are translated from Marthe Robert, *En haine du roman* (Balland, Paris, 1982), p. 14, taken from letters of 3 April and 11 December 1852.

14. Cf. Jean-Pierre Richard, *Littérature et sensation* (Seuil, Paris, 1954), p. 134ff.

15. Most unashamedly, for instance, in Victor Brombert, *The Novels of Flaubert* (Princeton University Press, Princeton, 1966), p. 91: 'ultimately, it does not matter whether we believe with Baudelaire that Flaubert infused his virile spirit into the veins of Emma, or whether we are convinced by Sartre's less flattering notion that in *Madame Bovary* Flaubert disguised himself as a woman.'

16. Charles Baudelaire, *Œuvres complètes*, ed. M. Ruff (Seuil, Paris, 1968), pp. 451–2.

17. For the latter reading see the convincing Ion Collas, *Madame Bovary: a Psychoanalytic Reading* (Droz, Paris, 1985).

18. Richard, *Littérature*, p. 152.

19. Pierre Drouin, 'Un nouveau type de couple', *Le Monde*, 4 April 1953. I am grateful to Claire Duchen for this wonderful citation.

20. For particularly tacky images of Emma Bovary as charming object, see R. P. Blackmur, *Eleven Essays in the European Novel* (Harcourt Brace, New York and Burlingame 1964), p. 58, 'the force we like to find in beauty out of place – in the gift of nature not used and therefore craving abuse'; and Mario Vargas Llosa, *The Perpetual Orgy* (Faber, London and Boston, 1986), p. 13, 'causes of her defiance that force me to admire that elusive little nobody'.

21. See D. A. Williams, *Psychological Determinism in Madame Bovary* (University of Hull Press, Hull, 1973), p. 48.

22. Gustave Flaubert, *Madame Bovary*, ed. Claudine Gothot-Mersch (Garnier, Paris, 1971), p. 331.

23. This note is quoted in Williams, *Psychological Determinism*, p. 31.

24. Oddly, though, in the first quotation the text has 'une enfant', the second follows 'votre enfant' by the masculine pronoun. Is this to stress the greater alienation of Rodolphe's written cliché, or the worse prospects of life saddled with a *girl*-child? Flaubert several times corrects a masculine to a feminine article for this malleable infant.

25. Elisabeth Badinter, *The Myth of Motherhood*, tr. Francine du Plessix Gray (Souvenir, London, 1982).

26. Tony Tanner, *Adultery in the Novel* (Johns Hopkins Press, Baltimore and London, 1979), pp. 261–3; Margaret Lowe, *Towards the Real Flaubert*, ed. A. W. Raitt (Clarendon, Oxford, 1984), pp. 70–1. Tanner leans on the pun 'tour-trou-rouet', Lowe on the pun 'rouet, Rouault, Rolet', neither of which is likely to have escaped the author.

27. Certain critics have commented on Anna's ambivalent relationship to a 'women's world'; see for instance John Bayley, *Tolstoy and the Novel* (Chatto & Windus, Edinburgh, 1966), p. 236; Ruth C. Benson, *Women in Tolstoy* (University of Illinois Press, Urbana, Chicago and London, 1973), p. 96; Black, *The Literature of Fidelity*, p. 122; and Barbara Heldt, *Terrible Perfection* (Indiana University Press, Bloomington and Indianapolis, 1987), p. 43. Quotations from Anna Karenina are again from tr. Rosemary Edmonds (Penguin, Harmondsworth, 1978); see note 25 in Chapter 3.

28. For a full analysis of the term 'cuckold' and an enlightening reading of the role of the husband in the adulterous triangle, see Alison Sinclair, *The Deceived Husband: the Literature of Infidelity and Psychoanalysis: a Kleinian Approach* (OUP, Oxford, forthcoming).

29. Judith Armstrong, *The Unsaid Anna Karenina* (Macmillan, Basingstoke and London, 1988), p. 95.

30. David van Leer, 'Hester's labyrinth', in Michael J. Colacurcio, ed., *New Essays on The Scarlet Letter* (CUP, Cambridge, 1985), p. 70.

31. Nathaniel Hawthorne, *The Scarlet Letter*, centenary edition, vol. I, eds W. Charvat and F. Bowers (Ohio State University Press, Columbus, 1962), p. 256.

32. Carol Bensick, 'His folly, her weakness: demystified adultery in *The Scarlet Letter*', in Colacurcio, *New Essays*, p. 149.

33. Louise DeSalvo, *Nathaniel Hawthorne* (Harvester, Brighton, 1987), pp. 66–9, points out that by making Hester's punishment lighter and less physical than what was usually meted out, Hawthorne exculpates not so much her as his male ancestors. For a description of the sadism of Puritan punishments see Frederick C. Crews, *The Sins of the Fathers* (OUP, New York, 1966), pp. 34ff.

34. See Hawthorne, *The Marble Faun*, centenary edition, vol. IV, eds W. Charvat and F. Bowers (Ohio State University Press, Columbus, 1968), p. 39. In this text, Miriam, also shockingly Oriental but a fully fledged visual artist, still finds time to sew. The narrator muses reassuringly: 'there is something extremely pleasant, and even touching – at least, of very sweet, soft, and

winning effect – in this peculiarity of needlework, distinguishing women from men. Our own sex is incapable of any such byplay aside from the main business of life; but women – be they of what earthly rank they may, however gifted with intellect or genius, or endowed with awful beauty – have always some little handiwork ready to fill the tiny gap of every vacant moment.' This enviable ability creates an 'electric line, stretching from the throne to the wicker chair of the humblest seamstress, and keeping high and low in a species of communion with their kindred beings' (p. 40). No such community of women across the class divide is available to Hester, however.

35. Every critic comments on Pearl, who becomes in their eyes anything from 'the most unpopular little girl in fiction' (F. O. Mathiessen, 'The Scarlet Letter', in Thomas J. Rountree, ed., *Critics on Hawthorne* (University of Miami Press, Coral Gables, 1972), p. 86) to 'the first genuine Miss America' (Hugo McPherson, *Hawthorne as Myth-Maker* (University of Toronto Press, Toronto, 1969), p. 189). For a summary, see Barbara Garlitz, 'Pearl: 1850–1955', *Proceedings of the Modern Language Association*, 72, 1957, pp. 689–99. For a biographical portrait of Una Hawthorne, see Raymona E. Hull, 'Una Hawthorne: a biographical sketch', in C. E. Frazer Clark Jr, ed., *The Nathaniel Hawthorne Journal 1976* (Information Handling Services, Englewood, 1978), pp. 86–119.

36. See Anne Marie McNamara, 'The character of flame: the function of Pearl in *The Scarlet Letter*', *American Literature*, 27, January 1956, pp. 537–53.

37. See Carol Delaney, 'Mortal flow: menstruation in Turkish village society', in Thomas Buckley and Alma Gottlieb, eds, *Blood Magic* (University of California Press, Berkeley, 1988), p. 92.

38. See Colacurcio, *New Essays*, pp. 121–2.

39. See Fiedler, *Love and Death in the American Novel* (Granada Paladin, London, [1960], 1970), p. 215: AD was the usual brand-mark for an adulterer, but A is more abstract, more malleable as a primal sign. Terence Martin, in *Nathaniel Hawthorne* (Twayne, Boston, 1983), p. 193, note 7, discerns another reason: 'had Hester worn the letters AD on her gown, Arthur Dimmesdale would probably have swooned in an ecstasy of guilt.'

40. Michael Minden, '*Effi Briest* and "die historische Stunde des Takts"', *Modern Language Review*, 76, no. 4, October 1981, p. 869.

41. For the comparison of maternal attitudes, see J. P. Stern, *Re-interpretations*, (Thames & Hudson, London, 1964), pp. 336–9, although Ani is not mentioned. On *Madame Bovary*, see for example Marianne Bonwit, '*Effi Briest* und ihre Vorgängerinnen Emma Bovary und Nora Helmer', *Monatshefte für deutschen Unterricht, deutsche Sprache und Literatur*, XL, no. 8, December 1948; Richard Brinkmann, *Theodor Fontane* (Piper, Munich, 1967), pp. 14–15; Lilian Furst, '*Madame Bovary* and *Effi Briest*', *Romanistisches Jahrbuch*, XII, 1961, pp. 124–35; and Juy-Wey Shieh, *Liebe, Ehe, Hausstand: die sprachliche und bildliche Darstellung des 'Frauenzimmers im*

Notes

Herrenhaus' in *Fontanes Gesellschaftsroman Effi Briest* (Peter Lang, Frankfurt, 1987), p. 142. On *Anna Karenina*, see Mary E. Gilbert, 'Fontanes *Effi Briest'*, *Der Deutschunterricht*, 11, no. 4, 1959, p. 70. The comparison with both texts is made by Stern, *Re-interpretations*, and by K. Richter, 'Poesie der Sünde: Ehebruch und gesellschaftliche Moral im Roman Theodor Fontanes', in Jörg Thunecke, ed., *Formen realistischer Erzählkunst* (Sherwood Press Agencies, Nottingham, 1979), pp. 44–51.

42. Despite informal consultation I am unable to discover a purely linguistic reason for Effi to have dropped the 'von' on her gravestone; as in French, the *particule* is normally omitted only when the surname is used alone.

43. Theodor Fontane, *Sämtliche Werke*, vol. VII, ed. Edgar Gross (Nymphenburger, Munich, 1959), p. 172.

44. On Effi's use of the exotic and its change into the uncanny, see the excellent Shieh, *Liebe*, pp. 90ff.

45. On the theme of swinging, see Peter Demetz, *Formen des Realismus: Theodor Fontane* (Hanser, Munich, 1964), pp. 209ff; Joachim Dyck and Bernhard Wurth, '"Immer Tochter der Luft": das gefährliche Leben der Effi Briest', *Psyche*, 39, no. 7, July 1985, pp. 617–33; and Robert L. Jamison, 'The fearful education of Effi Briest', *Monatshefte für deutschen Unterricht, deutsche Sprache und Literatur*, LXXIV, no. 1, Spring 1982, pp. 20–32. See also the fascinating Eva Cantarella, 'Dangling virgins: myth, ritual, and the place of women in ancient Greece', in Susan Rubin Suleiman, ed., *The Female Body in Western Culture* (Harvard University Press, Cambridge and London, 1986), pp. 57–67.

46. See Erike Swales, 'Private mythologies and public unease: on Fontane's *Effi Briest'*, *Modern Language Review*, 75, 1980, pp. 114–23.

47. Shieh, *Liebe*, p. 205; Jamison, 'The fearful education', p. 30. See also Donald C. Riechel, '*Effi Briest* and the calendar of fate', *The Germanic Review*, XLVIII, no. 3, May 1973, p. 199, note 17, who points out the similarity in the names of Annie and Nina.

48. François Mauriac, *Thérèse Desqueyroux* (Grasset, Paris, 1927), p. 109.

Notes to Chapter 5

1. Actually, blood need not and should not be shed at infantile circumcision, and other religions avoid even the mark, using running water instead. But the significant relation of blood to life-cycle rituals remains fundamental; Margaret Mead mentions it in *Male and Female* (Gollancz, London, 1949), pp. 180–1, and it is fully and powerfully argued in Bruno Bettelheim, *Symbolic Wounds* (Thames & Hudson, London, 1955).

2. Mary O'Brien, *The Politics of Reproduction* (Routledge & Kegan Paul, London, 1981), p. 47.

3. Myth of the Sinaugolo of New Guinea, quoted in Paula Weideger, *Female Cycles* (The Women's Press, London, 1978), pp. 118–19.
4. Penelope Shuttle and Peter Redgrove, *The Wise Wound* (Paladin, London, [1978], 1986), p. 29.
5. In theory but not in any other way; the mental confrontation with an ungendered human being seems almost impossible. An instructive parallel is available to the reader of Rose Macaulay's novel *The Towers of Trebizond* (Collins, London, 1956), in which the narrator Laurie is deliberately left without sex definition. In such a realist text, this tests the reader's powers of tolerant imagination to the utmost: we find ourselves looking to the conventions of discourse to guide us how to visualize this person. Such an experiment would of course be grammatically impossible in most languages.
6. See Sandra Bem, 'The measurement of psychological androgyny', *Journal of Consulting and Clinical Psychology*, 42, no. 2, 1974, pp. 155–62.
7. Ann Oakley, *From Here to Maternity* (Penguin, Harmondsworth, 1979), p. 120.
8. But in the 'News in brief' column of *The Guardian* of 22 August 1989 we read: 'couples in the US whose first child is a son are quicker to try for a second than parents who start with a daughter, according to researchers who say they had expected just the opposite.'
9. For the whole range, see Oakley, *From Here to Maternity*; for the first, Jane Lazarre, *The Mother Knot* (Virago, London, 1987); for the last, Irene Elia, *The Female Animal* (OUP, Oxford, 1985), pp. 177–82.
10. Carl Sagan, *Broca's Brain* (Hodder & Stoughton, London, 1974), pp. 301–14.
11. For useful studies, see June Statham, *Daughters and Sons* (Blackwell, Oxford, 1986) and the more practical Marianne Grabrucker, *There's a Good Girl*, tr. Wendy Philipson (The Women's Press, London, 1988). For a typical well-meaning but utterly uncritical approach, see Richard Green, *The 'Sissy Boy Syndrome' and the Development of Homosexuality* (Yale University Press, New Haven and London, 1987).
12. Jessica Benjamin, *The Bonds of Love* (Virago, London, 1990).
13. See Sara Ruddick, *Maternal Thinking* (Beacon, Boston, 1989). Ruddick is, like her inevitably somewhat idealized mother, a little too cheerful. But extraordinarily few theoretical books have been published describing anything but the haunted, Kleinian miasma of mothers' early relations with children. Those that do, and that also elaborate on the context of this eminently social relation, are sociologists and psychologists like Oakley and Statham.
14. A sober exposition can be found in J. Maynard Smith, *The Evolution of Sex* (CUP, Cambridge, 1978); two excellent ones in Elia, *The Female Animal*, and Sarah Blaffer Hrdy, *The Woman that Never Evolved* (Harvard University Press, Cambridge and London, 1981). Another, which offers an extraordinary mixture of tones, is Jeremy Cherfas and John Gribbin, *The Redundant*

Male (Bodley Head, London, 1984): despite their rather bold title, the analysis of the human female is so grotesquely sociobiologized that one might think culture had never existed. On the question of the near-redundancy of males, an article in the science section of *The New York Times* of 16 July 1991 reveals that it is now discovered that an identical gene inherited from one or other parent will have a different effect in the offspring: Jina Kolata, 'Biologists stumble across new pattern of inheritance', *Science Times*, p. C1. Thus despite the apocalyptic visions of reproductive technology, it seems that two parents are and will continue to be needed for the foreseeable future.

15. Maynard Smith, *The Evolution of Sex*, pp. 53 and 69.

16. See Michelle Stanworth, ed., *Reproductive Technologies* (Polity, Cambridge, 1987).

17. See Henrietta Moore, *Feminism and Anthropology* (Polity, Cambridge, 1988).

18. Elia, *The Female Animal*, p. 106.

19. Elaine Morgan, *The Descent of Woman* (Souvenir, London, 1972).

20. Tim Clutton-Brock, 'The red deer of Rhum', *Natural History*, 91, no. 11, November 1982, p. 45.

21. In Tim Clutton-Brock, 'Sex ratio variation in mammals', *The Quarterly Review of Biology*, 61, no. 3, September 1986, p. 339. He begins by announcing: 'for ease of comparison, we have transformed all sex ratio results into percentages of males and refer to this as the sex ratio throughout'; the sex ratio thus 'increases' or 'declines' (p. 357) according to male bias.

22. Robert L. Trivers, 'Parental investment and sexual selection', in B. Campbell, ed., *Sexual Selection and the Descent of Man* (Aldine, Chicago, 1972), p. 137.

23. Rosalind Coward, *Female Desire* (Paladin, London, 1984).

24. Mary Jane Sherfey, *The Nature and Evolution of Female Sexuality* (Random House, New York, 1966).

25. Charles Baudelaire, *Œuvres complètes*, ed. M. Ruff (Seuil, Paris, 1968), p. 46.

26. Clearly an important component of this phantasy is that the phallic transcendence carries a risk of castration. 'Taking off' is its own pun. The earth below (or any form of consummation/arrival) would be the dangerous feminine from which potency might not re-emerge.

27. Baudelaire, *Œuvres*, p. 123.

28. J. M. Barrie, *Peter Pan and Wendy* (1911) (Pavilion, London, 1988), p. 87.

29. Victor Hugo, *Les Contemplations*, ed. L. Cellier (Garnier, Paris, 1969), p. 462.

30. Leconte de Lisle, *Poésies complètes. I: Poèmes barbares* (Slatkine, Geneva, 1974), p. 193.

31. Albert Camus, *Le Mythe de Sisyphe* (Gallimard, Paris, 1942).

32. For a development of this argument and its connection to the aesthetics of violence, see my 'Who whom: violence, politics and the aesthetic', to appear

in Jana Howlett and Rod Mengham, eds, *The Violent Muse* (Manchester University Press, Manchester, forthcoming). References to sky-pilots are to Filippo Tommaso Marinetti, *L'Alcova di acciaio* (Serra e Riva, Milan, 1985), p. 21, and to Antoine de Saint-Exupéry, *Vol de nuit* (Gallimard, Paris, 1931).

33. David Halperin, *One Hundred Years of Homosexuality* (Routledge, New York, 1990), p. ix, and John J. Winkler, *The Constraints of Desire* (Routledge, New York, 1990).

34. Michel Foucault, *Histoire de la sexualité*, 3 vols (Gallimard, Paris, 1984); Jeffrey Weeks, *Sexuality and its Discontents* (Routledge & Kegan Paul, London, 1985); Halperin, *One Hundred Years*; and Eve Kosofsky Sedgwick, *Epistemology of the Closet* (Harvester Wheatsheaf, New York, 1991).

35. Judith Butler, *Gender Trouble* (Routledge, New York, 1990); Benjamin, *The Bonds of Love*.

36. See for example Ferenc Erös, 'The construction of Jewish identity in Hungary in the 1980s', unpublished conference paper 1991.

37. Jean Baker Miller, *Toward a New Psychology of Women* (Penguin, Harmondsworth, 1976).

38. Sedgwick, *Epistemology*, p. 4.

39. For an excellent analysis of the theory of the family, see Diana Gittins, *The Family in Question* (Macmillan, Basingstoke, 1985).

40. 'The dissolution of the Oedipus Complex' (1924), in *The Pelican Freud Library*, vol. 7, tr. J. Strachey, ed. A. Richards (Penguin, Harmondsworth, 1977), p. 321.

41. Bettelheim, *Symbolic Wounds*; Shuttle and Redgrove, *The Wise Wound*; Weideger, *Female Cycles*; Thomas Buckley and Alma Gottlieb, eds, *Blood Magic* (University of California Press, Berkeley, 1988).

42. Chris Knight, 'Menstrual synchrony and the Australian rainbow snake', in Buckley and Gottlieb, *Blood Magic*. See also Knight's *Blood Relations* (Yale University Press, New Haven, 1991).

43. For a useful analysis of this film, see Stephen Heath, *Questions of Cinema* (Indiana University Press, Bloomington, 1981), pp. 145–64.

44. Nancy Chodorow, *Feminism and Psychoanalytic Theory* (Polity, Cambridge, 1989); Benjamin, *The Bonds of Love*; Carol Gilligan, *In a Different Voice* (Harvard University Press, Cambridge, 1982); Evelyn Fox Keller, *Reflections on Gender and Science* (Yale University Press, New Haven, 1985).

45. Samuel Butler, *Life and Habit* (Trübner, London, 1878), p. 134: 'it has, I believe, been often remarked that a hen is only an egg's way of making another egg', quoted in Cherfas and Gribbin, *The Redundant Male*, p. 11. Patriarchy's exchange mechanism could neatly be phrased as using women as men's way of making more men; the reverse ought to set us thinking a bit. I am indebted to Cherfas and Gribbin also for the anti-Freudian aphorism: 'males are simply modified females tailored to a particular role in the reproductive process.'

46. Luce Irigaray, *Ce sexe qui n'en est pas un* (Minuit, Paris, 1977); Hélène Cixous, 'Sorties', in Catherine Clément and Hélène Cixous, eds, *La Jeune Née* (Union générale d'éditions, Paris, 1975).
47. Jean-Paul Sartre, *L'Etre et le néant* (Gallimard, Paris, 1943), pp. 663–90.

Selective Bibliography

Flaubert

Auerbach, Erich, *Mimesis* (1946), tr. W. R. Trask (Princeton University Press, Princeton, 1953)

Barnes, Hazel E., *Sartre and Flaubert* (University of Chicago Press, Chicago and London, 1981)

Bart, B. F., *Madame Bovary and the Critics* (New York University Press, New York, 1966)

Bem, Jeanne, *Clefs pour L'Education sentimentale* (Gunter Narr, Tübingen and Jean-Michel Place, Paris, 1981)

Bersani, Leo, *A Future for Astyanax* (Marion Boyars, London, 1978)

Black, Michael, *The Literature of Fidelity* (Chatto & Windus, London, 1975)

Blackmur, R. P., *Eleven Essays in the European Novel* (Harcourt Brace, New York and Burlingame, 1964)

Brombert, Victor, *The Novels of Flaubert* (Princeton University Press, Princeton, 1966)

Castex, Pierre-Georges, *Flaubert: L'Education sentimentale* (Société d'édition d'enseignement supérieur, Paris, 1980)

Cave, Terence, 'Introduction' to Flaubert, *Madame Bovary*, tr. G. Hopkins (OUP, Oxford and New York, 1981)

Collas, Ion K., *Madame Bovary: a Psychoanalytic Reading* (Droz, Paris, 1985)

Culler, Jonathan, *Flaubert: the Uses of Uncertainty* (Paul Elek, London, 1974)

Czyba, Lucette, *Mythes et idéologie de la femme dans les romans de Flaubert* (Presses universitaires de Lyon, 1983)

Drouin, Pierre, 'Un nouveau type de couple', *Le Monde*, 4 April 1953

Durry, Marie-Jeanne, *Flaubert et ses projets inédits* (Nizet, Paris, 1950)

Fairlie, Alison, *Flaubert: Madame Bovary* (Edward Arnold, London, 1962)

Flaubert, Gustave, *Madame Bovary*, ed. Claudine Gothot-Mersch (Garnier, Paris, 1971)

——, *Un Cœur simple, précédé des Mémoires d'un fou et de Novembre*, ed. R. Dumesnil (Editions du Rocher, Monaco, 1946)

Selective Bibliography

——, *La Première Education sentimentale*, ed. F.-R. Bastide (Seuil, Paris, 1963)
——, *L'Education sentimentale*, ed. P. M. Wetherill (Garnier, Paris, 1984)
——, *Correspondance*, vol. II, ed. J. Bruneau (Gallimard, Paris, 1980)
Ginsburg, Michal Peled, *Flaubert Writing* (Stanford University Press, Stanford, 1986)
Knight, Diana, *Flaubert's Characters* (CUP, Cambridge, 1985)
Lowe, Margaret, *Towards the Real Flaubert*, ed. A. W. Raitt (Clarendon, Oxford, 1984)
Richard, Jean-Pierre, *Littérature et sensation* (Seuil, Paris, 1954)
Robert, Marthe, *En haine du roman* (Balland, Paris, 1982)
Sartre, Jean-Paul, *L'Idiot de la famille*, 3 vols (Gallimard, Paris, 1971–2)
Schor, Naomi and Henry F. Majewski, eds., *Flaubert and Postmodernism* (University of Nebraska Press, Lincoln and London, 1984)
Sherrington, R. J., *Three Novels by Flaubert* (Clarendon, Oxford, 1970)
Starkie, Enid, *Flaubert: the Making of the Master* (Penguin, Harmondsworth, 1971)
——, *Flaubert the Master* (Weidenfeld & Nicolson, London, 1971)
Vargas Llosa, Mario, *The Perpetual Orgy* (Faber, London and Boston, 1986)
Vial, André, 'Flaubert, émule et disciple de Balzac', *Revue d'histoire littéraire de la France*, juillet–septembre 1948, 233–63
——, 'De *Volupté* à *L'Education sentimentale*', *Revue d'histoire littéraire de la France*, janvier–mars 1957, 44–65, and avril–juin 1957, 178–95
Williams, D. A., *Psychological Determinism in Madame Bovary* (University of Hull Press, Hull, 1973)

Fontane

Bance, Alan, *Theodor Fontane, the Major Novels* (CUP, Cambridge, 1982)
Bindokat, Karla, *Effi Briest: Erzählstoff und Erzählkunst* (Peter Lang, Frankfurt and Bern, 1984)
Bonwit, Marianne, '*Effi Briest* und ihre Vorgängerinnen Emma Bovary und Nora Helmer', *Monatshefte für deutschen Unterricht, deutsche Sprache und Literatur*, XL, no. 8, December 1948, 445–56
Brinkmann, Richard, *Theodor Fontane* (Piper, Munich, 1967)
Cantarella, Eva, 'Dangling virgins: myth, ritual and the place of women in ancient Greece', in Susan R. Suleiman, ed., *The Female Body in Western Culture* (Harvard University Press, Cambridge and London, 1986), 57–67
Demetz, Peter, *Formen des Realismus: Theodor Fontane* (Hanser, Munich, 1964)
Dyck, Joachim and Bernhard Wurth, '"Immer Tochter der Luft": das gefährliche Leben der Effi Briest', *Psyche*, 39, no. 7, July 1985, 617–33
Fontane, Theodor, *Sämtliche Werke*, vol. VII, ed. Edgar Gross (Nymphenburger, Munich, 1959)
Frei, Norbert, *Theodor Fontane: die Frau als Paradigma des Humanen* (Hain, Königstein, 1980)

Furst, Lilian R., '*Madame Bovary* and *Effi Briest*', *Romanistisches Jahrbuch*, XII, 1961, 124–35

Gilbert, Mary E., 'Fontanes *Effi Briest*', *Der Deutschunterricht*, 11, no. 4, 1959, 63–75

Hamann, Elisabeth, *Theodor Fontanes Effi Briest aus erzähltheoretischer Sicht* (Bouvier, Bonn, 1984)

Jamison, Robert L., 'The fearful education of Effi Briest', *Monatshefte für deutschen Unterricht, deutsche Sprache und Literatur*, LXXIV, no. 1, Spring 1982, 20–32

Minden, Michael, '*Effi Briest* and "die historische Stunde des Takts"', *Modern Language Review*, 76, no. 4, October 1981, 869–79

Lukács, Georg, *Deutsche Realisten des 19. Jahrhunderts* (Francke, Berlin, 1951)

Müller-Seidel, Walter, *Theodor Fontane* (Metzler, Stuttgart, 1975)

Nürnberger, Helmuth, *Fontane* (Rowohlt, Hamburg, 1968)

Pascal, Roy, *The German Novel* (Manchester University Press, Manchester, 1956)

Riechel, Donald C., '*Effi Briest* and the calendar of fate', *The Germanic Review*, XLVIII, no. 3, May 1973, 189–211

Shieh, Juy-Wey, *Liebe, Ehe, Hausstand: die sprachliche und bildliche Darstellung des 'Frauenzimmers im Herrenhaus' in Fontanes Gesellschaftsroman Effi Briest* (Peter Lang, Frankfurt, 1987)

Stern, J. P., *Re-interpretations* (Thames & Hudson, London, 1964)

Swales, Erika, 'Private mythologies and public unease: on Fontane's *Effi Briest*', *Modern Language Review*, 75, 1980, 114–23

Thunecke, Jörg, ed., *Formen realistischer Erzählkunst* (Sherwood Press Agencies, Nottingham, 1979)

Weber, Dietrich, '*Effi Briest* – "Auch wie ein Schicksal"', *Jahrbuch des Freien Deutschen Hochstifts*, 1966, 457–74

Hawthorne

Baym, Nina, *The Shape of Hawthorne's Career* (Cornell University Press, Ithaca and London, 1976)

Bell, Michael Davitt, *Hawthorne and the Historical Romance of Old England* (Princeton University Press, Princeton, 1971)

Bryson, Norman, 'Hawthorne's illegible letter', in Susanne Kappeler and Norman Bryson, eds, *Teaching the Text* (Routledge & Kegan Paul, London, 1983), 92–108

Cameron, Sharon, *The Corporeal Self* (Johns Hopkins University Press, Baltimore and London, 1981)

Carpenter, Frederick I., 'Scarlet A minus', *College English*, 5, no. 4, January 1944, 173–80

Colacurcio, Michael J., ed., *New Essays on The Scarlet Letter* (CUP, Cambridge, 1985)

Selective Bibliography

Crews, Frederick C., *The Sins of the Fathers* (OUP, New York, 1966)

DeSalvo, Louise, *Nathaniel Hawthorne* (Harvester, Brighton, 1987)

Donohue, Agnes McNeill, *Hawthorne. Calvin's Ironic Stepchild* (Kent State University Press, Kent, 1985)

Erlich, Gloria C., *Family Themes and Hawthorne's Fiction* (Rutgers University Press, New Brunswick, 1984)

Fetterley, Judith, *The Resisting Reader* (Indiana University Press, Bloomington and London, 1978)

Fiedler, Leslie, *Love and Death in the American Novel* (Granada Paladin, London, [1960], 1970)

Garlitz, Barbara, 'Pearl: 1850–1955', *Proceedings of the Modern Language Association*, 72, 1957, 689–99

Greiner, Donald J., *Adultery in the American Novel* (University of Southern Carolina Press, Columbia, 1985)

Hawthorne, Nathaniel, *The Scarlet Letter*, centenary edition, vol. I, eds W. Charvat and F. Bowers (Ohio State University Press, Columbus, 1962)

——, *The Marble Faun*, centenary edition, vol. IV, eds W. Charvat and F. Bowers (Ohio State University Press, Columbus, 1968)

Herzog, Kristin, *Women, Ethnics and Exotics* (University of Tennessee Press, Knoxville, 1983)

Hull, Raymona E., 'Una Hawthorne: a biographical sketch', in C. E. Frazer Clark Jr., ed., *The Nathaniel Hawthorne Journal 1976* (Information Handling Services, Englewood, 1978), 87–119

Irwin, John T., *American Hieroglyphs* (Yale University Press, New Haven and London, 1980)

James, Henry, *Hawthorne*, ed. Tony Tanner (Macmillan, London, [1879], 1967)

Leverenz, David, 'Mrs. Hawthorne's headache: reading *The Scarlet Letter*', in Shirley Nelson Garner, Claire Kahane and Madelon Sprengnether, eds, *The (M)Other Tongue* (Cornell University Press, Ithaca and London, 1985), 194–216

Martin, Terence, *Nathaniel Hawthorne* (Twayne, Boston, 1983)

McNamara, Anne Marie, 'The character of flame: the function of Pearl in *The Scarlet Letter*', *American Literature*, 27, January 1956, 537–53

McPherson, Hugo, *Hawthorne as Myth-Maker* (University of Toronto Press, Toronto, 1969)

Rountree, Thomas J., ed., *Critics on Hawthorne* (University of Miami Press, Coral Gables, 1972)

Sundquist, Eric J., *Home as Found* (Johns Hopkins University Press, Baltimore and London, 1979)

Thompson, G. R. and Virgil L. Lokke, *Ruined Eden of the Present* (Purdue University Press, West Lafayette, 1981)

Warren, Joyce W., *The American Narcissus* (Rutgers University Press, New Brunswick, 1984)

Maupassant

Artinian, Artine, *Maupassant Criticism in France 1880–1940* (King's Crown, Morningside Heights, 1941)

Besnard-Courodon, Micheline, *Etude thématique et structurale de l'œuvre de Maupassant* (Nizet, Paris, 1973)

Bonnefils, Philippe, *Comme Maupassant* (Presses universitaires de Lille, Lille, 1981)

Boyd, Ernest, *Guy de Maupassant* (Knopf, London, 1926)

Donaldson-Evans, Mary, 'Maupassant *ludens*: a re-examination of *Pierre et Jean*', *Nineteenth-Century French Studies*, 9, Fall–Winter 1980–81, 204–19

——, 'The sea as symbol: a key to the structure of Maupassant's *Pierre et Jean*', *Nineteenth-Century French Studies*, 17, no, 1, 1978, 36–43

Freimanis, Dzintars, 'More on the meaning of *Pierre et Jean*', *French Review*, 38, no. 3, January 1965, 326–31

Gaudefroy-Demombynes, Lorraine Nye, *La Femme dans l'œuvre de Maupassant* (Université de Paris, Paris, 1943)

Grant, Elliott M., 'On the meaning of Maupassant's *Pierre et Jean*', *French Review*, 36, no. 5, April 1963, 469–73

Halperin, Josef, *Maupassant der Romancier* (Artemis, Zurich and Stuttgart, 1961)

Ignotus, Paul, *The Paradox of Maupassant* (University of London Press, London, 1966)

James, Henry, *Partial Portraits* (Greenwood, Westport, [1888], 1970)

Kelly, Dorothy, *Fictional Genders* (University of Nebraska Press, Lincoln and London, 1989)

Lecarme, Jacques and Bruno Vercier, eds, *Colloque de Cerisy: Maupassant* (Presses universitaires de Vincennes, Saint-Denis, 1988)

Lethbridge, Robert, *Maupassant: Pierre et Jean* (Grant & Cutler, London, 1984)

Maupassant, Guy de, *Pierre et Jean*, ed. Pierre Cogny (Garnier, Paris, 1959)

——, 'Préface' to Abbé Prévost, *Manon Lescaut* (Boudet, Paris, 1889)

Rolland, Joachim, *Guy de Maupassant* (Revue des études littéraires, Paris, 1924)

Ropars-Wuilleumier, Marie-Claire, 'Lire l'écriture', *Esprit*, 12, December 1974, 800–33

Sachs, Murray, 'The meaning of Maupassant's *Pierre et Jean*', *French Review*, 34, no. 3, January 1961, 244–50

Schasch, Nafissa A.-F., *Guy de Maupassant et le fantastique ténébreux* (Nizet, Paris, 1983)

Schmidt, Albert-Marie, *Maupassant par lui-même* (Seuil, Paris, 1962)

Schor, Naomi, *Breaking the Chain* (Columbia, New York, 1985)

Segal, Naomi, 'The adulteress's child – a sidelight on *Pierre et Jean*', *French Studies Bulletin*, 17, Winter 1985–86, 6–8

Simon, Ernest, 'Descriptive and analytical techniques in Maupassant's *Pierre et Jean*', *Romanic Review*, 51, no. 1, February 1960, 45–52

Selective Bibliography

Smith, Maxwell A., 'Maupassant as a novelist', *Tennessee Studies in Literature*, 1, 1956, 43–49
Steegmuller, Francis, *Maupassant* (Macmillan, London, 1949)
Sullivan, Edward, *Maupassant the Novelist* (Kennikat, Port Washington and London, 1972)
Togeby, Knud, *L'Œuvre de Maupassant* (Danish Science Press, Copenhagen, and Presses universitaires de France, Paris, 1954)
Vial, André, *Guy de Maupassant et l'art du roman* (Nizet, Paris, 1954)

Stendhal

Alter, Robert and Carol Cosman, *Stendhal* (Allen & Unwin, London, 1980)
Andrieu, René, *Stendhal ou le bal masqué* (Lattes, Paris, 1983)
Auerbach, Erich, *Mimesis* (1946), tr. W. R. Trask (Princeton University Press, Princeton, 1953)
Bersani, Leo, *Balzac to Beckett* (OUP, New York, 1970)
Bertelà, Maddalena, *Stendhal et l'autre* (L. S. Olschki, Florence, 1985)
Berthier, Philippe, ed., *Stendhal, l'écrivain, la société, le pouvoir* (Presses universitaires de Grenoble, Grenoble, 1984)
Blin, Georges, *Stendhal et les problèmes du roman* (Corti, Paris, 1954)
Brombert, Victor, *Stendhal et la voie oblique* (Yale University Press, New Haven, and Presses universitaires de France, Paris, 1954)
——, ed., *Stendhal: a Collection of Critical Essays* (Prentice-Hall, Englewood Cliffs, 1962)
Chaitin, Gilbert, *The Unhappy Few* (Indiana University Press, Bloomington, 1972)
Crouzet, Michel, *Stendhal et le langage* (Gallimard, Paris, 1981)
Didier, Béatrice, *Stendhal autobiographe* (Presses universitaires de France, Paris, 1983)
Felman, Shoshana, *La 'Folie' dans l'œuvre de Stendhal* (Corti, Paris, 1971)
Girard, René, *Mensonge romantique et vérité romanesque* (Livre de poche, Paris, 1961): translated as *Deceit, Desire and the Novel* by Y. Freccero (Johns Hopkins Press, Baltimore, 1965)
Gracq, Julien, *Proust considéré comme terminus; suivi de Stendhal, Balzac, Flaubert, Zola* (Corti, Paris, 1980)
Hemmings, F. W. J., *Stendhal* (Clarendon, Oxford, 1964)
Jameson, Storm, *Speaking of Stendhal* (Gollancz, London, 1979)
Jefferson, Ann, *Reading Realism in Stendhal* (CUP, Cambridge, 1988)
Jones, Grahame C., *L'Ironie dans les romans de Stendhal* (Editions du grand chêne, Lausanne, 1966)
Landry, François, *L'Imaginaire chez Stendhal* (L'Age d'homme, Lausanne, 1982)
Litto, Victor del, *La Vie de Stendhal* (Editions du sud, Paris, 1965)
Lukács, Georg, *Studies in European Realism*, tr. E. Bone (Merlin, London, 1950)

Martino, Pierre, *Stendhal* (Boivin, Paris, [1914], 1934)
May, Gita, *Stendhal and the Age of Napoleon* (Columbia, New York, 1977)
Moretti, Franco, *The Way of the World* (Verso, London, 1987)
Mossman, Carol, *The Narrative Matrix* (French Forum, Lexington, 1984)
Mouillaud, Geneviève, *Le Rouge et le noir de Stendhal* (Larousse, Paris, 1973)
Pearson, Roger, *Stendhal's Violin* (Clarendon, Oxford, 1988)
Richard, Jean-Pierre, *Littérature et sensation* (Seuil, Paris, 1954)
Rioux, Jean-Claude, *Le Symbolisme stendhalien* (Arts-Cultures-Loisirs, Nantes, 1986)
Robert, Marthe, *Roman des origines et origine du roman* (Grasset, Paris, 1972)
Simons, Madeleine Anjubault, *Sémiotisme de Stendhal* (Droz, Geneva, 1986)
Stendhal, *Le Rouge et le noir*, ed. P. Castex (Garnier, Paris, 1973)
——, *La Chartreuse de Parme*, ed. V. del Litto (Librairie générale française, Paris, 1972)
——, *Vie de Henry Brulard*, ed. H. Martineau (Garnier, Paris, 1953)
Vigneron, Robert, *Etudes sur Stendhal et sur Proust* (Nizet, Paris, 1978)
Wood, Michael, *Stendhal* (Paul Elek, London, 1971)

Tolstoy

Armstrong, Judith, *The Unsaid Anna Karenina* (Macmillan, Basingstoke and London, 1988)
Aucouturier, Michel, ed., *Cahiers Léon Tolstoï I: Anna Karénine* (Institut d'Etudes slaves, Paris, 1984)
Bayley, John, *Tolstoy and the Novel* (Chatto & Windus, Edinburgh, 1966)
Benson, Ruth C., *Women in Tolstoy* (University of Illinois Press, Urbana, Chicago, London, 1973)
Black, Michael, *The Literature of Fidelity* (Chatto & Windus, London, 1975)
Bonamour, Jean, ed., *Colloque international Tolstoï 1978* (Institut d'Etudes slaves, Paris, 1980)
Boyd, Alexander, *Aspects of the Russian Novel* (Chatto & Windus, London, 1972)
Calder, Angus, *Russia Discovered* (Heinemann, London, 1976)
Christian, R. F., *Tolstoy* (CUP, Cambridge, 1969)
Davie, Donald, ed., *Russian Literature and Modern English Fiction* (University of Chicago Press, Chicago and London, 1965)
Eikhenbaum, Boris, *Tolstoi in the Seventies*, tr. Albert Kaspin (Ardis, Ann Arbor, 1982)
Engel, Barbara A., *Mothers and Daughters* (CUP, Cambridge, 1983)
Gunn, Elizabeth, *A Daring Coiffeur* (Chatto & Windus, London, 1971)
Hardy, Barbara, *The Appropriate Form* (Athlone, London, [1964], 1971)
Heldt, Barbara, *Terrible Perfection* (Indiana University Press, Bloomington and Indianapolis, 1987)

Selective Bibliography

Jackson, Robert L., 'Chance and design in *Anna Karenina*', in Peter Demetz, Thomas Greene and Lowry Nelson Jr., eds, *The Disciplines of Criticism* (Yale University Press, New Haven and London, 1968), 315–29

Jones, Malcolm, ed., *New Essays on Tolstoy* (CUP, Cambridge, 1978)

Leavis, F. R., *'Anna Karenina' and other Essays* (Chatto & Windus, London, 1967)

Lubbock, Percy, *The Craft of Fiction* (Jonathan Cape, London, 1921)

Lukács, Georg, *Studies in European Realism*, tr. E. Bone (Merlin, London, 1950)

Matlaw, Ralph E., ed., *Tolstoy: a Collection of Critical Essays* (Prentice-Hall, Englewood Cliffs, 1967)

Reeve, F. D., *The Russian Novel* (Frederick Muller, London, 1967)

Sémon, Marie, *Les Femmes dans l'œuvre de Léon Tolstoï* (Institut d'Etudes slaves, Paris, 1984)

Steiner, George, *Tolstoy or Dostoevsky* (Knopf, New York, 1959)

Stenbock-Fermor, Elisabeth, *The Architecture of Anna Karenina* (Peter de Ridder, Lisse, 1975)

Tolstoy, Leo, *Anna Karenin*, tr. R. Edmonds (Penguin, Harmondsworth, 1978)

Trilling, Lionel, *The Opposing Self* (OUP, Oxford, [1955], 1980)

Troyat, Henri, *Tolstoy*, tr. N. Amphoux (Penguin, Harmondsworth, 1967)

Wasiolek, Edward, *Tolstoy's Major Fiction* (University of Chicago Press, Chicago and London, 1978)

Williams, Raymond, *Modern Tragedy* (Chatto & Windus, London, [1966], 1979)

General

Allatt, Patricia, Teresa Keil, Alan Bryman and Bill Bytheway, eds, *Women and the Life Cycle* (Macmillan, Basingstoke and London, 1987)

Arcana, Judith, *Our Mothers' Daughters* (The Women's Press, London, [1979], 1984)

——, *Every Mother's Son* (The Women's Press, London, 1983)

Archer, John and Barbara Lloyd, *Sex and Gender* (CUP, Cambridge, 1982)

Arditti, Rita, Renate Duelli-Klein and Shelley Minden, *Test-Tube Women* (Pandora, London, Boston, Melbourne and Henley, 1984)

Armstrong, Judith, *The Novel of Adultery* (Macmillan, London, 1976)

Auerbach, Erich, *Mimesis*, tr. W. Trask (Princeton University Press, Princeton, 1953)

Badinter, Elisabeth, *The Myth of Motherhood*, tr. Francine du Plessix Gray (Souvenir, London, 1982)

Bal, Mieke, *Lethal Love* (Indiana University Press, Bloomington, 1987)

Bargate, Verity, *No Mama No* (Fontana, London, 1979)

Barrie, J. M., *Peter Pan and Wendy* (1911) (Pavilion, London, 1988)

Baudelaire, Charles, *Œuvres complètes*, ed. M. Ruff (Seuil, Paris, 1968)

Beauvoir, Simone de, *Le Deuxième Sexe*, 2 vols (Gallimard, Paris, 1949)

Belotti, Elena Gianini, *Little Girls*, tr. Lisa Appignanesi et al. (Writers and Readers, London, 1975)

Bem, Sandra, 'The measurement of psychological androgyny', *Journal of Consulting and Clinical Psychology*, 42, no. 2, 1974, 155–62

Benjamin, Jessica, *The Bonds of Love* (Virago, London, 1990)

Bernheimer, Charles and Claire Kahane, eds, *In Dora's Case* (Virago, London, 1985)

Bettelheim, Bruno, *Symbolic Wounds* (Thames & Hudson, London, 1955)

Blackie, Penny, *Becoming a Mother after Thirty* (Blackwell, Oxford, 1986)

Boulton, Georgina, *On Being a Mother* (Tavistock, London, 1983)

Bradley, Ben, *Visions of Infancy* (Polity, Cambridge, 1989)

Brennan, Teresa, ed., *Between Feminism and Psychoanalysis* (Routledge, London and New York, 1989)

——, *The Interpretation of the Flesh* (Routledge, London, forthcoming)

Breton, André, *Nadja* (Gallimard, Paris, 1964)

Brown, F., S. R. Driver and C. A. Briggs, *A Hebrew and English Lexicon of the Old Testament* (Clarendon, Oxford, [1907], 1959)

Buckley, Thomas and Alma Gottlieb, eds, *Blood Magic* (University of California Press, Berkeley, 1988)

Burgin, Victor, James Donald and Cora Kaplan, eds, *Formations of Fantasy* (Methuen, London and New York, 1986)

Butler, Judith, *Gender Trouble* (Routledge, New York, 1990)

Butler, Samuel, *Life and Habit* (Trübner, London, 1878)

Camus, Albert, *Le Mythe de Sisyphe* (Gallimard, Paris, 1942)

——, *La Chute* (Gallimard, Paris, 1956)

Carter, Jenny and Thérèse Duriez, *With Child* (Mainstream, Edinburgh, 1986)

Cartledge, Sue and Joanna Ryan, *Sex and Love* (The Women's Press, London, 1983)

Chatman, Seymour, *Story and Discourse* (Cornell University Press, Ithaca and London, 1978)

Cheal, David, *Family and the State of Theory* (Harvester Wheatsheaf, New York and London, 1991)

Cherfas, Jeremy and John Gribbin, *The Redundant Male* (Bodley Head, London, 1984)

Chernin, Kim, *In my Mother's House* (Virago, London, 1985)

——, *The Hungry Self* (Virago, London, 1986)

Chesler, Phyllis, *Women and Madness* (Avon, New York, 1972)

——, *Sacred Bond* (Virago, London, 1990)

Chodorow, Nancy, *The Reproduction of Mothering* (University of California Press, Berkeley, Los Angeles and London, 1978)

——, *Feminism and Psychoanalytic Theory* (Polity, Cambridge, 1989)

Chopin, Kate, *The Awakening* (The Women's Press, London, 1978)

Clément, Catherine and Hélène Cixous, *La Jeune Née* (Union générale d'éditions, Paris, 1975)

Clutton-Brock, Tim, 'Sons and daughters', *Nature*, 298, 1 July 1982, 11–13
——, 'The red deer of Rhum', *Natural History*, 91, no. 11, November 1982, 42–6
——, 'Sex ratio variation in mammals', *The Quarterly Review of Biology*, 61, no. 3, September 1986, 339–74
Collange, Christiane, *Moi, ta mère* (Fayard, Paris, 1985)
Coward, Rosalind, *Female Desire* (Paladin, London, 1984)
Dally, Ann, *Inventing Motherhood* (Burnett, London, 1982)
Dejean, Joan, *Fictions of Sappho 1546–1937* (University of Chicago Press, Chicago and London, 1989)
Dinnerstein, Dorothy, *The Rocking of the Cradle and the Ruling of the World* (The Women's Press, London, [1976], 1987)
Dowrick, Stephanie and Sibyl Grundberg, eds, *Why Children?* (The Women's Press, London, 1980)
Duchen, Claire, *Feminism in France from May '68 to Mitterrand* (Routledge and Kegan Paul, London, Boston and Henley, 1986)
Eichenbaum, Luise and Susie Orbach, *Understanding Women* (Penguin, Harmondsworth, 1983)
Eisenstein, Hester and Alice Jardine, eds, *The Future of Difference* (Hall, Boston, 1980)
Elia, Irene, *The Female Animal* (OUP, Oxford, 1985)
Emlen, Stephen T. and Lewis W. Oring, 'Ecology, sexual selection and the evolution of mating systems', *Science*, 197, no. 4300, 15 July 1977, 215–23
Ernst, Sheila and Marie McGuire, eds, *Living with the Sphinx* (The Women's Press, London, 1987)
Erös, Ferenc, 'The construction of Jewish identity in Hungary in the 1980s', unpublished conference paper 1991
Felman, Shoshana, *Literature and Psychoanalysis* (Johns Hopkins Press, Baltimore and London, 1977)
Feminist Review, *Sexuality: a Reader* (Virago, London, 1987)
Flax, Jane, *Thinking Fragments* (University of California Press, Berkeley, Los Angeles and Oxford, 1990)
Forrester, John, *The Seductions of Psychoanalysis* (CUP, Cambridge, 1990)
Foucault, Michel, *Histoire de la sexualité*, 3 vols (Gallimard, Paris, 1984)
Freedman, H. and M. Simon, eds, *Midrash Rabbah I: Genesis* (Soncino, London, [1939], 1961)
——, eds, *Midrash Rabbah VIII: Ruth, Ecclesiastes* (Soncino, London, [1939], 1961)
Freud, Sigmund, *The Pelican Freud Library*, 15 vols, tr. J. Strachey, ed. A. Richards (Penguin, Harmondsworth, 1973–86)
Fuchs, Esther, 'The literary characterization of mothers and sexual politics in the Hebrew Bible', in Adela Yarbro Collins, ed., *Feminist Perspectives on Biblical Scholarship* (Scholars Press, Chico, 1985)
Gallop, Jane, *Thinking Through the Body* (Columbia, New York, 1988)

Garner, Shirley Nelson, Claire Kahane and Madelon Sprengnether, eds, *The (M)Other Tongue* (Cornell University Press, Ithaca and London, 1985)

Gavron, Hannah, *The Captive Wife* (Routledge and Kegan Paul, London, [1966], 1983)

Gieve, Katharine, ed., *Balancing Acts* (Virago, London, 1989)

Gilligan, Carol, *In a Different Voice* (Harvard University Press, Cambridge, 1982)

Gittins, Diana, *The Family in Question* (Macmillan, Basingstoke, 1985)

Goncourt, Edmond et Jules de, *Germinie Lacerteux* (Union générale d'éditions, Paris, 1979)

Grabrucker, Marianne, *There's a Good Girl*, tr. Wendy Philipson (The Women's Press, London, 1988)

Green, Richard, *The 'Sissy Boy Syndrome' and the Development of Homosexuality* (Yale University Press, New Haven and London, 1987)

Halperin, David, *One Hundred Years of Homosexuality* (Routledge, New York, 1990)

Hardyment, Christina, *From Mangle to Microwave* (Polity, Cambridge, 1988)

Hare, David, *Paris by Night* (Faber, London, 1988)

Heath, Stephen, *Questions of Cinema* (Indiana University Press, Bloomington, 1981)

Herman, Nini, *Too Long a Child* (Free Association, London, 1989)

Hinde, Robert A., *Individuals, Relationships and Culture* (CUP, Cambridge, 1987)

Hirsch, Marianne, *The Mother/Daughter Plot* (Indiana University Press, Bloomington, 1989)

Hrdy, Sarah Blaffer, *The Woman that Never Evolved* (Harvard University Press, Cambridge and London, 1981)

Hugo, Victor, *Les Contemplations*, ed. L. Cellier (Garnier, Paris, 1969)

Jacobus, Mary, *Reading Woman* (Methuen, London, 1986)

Irigaray, Luce, *Ce sexe qui n'en est pas un* (Minuit, Paris, 1977)

——, *Sexes et parentés* (Minuit, Paris, 1987)

Jardine, Alice and Paul Smith, eds, *Men in Feminism* (Methuen, New York and London, 1978)

Jones, A., ed., *The Jerusalem Bible* (Darton, Longman & Todd, London, [1966], 1968)

Joyce, James, *A Portrait of the Artist as a Young Man* (1916) (Panther, London, 1977)

Kartun-Blum, Ruth, '"Where does this wood in my hand come from?": the binding of Isaac as a test-case in modern Hebrew poetry', *Prooftexts*, 8, 1988, 293–310

Kehoe, Monika, ed., *Historical, Literary, and Erotic Aspects of Lesbianism* (Harrington Park, New York and London, 1986)

Keller, Evelyn Fox, *Reflections on Gender and Science* (Yale University Press, New Haven, 1985)

Kelly, Mary, *Post-Partum Document* (Routledge and Kegan Paul, London, 1983)

Kitzinger, Sheila, *The Experience of Childbirth* (Penguin, Harmondsworth, [1962], 1972)

Knight, Chris, *Blood Relations* (Yale University Press, New Haven, 1991)

Kofman, Sarah, *L'Enigme de la femme* (Galilée, Paris, 1983)

Kolata, Jina, 'Biologists stumble across new pattern of inheritance', *The New York Times*, 16 July 1991

Kristeva, Julia, *Pouvoirs de l'horreur* (Seuil, Paris, 1980)

Laplanche, J., and J.-B. Pontalis, eds, *The Language of Psychoanalysis*, tr. D. Nicholson-Smith (Hogarth, London, 1973)

Lawson, Annette, *Adultery* (Blackwell, Oxford, 1988)

Lazarre, Jane, *On Loving Men* (Virago, London, 1981)

——, *The Mother Knot* (Virago, London, 1987)

Leconte de Lisle, *Poésies complètes. I: Poèmes barbares* (Slatkine, Geneva, 1974)

Lepape, Jean, 'Oshima', *Cahiers du cinéma*, 285, février 1978, p. 72

Lips, M., *Le Style indirect libre* (Payot, Paris, 1926)

Macaulay, Rose, *The Towers of Trebizond* (Collins, London, 1956)

MacCannell, Juliet Flower, *The Regime of the Brother* (Routledge, London and New York, 1991)

Mahony, Pat, *Schools for the Boys?* (Hutchinson, London, 1985)

Malos, Ellen, ed., *The Politics of Housework* (Allison & Busby, London and New York, 1980)

Margolis, Maxine L., *Mothers and Such* (University of California Press, Berkeley, Los Angeles and London, 1984)

Marinetti, Filippo Tommaso, *L'Alcova di acciaio* (Serra e Riva, Milan, 1985)

Martin, Emily, *The Woman in the Body* (Open University Press, Milton Keynes, 1987)

Mauriac, François, *Thérèse Desqueyroux* (Grasset, Paris, 1927)

——, *La Fin de la nuit* (Grasset, Paris, 1935)

McConville, Brigid, *Mad to be a Mother* (Century, London, 1987)

McCormick, Ruth, 'In the realm of the senses', *Cinéaste*, VII, no. 4, Winter 1976–77, 32–34

Mead, Margaret, *Male and Female* (Gollancz, London, 1949)

Miller, Jean Baker, *Toward a New Psychology of Women* (Penguin, Harmondsworth, 1976)

Miller, Nancy K., ed., *The Poetics of Gender* (Columbia, New York, 1986)

Moore, Henrietta, *Feminism and Anthropology* (Polity, Cambridge, 1988)

Morgan, Elaine, *The Descent of Woman* (Souvenir, London, 1972)

Oakley, Ann, *From Here to Maternity* (Penguin, Harmondsworth, 1979)

——, *The Captured Womb* (Blackwell, Oxford, 1984)

O'Brien, Mary, *The Politics of Reproduction* (Routledge & Kegan Paul, London, 1981)

Olivier, Christiane, *Enfants de Jocaste* (Denoel, Paris, 1980)

Olsen, Tillie, ed., *Mother to Daughter, Daughter to Mother* (Virago, London, 1985)

Pascal, Roy, *The Dual Voice* (Manchester University Press, Manchester, 1977)

Payne, Karen, ed., *Between Ourselves* (Picador, London, 1984)

Plaut, W. Gunther, ed., *The Torah: a Modern Commentary* (Union of American Hebrew Congregations, New York, 1981)

Plaza, Monique, 'The mother/the same: hatred of the mother in psychoanalysis', *Feminist Issues*, Spring 1982, 75–99

Pound, Ezra, *Selected Poems* (Faber, London, [1928], 1968)

Reiter, Rayna R., ed., *Toward an Anthropology of Women* (Monthly Review, New York and London, 1975)

Rhode, Deborah L., ed., *Theoretical Perspectives on Sexual Difference* (Yale University Press, New Haven and London, 1990)

Rich, Adrienne, *Of Woman Born* (Virago, London, 1977)

——, *Blood, Bread and Poetry* (Virago, London, 1987)

Riley, Denise, *War in the Nursery* (Virago, London, 1983)

Roith, Estelle, *The Riddle of Freud* (Tavistock, London and New York, 1987)

Rose, Jacqueline, *Sexuality in the Field of Vision* (Verso, London and New York, 1986)

Rougemont, Denis de, *L'Amour et l'Occident* (Plon, Paris, 1939)

Ruddick, Sara, *Maternal Thinking* (Beacon, Boston, 1989)

Sagan, Carl, *Broca's Brain* (Hodder & Stoughton, London, 1974)

Saint-Exupéry, Antoine de, *Vol de nuit* (Gallimard, Paris, 1931)

Sartre, Jean-Paul, *L'Etre et la néant* (Gallimard, Paris, 1943)

Sayers, Janet, *Sexual Contradictions* (Tavistock, London and New York, 1986)

Scholes, Robert and Robert Kellogg, *The Nature of Narrative* (OUP, Oxford, 1966)

Sedgwick, Eve Kosofsky, *Between Men* (Columbia, New York, 1985)

——, *Epistemology of the Closet* (Harvester Wheatsheaf, New York, 1991)

Segal, Lynne, *Is the Future Female?* (Virago, London, 1987)

——, *Slow Motion* (Virago, London, 1990)

Segal, Naomi, *The Unintended Reader* (CUP, Cambridge, 1986)

——, *Narcissus and Echo* (Manchester University Press, Manchester, 1988)

——, '*Style indirect libre* to stream-of-consciousness: Flaubert, Joyce, Schnitzler, Woolf', in Peter Collier and Judy Davies, eds, *Modernism and the European Unconscious* (Polity, Cambridge, 1990), 94–114

——, 'Who whom: violence, politics and the aesthetic', in Jana Howlett and Rod Mengham eds, *The Violent Muse* (Manchester University Press, Manchester, forthcoming).

Sharpe, Sue, *Double Identity* (Penguin, Harmondsworth, 1984)

Sherfey, Mary Jane, *The Nature and Evolution of Female Sexuality* (Random House, New York, 1966)

Showalter, Elaine, *The Female Malady* (Virago, London, 1987)

——, ed., *Speaking of Gender* (Routledge, London, 1989)

Shuttle, Penelope and Peter Redgrove, *The Wise Wound* (Paladin, London, [1978], 1986)

Sinclair, Alison, *The Deceived Husband: the Literature of Infidelity and Psychoanalysis: a Kleinian Approach* (OUP, Oxford, forthcoming)

Smith, J. Maynard, *The Evolution of Sex* (CUP, Cambridge, 1978)

Spender, Dale and Elizabeth Sarah, *Learning to Lose* (The Women's Press, London, 1980)

Stanworth, Michelle, ed., *Reproductive Technologies* (Polity, Cambridge, 1987)

Statham, June, *Daughters and Sons* (Blackwell, Oxford, 1986)

Steedman, Carolyn, Cathy Urwin and Valerie Walkerdine, eds, *Language, Gender and Childhood* (Routledge & Kegan Paul, London, 1985)

Still, Judith, 'A feminine economy: some preliminary thoughts', in Helen Wilcox, Keith McWatters, Ann Thompson and Linda R. Williams, eds, *The Body and the Text* (Harvester Wheatsheaf, New York, 1990), 49–60

Stoller, Robert J., *Presentations of Gender* (Yale University Press, New Haven and London, 1985)

Suleiman, Susan Rubin, ed., *The Female Body in Western Culture* (Harvard University Press, Cambridge and London, 1986)

Tanner, Tony, *Adultery in the Novel* (Johns Hopkins Press, Baltimore and London, 1979)

Thorne, Barrie and Marilyn Yalom, eds, *Rethinking the Family* (Longman, New York, 1982)

Tobin, Patricia Drechsel, *Time and the Novel* (Princeton University Press, Princeton, 1978)

Trible, Phyllis, *God and the Rhetoric of Sexuality* (Fortress, Philadelphia, 1978)

Trivers, Robert L., 'Parental investment and sexual selection', in B. Campbell, ed., *Sexual Selection and the Descent of Man* (Aldine, Chicago, 1972), 136–79

Vance, Carol S., *Pleasure and Danger* (Routledge and Kegan Paul, London, 1984)

Watson, James D., 'The future of asexual reproduction', *Intellectual Digest*, October 1971

Waugh, Evelyn, *A Handful of Dust* (Penguin, Harmondsworth, 1951)

Weedon, Chris, *Feminist Practice and Poststructuralist Theory* (Blackwell, Oxford, 1987)

Weeks, Jeffrey, *Sexuality and its Discontents* (Routledge & Kegan Paul, London, 1985)

Weideger, Paula, *Female Cycles* (The Women's Press, London, 1978)

Wilcox, Helen, Keith McWatters, Ann Thompson and Linda R. Williams, eds, *The Body and the Text* (Harvester Wheatsheaf, New York, 1990)

Williams, G. C., 'The Question of adaptive sex ratio in outcrossed vertebrates', *Proceedings of the Royal Society, Series B*, 205, 1979, 567–80

Winkler, John J., *The Constraints of Desire* (Routledge, New York, 1990)

Winnicott, Donald, 'The theory of the parent–infant relationship', *International Journal of Psycho-analysis*, 41, 1960, 585–95

——, *Playing and Reality* (Penguin, Harmondsworth, [1971], 1985)

Zaretsky, Eli, *Capitalism, the Family and Personal Life* (Pluto, London, 1976)

Zipes, Jack, *Don't Bet on the Prince* (Gower, Aldershot, 1986)

Index

Index

DEMCO 38-297